Chinese Law of Personality Rights I

This volume is a collection of up-to-date, authoritative essays on China's Law of Personality Rights, its impact in practice and its legal background.

The Law of Personality Rights was enacted in China in May 2020, the first time that the Law has been legislated as an independent part of the Civil Code of the People's Republic of China, marking an unprecedented step in protecting the personality rights of citizens. As the first volume of a two-volume set that elucidates the theory, practice and codification experience of the Law in China, the book examines the basis for the Law as a standalone part of the Civil Code, its overall framework and the delimitation and formation of the Law. In terms of practical aspects, the contributors delve into institutional arrangements, the relationship between human rights and personality rights, and the relationship with laws on tort liability, as well as those pertaining to marriage and the family.

The book will be an essential reference to scholars and students studying civil law, continental law, Chinese law and the legal protection of personality rights.

Wang Liming is a professor in the Law School at Renmin University of China, vice president of the Chinese Law Society, president of the Chinese Civil Law Society and researcher at the Research Center for Civil and Commercial Law of Renmin University of China. He is the Changjiang Distinguished Professor, a scholar award programme of the Ministry of Education, China.

Shi Jiayou is a professor in the Law School at Renmin University of China, executive director of the Research Centre for Civil and Commercial Law, director of the Francophone Legal Research Centre, visiting professor at the University of Paris II, University of Paris VIII, University of Geneva, University of Ottawa and so on.

China Perspectives

The *China Perspectives* series focuses on translating and publishing works by leading Chinese scholars, writing about both global topics and China-related themes. It covers Humanities & Social Sciences, Education, Media and Psychology, as well as many interdisciplinary themes.

This is the first time any of these books have been published in English for international readers. The series aims to put forward a Chinese perspective, give insights into cutting-edge academic thinking in China, and inspire researchers globally.

To submit proposals, please contact the Taylor & Francis Publisher for China Publishing Programme, Lian Sun (Lian.Sun@informa.com)

Titles in law currently include:

Building the Rule of Law in China
Procedure, Discourse and Hermeneutic Community
Weidong Ji

Deciphering Intellectual Property Law and Its Conflict/Reconciliation with Competition Law
Kongzhong Liu

The Crisis of Distribution (Set: The Crisis of Distribution and the Regulation of Economic Law)
Theoretical Analysis from Economic Law
Shouwen Zhang

Distributive Institutions (Set: The Crisis of Distribution and the Regulation of Economic Law)
The View of Economic Law
Shouwen Zhang

Chinese Law of Personality Rights I
Theory and Practice
Edited by Wang Liming and Shi Jiayou

For more information, please visit https://www.routledge.com/China-Perspectives/book-series/CPH

Chinese Law of Personality Rights I

Theory and Practice

Edited by
Wang Liming and Shi Jiayou

Routledge
Taylor & Francis Group
LONDON AND NEW YORK

The publication of this book is sponsored by the B&R Book Program.

First published in English 2023
by Routledge
4 Park Square, Milton Park, Abingdon, Oxon OX14 4RN

and by Routledge
605 Third Avenue, New York, NY 10158

Routledge is an imprint of the Taylor & Francis Group, an informa business

English Version by permission of China Renmin University Press.

British Library Cataloguing-in-Publication Data
A catalogue record for this book is available from the British Library

Library of Congress Cataloging-in-Publication Data
A catalog record has been requested for this book

ISBN: 978-1-032-29128-4 (hbk)
ISBN: 978-1-032-29136-9 (pbk)
ISBN: 978-1-003-30016-8 (ebk)

DOI: 10.4324/9781003300168

Typeset in Times New Roman
by Deanta Global Solutions, Chennai, India

Contents

Contributors

Shi Jiayou is a researcher at the Research Center for Civil and Commercial Legal Sciences of Renmin University of China (RUC) and a professor and doctoral supervisor at the Law School of RUC, mainly engaged in research on civil law.

Sun Ruojun is a researcher at the Research Center for Civil and Commercial Law of Renmin University of China, a professor and doctoral supervisor at the School of Law of RUC, mainly engaged in the research of civil law and marriage and family law.

Wang Liming is a professor and doctoral supervisor at the Law School of Renmin University of China, vice president of the Chinese Law Society, president of the Chinese Civil Law Research Association and a researcher at the Research Center for Civil and Commercial Law of Renmin University of China.

Yang Lixin is a researcher at the Research Center for Civil and Commercial Law of Renmin University of China, and a professor and doctoral supervisor at the Law School of Renmin University of China, mainly engaged in research on civil law.

Zhang Xinbao is a researcher at the Research Center for Civil and Commercial Law of Renmin University of China, a professor and doctoral supervisor at the Law School of Renmin University of China, mainly engaged in the research on civil law.

Preface

The original intention of the Communist Party of China (CPC) in power and our goal in the new era is to seek happiness for the people and pursue rejuvenation for the nation. The report made by the 19th CPC National Congress proposed protecting people's personal rights, property rights and personality rights. Personality rights were first written into the report by the CPC National Congress, which is of far-reaching significance. This fully reflects the respect and protection of human rights by our Party and highlights the thought of people-centred development. Strengthening the protection of personality rights reflects the unremitting pursuit of people's all-round development and indicates an important measure to deliver a good and happy life to the people.

The personality right, related to the personal dignity of everyone, is a kind of basic civil right enjoyed by citizens. However, the system of personality rights is the latest among the sub-divisions of civil law. According to the textual research on the history of law, the systematic theory of personality rights appeared in Germany in the middle and late 19th century and then spread to France, Switzerland and other European countries. In the United States, on the other side of the ocean, Samuel D. Warren and Louis D. Brandeis had The Right to Privacy published in 1890, which laid the foundations for the American system of privacy protection. In terms of legislation, the Civil Code of Switzerland in 1907 can be regarded as the foundation for the modern legislation of personality rights. Since then, great progress has been made in theory as well as in the legislation and judicial practice of personality rights all over the world. The legislation of personality rights in China began with the General Principles of the Civil Law in 1986, in which Section 4 Personal Rights is specifically included in Chapter 5 Civil Rights. The General Principles of the Civil Law stipulates the right to life and health, name, portrait, reputation and honour, and recognises some of the legal persons' personality rights (such as name, reputation, etc.), which indicates a historic initiative of civil legislation in New China. The General Principles of the Civil Law, based on the reality of China's reform and opening-up, and on the drafters' profound reflection on historical events such as the Cultural Revolution that seriously infringed upon the people's right to personality, contains practical and forward-looking provisions on personality rights protection, which has laid a solid legislative foundation for personality rights protection in China. Since then, in accordance with the provisions of the General Principles of the Civil Law, the Supreme People's Court has drafted a number of judicial interpretations on the right to reputation, mental damage, personal damage, protection of the personality interests of the deceased and protection of property for personhood. People's courts at all levels have also made creative judgments on a large number of precedents on the protection of personality rights. This shows that the administration of justice has contributed much to the development of the personality rights system, which is also consistent with the experience in comparative law.

In the new era of building socialism with Chinese characteristics, China is facing transformed principal social contradictions. Thanks to the development since the reform and opening-up initiated 40 years ago, China, the second-largest economy in the world, has continuously met the basic needs of more than 1 billion people, and the people's living conditions have been greatly improved. Overall, China has become a moderately prosperous country and will be one in an all-round way in the future. In this context, people have more needs in their material and spiritual life, especially in a democracy, the rule of law, fairness, justice, security and the environment. When their basic needs are met, people will pursue a higher level of spiritual life and hope to live a more dignified and decent life. According to Maslow's hierarchy of needs, people have fewer demands for spiritual personality rights such as privacy when their basic material needs have not been met; they have increasingly stronger cultural and spiritual needs when their survival needs are met. Therefore, in terms of people's wellbeing, the report made by the 19th National Congress of the CPC proposed protecting the legitimate rights and interests of citizens and especially emphasised the protection of personality rights. This highlights the important value of the protection of personality rights as an important part of people's happy lives.

Personal dignity, whose protection is the essential value of the personality rights system, means everyone as a human deserves social status and the most basic respect from others and society. It is the value basis of specific personality rights, the provisions of which should be designed to protect the individual's personal dignity. Personal dignity is embodied in personal interests such as life, health, reputation and portrait that individuals enjoy. As society develops, the protection of personal life of peace, private space and independent decision-making of personal information is being strengthened, which demonstrates the concept of personal dignity. An important task in state affairs management in accordance with law is to protect personality rights and safeguard personal dignity. Therefore, it is necessary to add the compilation of personality rights to the civil code if we are to implement the guideline of protecting people's personality rights in the report made by the 19th CPC National Congress and in other documents and act in line with the provision stipulated in the constitution that the personal dignity of citizens is inviolable.

There is a sufficient scientific basis for the compilation of personality rights as a separate part of the civil code. The separate compilation of personality rights is in line with the latest development trend of the civil law and with the scientific and systematic nature of the civil code. The claim of the personality right, independent of the claim of infringement, does not take fault and damage as the elements. The personality right has a traditional defensive function and endows the individual with the right to make active use of it. The legislation of personality rights emphasises both the relief after infringement and the prevention of damage in advance; that is, the obligee is allowed to take reasonable measures to prevent infringement in advance. Therefore, the specific provisions of the concept, effectiveness, exercise elements and rights conflict of personality rights that are established in the separate part of the civil code help the accuracy and unity of the application of law and meet the challenges and needs posed to law in the development of the Internet, advanced technology and big data. Based on the summary of more than 30 years of experience in the implementation of the General Principles of the Civil Law, the compilation of personality rights as a separate part is also the product and innovation of China's civil law adapting to the new era.

The Law School of Renmin University of China has always paid attention to the integration of theoretical legal research and legal practice. It seeks to make a constructive and pragmatic response, based on China's reality and the beneficial experience from comparative law to the needs for China's rule of law practice. As far as the Law of Personality Rights is concerned, the Law School of Renmin University of China has been engaged in relevant research for a long time. Since the 1990s, it has published many monographs and teaching materials on the Law of Personality Rights and hundreds of high-level papers. In recent years, the Law School of Renmin University of China has also initiated courses on the Law of Personality Rights for undergraduates and postgraduates and summarised relevant judicial precedents. Thanks to long-term teaching and research, we established the Research Group on the Separate Legislation of Personality Rights in China's Civil Code in 2016. The research group has organised many discussions and investigations in Beijing, Suzhou, Wuhan, Guangzhou and other places. At the beginning of 2017, the research group submitted to the legislature the Proposal Draft by the Scholars on the Compilation of Personality Rights in the Civil Code of China, which serves as a reference for the legislature to compile the official draft of personality rights in the civil law. Some teachers at the Law School of Renmin University of China also participated in the provision drafting and demonstration of the official draft of personality rights in the civil code.

This book brings together the thoughts of our teachers on the legislation of personality rights as a separate part of the civil code in recent years, which also reflects, to a certain extent, the exploration by Chinese civil law scholars into the legislation of personality rights. Some of the thoughts, although not very mature, do reflect the subjective consciousness of Chinese scholars considering the context in China and committing to solving problems facing China. This subjective consciousness should run through not only the legislative design of personality rights but also the interpretation and application of personality rights in the future civil code.

Let's pool all wisdom to create a great code. The historical task to promote the compilation of the civil code falls on our generation. It is a great honour for each of us civil law scholars to participate in it personally. Let's work together to formulate a scientific civil code for the 21st century to solve practical problems facing China and to provide Chinese wisdom and solutions for the personality rights protection facing mankind in the new era.

Such is the preface!

Wang Liming

1 On the Reasons for the Separate Compilation of the Law of Personality Rights[1]

By Wang Liming

The prosperity of the personality rights system is the most important development in modern civil law. The protection of personality rights has generally been strengthened in China and beyond. The proposed compilation of personality rights as a separate part of the civil code in China aims to respond to scientific and technological progress as well as social development and comprehensively protect personal dignity. The compilation of personality rights as a separate part of the civil code helps improve China's civil law system and solve the difficulties in the norms of personality rights in civil law. With sufficient practical and value basis, the compilation of personality rights as a separate part of the civil law can solve the practical problems facing China in the protection of personality rights. The separate compilation of personality rights will enable China's civil code to truly become a scientific civil code that can stand out among the civil codes in the world for the 21st century.

1.1 The Separate Compilation of the Law of Personality Rights Aims to Effectively Respond to Scientific and Technological Progress as well as Social Development

1.1.1 The Development of Technology and the Internet Generates the Practical Problem of Personality Right Protection

In the 21st century, the era of the Internet, advanced technology and an information explosion, modern science and technology are value neutral[2] and the rapid development of science and technology is a double-edged sword. On the one hand, it has brought great benefits to mankind and transformed the way of human production and life. On the other hand, once abused, science and technology may damage personal privacy, personal information, human life and health and human well-being. With the development of biotechnology, for example, there are increasingly common problems such as surrogacy and DNA identification errors. In responding to the practical threat resulting from the development of modern science and technology to personal privacy and other personality rights, American scholar Froomkin proposed the concept of zero privacy. He argues that all kinds of high-tech and Internet inventions have brought great benefits

DOI: 10.4324/9781003300168-1

to humankind but have a common side effect, a great threat to the protection of privacy.[3] The Internet, satellite technology, biometric technology and monitoring technology, for example, are becoming tools for personal information collection. As unmanned aerial vehicle (UAV) technology develops, imaginary surveillance through a fly carrying a camera to other people's homes in science fiction has become a reality. All kinds of high-tech inventions have made it so that mankind has nowhere to hide. Therefore, the most severe challenge faced by the modern legal system is how to strengthen the protection of personality rights and interests such as privacy.[4]

The development of Internet technology has posed great challenges to the protection of personality rights, especially the right to privacy. In fact, when discussing the right to privacy in the early 20th Century, Samuel D. Warren and Louis Brandies warned, "Numerous mechanical devices threaten to make good the prediction that what is whispered in the closet shall be proclaimed from the housetops."[5] As the Internet thrives, various cyber manhunts are flooding, there is frequent hacking of private email, stealing of information, trafficking in personal information and eavesdropping on conversations, and it is very common to illegally disclose text messages and WeChat records through the Internet. Such acts contaminate cyberspace and infringe other people's personality rights. In the famous Internet rumour case of a woman with AIDS, for example, the perpetrator infringed the personality rights and interests of others by spreading rumours on the Internet. The freedom of Internet use makes it easy to infringe a person's right to personality through the Internet. In addition, the infinite and boundless nature of the Internet audience also infinitely amplifies the consequences of infringement on the right to personality. In other words, once released, information can be transmitted all over the world in an instant, multiplying the damage infinitely, which also makes recovery from the damage extremely difficult. Therefore, in the Internet age, the most severe challenge faced by the modern legal system is how to curb online infringement of personality rights.

The development of modern science and technology has brought us into a big data era and information society. The boom of big data highlights the economic value contained in personal information. Big data technology can be commercialised when fragmented personal information is integrated and massive information is analyzed and processed. The development of big data technology, however, also involves the protection of personality rights and interests, especially the protection of privacy and independent decision-making regarding personal information.[6] According to the *Survey on the Protection of the Rights and Interests of Chinese Internet Users* (2015), in the past year, Internet users suffered a total loss of about 80.5 billion yuan, 124 yuan per capita, due to personal information disclosure, spam, and fraud. About 45 million Internet users have sustained an economic loss of more than 1000 yuan. In fact, this has generated the practical problem of personal network information security. Therefore, it is necessary to standardise the collection and utilisation of personal information and balance the relationship between personality rights and interest protection and personal information utilisation, as well as between personal information protection and data capitalisation.

Human embryos, surrogacy, cosmetic surgery, organ transplantation, human organ donation and biological experiments generated by biotechnology have posed a threat to the protection of human subject status and personal dignity. There are more prominent concerns about humans being reduced from subjects to objects.[7] The development of artificial intelligence has also generated the need for the protection of personality rights. As artificial intelligence can talk and communicate with people like a human by imitating other people's voices and body movements, many artificial intelligence systems now have implanted some people's voices, expressions and body movements into their internal systems, but the imitation of others' voices without their permission may infringe on their personality rights. Besides, the illegal use of optical technology, voice control and face recognition technology makes the protection of voice and portrait increasingly important. For example, the development of optical technology promotes the improvement of camera technology as well as the resolution of pictures so that pictures taken at night are as clear as those taken in the daytime; this makes it easier to use a person's portrait. For another example, the significant development of facial recognition technology, retinal recognition and other technologies in China makes the confirmation of personal identity easier. These technologies, once abused, may pose a major threat to the protection of personality rights and interests. In particular, as 5G technology and artificial intelligence develop, face recognition and cloud computing make people in public places visible. According to an article in *The Economist*, face recognition technology can be used to identify a person simply and even his or her sexual preferences (homosexual or heterosexual) according to his or her facial image.[8] The visual accuracy of the current technology can be as high as 81%, even 91% in some places.[9]

At the beginning of this century, Yang Xiaokai, a famous foreign economist of Chinese origin, noted that China's advantage of backwardness might be transformed into a disadvantage if it only pays attention to technological imitation and ignores system construction.[10] Therefore, we cannot only focus on the application of technology or ignore its possible negative effects. In terms of Internet technology, for example, we have greatly benefited from the Internet but have yet to pay due attention to its negative effects. As advanced technology and the Internet develop, the most severe challenge facing the modern civil law system is the protection of personality rights in the Internet era. Therefore, civil law for the 21st century needs to keep pace with the times and make the protection of personality rights a priority.

1.1.2 The Development of the Market Economy and the Change of Business Model Poses a Challenge to Personality Right Protection

The development of the market economy and the change in the business model, such as online marketing, have profoundly changed our mode of consumption while posing a threat to personal information security and privacy protection.

The collection and utilisation of personal information have greatly promoted socio-economic development. According to statistics, the global big data market increased by 16.5% in 2016 and is expected to maintain a growth rate of about 15% for three years running.[11] Thanks to the rapid development of e-commerce, online shopping has become an essential part of the daily life of ordinary people. E-commerce has generated many new advertising modes. For example, businesses post tailored advertising according to consumers' specific consumption habits. This means that the analysis of consumers' consumption habits will inevitably involve the collection and utilisation of massive consumer information, which will also pose challenges to the protection of personal rights and interests such as personal privacy. According to the 2014 report on the network security of consumers' personal information released by the China Consumers' Association, there is an increase in the stealing and illegal use of consumers' personal information through computer networks. Consumers have suffered huge losses; about two-thirds of consumers have suffered personal information leaks.[12] As is shown in a report on research and analysis of network privacy security and network fraud (the first quarter of 2017) jointly released by the Tencent Centre for Social Research and Data Centre of the China Internet (DCCI), there is cross-border collection of personal information in mobile apps; 96.6% of Android apps and 69.3% of IOS apps have had improper access to users' mobile phone privacy, and 25.3% of Android apps have obtained users' rights to mobile phone privacy without their permission. These acts have become the main source of network fraud.[13] The infringement of personal privacy remains very easy, but the protection of rights is very difficult in cyberspace.

Due to the person data collection in the Internet, especially in the parts of e-commerce, express delivery, the invasion of privacy occurs more frequently and the protection of it sharpens. Some businesses collect or use personal information in violation of the regulation or agreement, which actually constitutes an infringement on the right to personal information. For example, when lending money to a borrower, some small online loan companies will require the borrower to provide his or her account number and password to apps often used in his or her daily life for them to log in and learn about the borrower's daily consumption and judge whether the borrower has the ability to repay the loan. The borrower has to agree to these conditions to obtain the loan. However, the personal privacy of the borrower will be completely exposed to the small loan company once it is allowed to log into the borrower's apps. If the small loan company does not pay attention to protecting the borrower's privacy or even maliciously uses and resells the information to others, the borrower will have no privacy, with his or her personal life completely exposed. Also, some network companies engage in illegal lending to college students and require borrowers, especially female college students, to provide them with nude photos and leave ID cards as a guarantee. Once the borrower cannot repay the loan on time, the small loan company will immediately publish the photos on the Internet.[14] Some online loan companies even maliciously sell or transfer nude photos of their borrowers, causing a very bad social impact. The establishment of a credit investigation system and blacklist system also pose challenges to the protection of personal information. Various ratings and blacklists established by enterprises can damage others' reputations and credit and affect their normal business activities due to inaccurate evaluation resulting from information distortion.

On top of that, the change to the modern business model also requires strengthening the protection of enterprise credit and goodwill. The infringement on goodwill through online rumours, for example, has become a common means of vicious competition.[15] In the Internet era, the development of the me-media enables every one of us to become a publisher and disseminator of information by means of Internet forums, blogs, microblogs, WeChat and so on. Everyone can evaluate people and things, and there is no lack of improper remarks and untruths in this massive evaluation. This has made it necessary to make special legal rules for such acts to define the actor's liability without curbing individual freedom so as to prevent infringement.

1.1.3 The Transformation of Social Forms have Highlighted the Significance of Personality Right Protection

China is experiencing a transformation from an agricultural society to an industrial and information society. In fact, this transformation also means a change from a familiar ties-based society to an estranged ties-based society, which is embodied in the network society, science and technology community, media circle, consumer society, risk society, business community and so on. These social changes are involved in so many aspects of social life that they no longer require negative and simple protection but a comprehensive standardisation of the right to personality in law. In traditional society, for example, there was no awareness of privacy, but in an estranged ties-based society, privacy protection, especially protection of the peace of private life and independent arrangements for our own affairs, is increasingly important. With the advent of the information society, the value of personal information protection and independent decision-making on personal information is becoming increasingly prominent.[16] Even a specific type of personality right involves more problems and is becoming increasingly more complex in modern society. Therefore, it is necessary to make more detailed rules for personality rights law. The right to the body stipulated in Article 110 of the General Rules of the Civil Law, for instance, may involve medical treatment, organ transplantation, human donation, biological experiments, genetic examination and identification, surrogacy, institutional imprisonment, spiritual evaluation and so on in modern society. All this makes it necessary to make more complex adjustments to more aspects of the personality right. This can only be better implemented and realised through the separate compilation of the personality rights in the civil code.

1.2 The Separate Compilation of the Law of Personality Rights Aims to Maintain Personal Dignity and Comprehensively Protect Personality Rights

1.2.1 The Separate Compilation of the Law of Personality Rights Aims to Maintain Personal Dignity

It is an important goal of the legal system to safeguard personal dignity. The 21st century has witnessed human well-being greatly improved thanks to the development of science and technology as well as globalisation. People will have a stronger demand for dignity when their basic material life is guaranteed. Thanks to the 30 years of development since the reform and opening up, China has become the second-largest economy in the world, and the living standards of the people have been greatly improved. In this context, we should give people not only a rich life but also a life with dignity. People yearn for a better and happy life not only with sufficient food and warm clothes but also a sense of security among the elderly and with housing and medical treatment. In particular, people aspire to live with dignity. Therefore, the comprehensive compilation of personality rights as a separate part of the civil code aims essentially to protect personality rights across the board and give people a dignified life.

The compilation of personality rights as a separate part of the civil code helps proclaim the concept and value of personal dignity protection. Legally, personal dignity, the core element of the protection of personality rights in civil law, can't be reduced.[17] The fundamental purpose of the legal system of personality rights is to protect personal dignity, which is reflected by specific personality rights. One's reputation, portrait and privacy, for instance, directly embody the value of personal dignity, so do even some new types of personality rights. Personal information, for example, digital images of individuals,[18] shows that individuals have an equal right to dispose of their personal information, thus highlighting their personal dignity. China's traditional parade through the street as a punishment to warn others actually serves as a kind of shock and awe by undermining human dignity. This practice still happens from time to time today and is often seen in the newspapers. It is also very common to disclose private information and fabricate all kinds of news to wantonly slander others on the Internet. Actually, some violations of personality rights, including insulting and slandering, damaging portraits, publicising privacy and divulging the personal information of others, have damaged people's personal dignity to varying degrees. Therefore, Article 109 of the General Rules of the Civil Law of China lays a value foundation for the compilation of the right to personality as a separate part of the civil code. It is stipulated in this article that the personal freedom and dignity of natural persons are protected by law. This article specifies the personal freedom and personal dignity from the macro perspective for the first time, which is arguably a response to the violations of personal dignity in reality. Besides, this provision declares that the legislative purpose and fundamental value of the personality rights system are to respect and protect personal freedom and dignity. This provision, with distinctive characteristics of the times, embodies the humanistic spirit and care in China's modern civil legislation.

1.2.2 The Separate Compilation of the Law of Personality Rights Aims to Comprehensively Protect Personality Rights

The compilation of the law of personality rights as a separate part of the civil code is about reserving certain space for the protection of various personality rights and interests by constructing the personality rights system. According to comparative law, an important development trend in the legislative and judicial practice of various countries is to strengthen the protection of personality rights. For example, there are more than ten articles on personality rights in the Civil Code of Quebec (1991) and the Civil Code of Romania (2009). In the Civil Code of Ethiopia, personality rights are specifically stipulated in 24 articles from Article 8 to Article 31 in Section 2 of Chapter 1. The New Civil Code of Brazil stipulates personality rights in 11 articles from Article 11 to Article 21 in Chapter 2 (Personality Rights), Part 1, subsection 1. The New Civil Code of the Republic of Peru specifically stipulates the right to personality in 16 articles from Article 3 to Article 18 in subsection 2 of Part 1 (Natural Persons) and specifies the right to a name from Article 19 to Article 32 in subsection 3, totalling 30 articles. The revised Civil Code of France (1970) stipulates Article 9 on privacy protection as a new article,[19] which means the protection of the right to privacy is stipulated as a basic principle. In addition to the civil code, there are increasingly more international conventions on the protection of personality rights, such as the *International Covenant on Civil and Political Rights*, which contains a large number of chapters stipulating specific personality rights. It can be seen that the latest legislative trend is to further strengthen the protection of personality rights.

In view of developing world trends and the realities in China, several provisions of the General Rules of the Civil Law in China are too principled and simple to comprehensively protect personality rights and interests. In addition, although the General Rules of the Civil Law completes the confirmation of the types of personality rights to a certain extent by listing various specific personality rights in Article 110, it does not specify the specific contents of personality rights, specifically the behavioural obligations that the obligor should undertake, the specific rules that should be followed to respect the right to personality, the coordination of the relationship between various interests in the exercising of rights, as well as rules for protecting infringed personality rights. Therefore, the General Rules of the Civil Law has not really completed the task of confirming personality rights. Every single rights of a person can be typed independently with all of them forming a whole system called personality right. For example, the right to privacy can be divided into the right to peace of life, freedom of communication, independent decision-making on private information and so on. The right to privacy stipulated in Article 110 of the General Rules of the Civil Law is far from being specific for its content is complex, and personality rights cannot be really confirmed. Therefore, it is necessary to expand this article on the specific provisions of the civil code and build a complete personality rights system on this basis.

In fact, the General Provisions of the Civil Law of China issued in 1986 stipulates personality rights among civil rights in nine articles in a separate section (Section 4 of Chapter 5), and the personality rights involved are even more detailed and comprehensive than those in the General Rules of the Civil Law. Since the General Principles of the Civil Law was promulgated more than 30 years ago, China has made great progress in the system of personality rights protection. However, it should be noted that the provisions in the General Principles of the Civil Law are simpler and need to be strengthened to better conform to the realities of the following aspects. First, the right to body, especially involving the donation of human organs, the disposal of the remains, human medical experiments, compulsory medical treatment of psychiatric patients, as well as frequent sexual harassment by means of words and actions, which is absent from the General Principles of the Civil Law, needs to be stipulated in the law. Second, the right to name should be strengthened. The right to name stipulated in the General Principles of the Civil Law of China is too simple to meet the growth of new types of cases in judicial practice. It is necessary to include the right to name in the civil code because China's legislature has made a special legislative interpretation on its protection, and the Supreme People's Court has also made relevant judicial interpretations on the change of name. In addition, it is necessary to stipulate legally the registration and transfer of the name of legal persons and non-legal persons, as well as the protection of the abbreviations of names. Third, in terms of the protection of the right to portrait, Article 100 of the General Principles of the Civil Law takes profitability as the element of infringement, which is not conducive to the protection of the interests of the portrait rightsholder. There are no provisions on the rational use of the portrait, the conflict between the right to portrait and the intellectual property right, as well as the image and voice other than the portrait. Fourth, the right to reputation is stipulated only in one article of the General Principles of the Civil Law, while the Supreme People's Court has made a large number of interpretations and replies to it, including the exercise of the right to reputation, the conflict between freedom of speech and the right to reputation, the protection of the reputation of the deceased and the criticism and supervision of state organs. In particular, the prevention of the spread of Internet rumours by legal means is of great importance in cyberspace. It should also be noted that the right to credit is not stipulated in either the General Principles of the Civil Law or the General Rules of the Civil Law. Some people believe that the right to credit falls under the right to reputation, and there is no need to stipulate it independently. However, the author believes that the right to credit differs from the right to reputation. For instance, a false credit evaluation made by a credit investigation institution will take a great toll on the financial activity and consumption of individuals, but it will not necessarily affect the victim's social status or naturally infringe on his right to reputation. Fifth, the right to personal information should be included. The General Principles of the Civil Law do not provide for the right to privacy or the right to personal information. The development trend of modern civil law is to strengthen the protection of the right to personal information. Therefore, it is necessary to stipulate the right to personal information in a separate part of the civil code. Sixth, the licensed use of personality rights and interests is not stipulated in the General Principles of the Civil Law. However, as its commercial use develops, more attention has been paid to the property interests of personality rights, which makes the commercial utilisation of personality rights and interests more important.[20] Therefore, it needs to be clearly stipulated in the civil code. These problems have not been solved in either the General Principles of the Civil Law or the General Rules of the Civil Law and need to be put in place through specific norms in the civil code. Only the compilation of personality rights as a separate part of the civil code can provide enough legislative space to solve the above problems.

It should also be noted that the open system of personality rights is constantly developing in the type and content of personality rights.[21] Therefore, personality rights should be stipulated legally as a separate part of civil law to reserve space for the development of this system. In particular, as the development of science and technology will continue to have an impact on the relationship between people and our complex modern society, people will have more demands for their own development and have stronger subjective consciousness. In this context, as personality rights will continue to evolve in type and content, it is necessary for the law to recognise new types of personality rights and interests,[22] and there may be more types of personality rights in the civil code in the future. The compilation of personality rights as a separate part of the civil code makes them more likely to be open to keeping pace with the times because, in a separate part of personality rights, judges can confirm new legal interests of personality rights by applying references and analogies to the provisions of existing personality rights.

1.3 The Separate Compilation of Personality Rights Aims to Improve the Civil Code System

The civil code system includes the substantive system, also known as the internal system,[23] which refers to the values and principles implemented in the law with internal unity, and the institutional system, also known as external systematics, which refers to the arrangement of chapters and basic systems. The separate compilation of personality rights fully shows the spirit and value of humanistic care in civil law. As Montesquieu noted, in the motherly eyes of civil law, every individual is the whole country.[24] The General Rules of the Civil Law of China, when stipulating civil rights, places the protection of personal freedom and dignity in Article 1 of Chapter 5. This is actually a formal declaration of personal dignity protection and grants personal dignity a basic position in the protection of various rights. This is of paramount significance as that embodies the fundamental purpose of the protection of all personal rights and property rights. The separate compilation of personality rights prior to all other parts conform with the legislative concept of the General Rules of the Civil Law and is a declaration to protect the value of human dignity. This also helps highlight the responsibility of the civil code to respect, care for and protect people, which is consistent with the spirit of humanistic care in the 21st century.

The compilation of personality rights as a separate part of the civil code highlights the essence of civil law as human law, which helps change the systematic defect of valuing objects over people in traditional civil law. In terms of the classical civil code system, both the mode of Institutiones and the mode of the Digest or Pandects focus on property relations. The provisions concerning humans are made from the perspective of a subject, focusing on solving the qualification and ability of the subject to participate in legal relations while ignoring the independent status of the personality right and the value of a human's status.[25] The right to personality is about confirming the rights that people enjoy as an inseparable part of themselves. Although the civil law burdens itself to protect personal rights and property rights, the civil law of traditional civil law jurisdictions only stipulates the property right (real right, creditor's right) and the right to identity (provisions on relatives and inheritance) in specific provisions, and ignores the personality right, the most important right in the personal rights. This shows that there is a major systematic defect of valuing objects over people in traditional civil law.[26] If the right of personality cannot be compiled as a separate part, the specific provisions are obviously dominated by property law, which will give people the impression that civil law is about property. Therefore, the personality right should be compiled as a separate part of the civil code and put before other parts. When stipulating specific personality rights, the civil code should also stipulate the general personality right to protect various personality rights and interests across the board and make up for the defect of the traditional civil code system. The compilation of personality rights as a separate part of the civil code will be an important highlight for the civil code of China and is also a historical opportunity we will encounter.

The compilation of personality rights as a separate part of the civil code also conforms to the adjustment object established in the General Rules of the Civil Law. It is stipulated in Article 2 of the General Rules of the Civil Law of China that civil law regulates the personal relationship and property relationship between natural persons, legal persons and unincorporated organisations, all as equal subjects. Compared with Article 2 of the General Principles of the Civil Law, this article puts the personal relationship before the property relationship, highlighting the importance of the former. This shows that the civil code of China requires further strengthening of the protection of personal rights and interests, which should be reflected in the specific provisions of the civil code. The provisions on personality rights in the General Rules of the Civil Law actually lay the foundation for the compilation of personality rights as a separate part of the civil code. On the one hand, the General Rules of the Civil Law highly generalises general and specific personality rights in Article 109 and Article 110 but doesn't stipulate their specific contents, which needs to be stipulated in the specific provisions of the civil code. On the other hand, the civil rights stipulated in the General Rules of the Civil Law actually need to be detailed in specific provisions and special laws. Real rights and creditor's rights, for example, are protected through specific provisions; the right to identity through marriage and family law and other investment rights are protected through special laws such as company law. However, there have been no detailed rules for the protection of personality rights so far, which makes it difficult to achieve the legislative purpose of the General Rules of the Civil Law.

The separate compilation of personality rights also aims to improve the system of personality rights itself. To be compiled as a separate part of the civil code, personality rights should have a perfect internal logical system composed of the general and specific provisions of personality rights, where detailed provisions are made on the protection, restriction and utilisation of personality rights. The system of personality rights helps protect and utilise personality rights, and based on these existing norms, more detailed provisions can be further developed through trial practice. Deficient norms of personality rights can hardly provide a unified normative basis for trial practice, develop a unified practical point of view, or then realise the self-development of personality right norms.

1.4 The Separate Compilation of the Law of Personality Rights Aims to Improve the Provisions of Personality Rights in the Civil Code

1.4.1 The Separate Compilation of the Law of Personality Rights Aims to Improve the Rules of Personality Rights in the General Rules of the Civil Law

The General Rules of the Civil Law attaches great importance to the protection of the right to personality. Although it contains few articles on the right to personality (including Articles 109, 110, 111 and 185), the General Rules of the Civil Law stipulates the right to personality before all other civil rights and declares the value of the protection of the right to personality—personal freedom and dignity—and establishes the general right to personality through this system to provide a legal basis for the protection of personality rights. In addition, the General Rules of the Civil Law specifically lists in Article 110 the right to life, the right to body, the right to health, the right to name, the right to personal image, the right to reputation, the right to honour, the right to privacy, the right to marital autonomy, as well as personality rights such as the right to name, the right to reputation and the right to honour enjoyed by legal persons and unincorporated organisations. The provisions of personality rights in the three articles need to be further detailed. Although only four articles are allocated for the provisions of personality right protection, the General Rules of the Civil Law puts them at the top of all civil rights, which highlights the significance of personality right protection. Other provisions of civil rights in the General Rules of the Civil Law will be improved in detail in the specific provisions of the civil code. Therefore, the provisions of the General Rules of the Civil Law actually lay a foundation for the independent compilation of personality rights.

First, the types of personality rights need to be further improved. The General Rules of the Civil Law specifically lists in Article 110 specific personality rights enjoyed by natural persons, legal persons and unincorporated organisations. Although this list is arguably comprehensive, still some are omitted, such as the right to credit. In many disputes involving credit in practice, some enterprises and institutions rate credit at will, conduct biased credit ratings, or disclose untrue personal information, which also infringes on the credit right of others to a certain extent.[27] Another example is that although it stipulates the rules for the protection of personal information and affirms it as a kind of personality interest, Article 111 of the General Rules of the Civil Law does not stipulate it as a specific personality right. According to comparative law, the right to personal information is stipulated by most countries. The stipulation of the right to personal information in the specific provisions of the civil code of China helps strengthen the protection of personal information.

Second, the personality right needs to be further detailed. As mentioned above, the General Rules of the Civil Law only lists specific personality rights but does not detail them. In fact, each specific personality right is very rich in content. The right to privacy, for example, can be further divided into the right to be alone, the right to privacy of personal life, freedom of communication, peace of private life, residential privacy and so on. The privacy of personal life can be further classified into physical privacy, family privacy, personal information privacy, health privacy, gene privacy and so on. Different types of privacy may differ in the content of rights and the constituent elements of infringement. Another example is whether the protection of the right to name can be extended to pen names, aliases, stage names and so on needs to be stipulated by law. Be it the personality right of natural persons or legal persons and unincorporated organisations, and be it specific personality rights or general personality rights, they contain rich and complex content. In this sense, only by formulating the law of personality rights can we fully confirm specific personality rights and reflect the need to exercise and protect privacy rights.

Third, the rules for the use and exercise of personality rights need to be further improved. As the economy and society develop, there is the increasingly common and obvious commercial utilisation of personality rights. Therefore, the part of personality rights in the civil code of China should provide for the utilization and exercise of personality rights by not only listing and commending various rights and functions but also specifying their exercise and performance effects. Although the right to personality cannot be transferred in principle, the obligee of some personality rights can authorize others to utilize their personality rights.[28] For instance, the right to portrait can be transferred, so can be the right to name of a legal person. In particular, when the right to personal information is stipulated in future personality rights law, the rules for utilising this right must also be stipulated. Article 110 of the General Rules of the Civil Law only lists specific personality rights enjoyed by the civil subject but does not stipulate the specific use of these rights and functions, which needs to be detailed in the separate personality rights in the civil code in the future.

Fourth, the restrictive rules for the personality right need to be stipulated. As a kind of specific right, the personality right can be limited to a certain extent for the purpose of maintaining the public interest. Except for the inherently unrestricted right to life and health, many personality rights should be limited in accordance with the law to varying degrees. For example, the rule that the right to privacy of public figures should be restricted was established in China's judicial practice a long time ago, but how it is restricted and to what extent it is restricted need to be detailed legally. The separate part of personality rights in the civil code should contain the restrictive rules of personality rights to better coordinate thc conflict between various rights.

Fifth, the obligor should undertake corresponding obligations. The legal rules of personality rights should confirm the rights of the obligee and stipulate the obligations of the obligor. For example, in terms of the protection of personal information, in addition to the provisions on the right to personal information enjoyed by individuals, the legislature should also provide for the obligations of information collectors to maintain the security of the information, especially the obligations of relevant subjects in personal information collection and utilisation. The General Rules of the Civil Law of China stipulate in Article 111 the obligations of relevant subjects to maintain information security, as well as the legal collection and use of personal information. But how to perform the obligation to maintain information security and how to define the legal collection and use of personal information are not detailed. This calls for specific stipulation in the separate personality rights of the civil code.

It is of great significance that in the chapter on civil rights, the General Rules of the Civil Law specifically stipulates personality rights prior to the right to property, which highlights the importance of personality rights. However, only a few articles for the provisions of personality rights are not enough to form a system for personality rights protection. If personality rights cannot be compiled independently in the civil code in the future, it will be difficult to comprehensively protect personality rights, and it will be impossible to show the progress in the protection of personality rights in China for decades.

1.4.2 Separate Provisions on Contract Cannot Solve the Utilisation of Personality Rights

The commercial utilisation of personality rights, as an important development trend of the system of personality rights, has emerged as a new field of personality right protection in civil law.[29] The commercial utilisation of personality rights cannot be adjusted completely through tort liability law just because that is usually realised through contract. Although the commercial utilisation of personality rights is mainly realised through contract, it does not mean that it can be completely stipulated in the contract law rather than be stipulated in the separate part of personality rights. The main reasons are as follows.

First, the commercial use of personality rights is not purely about the contract but also about the exercise of personality rights. Traditionally, personality rights only have the effect of negative defence and do not have the function of positive utilisation. In the civil law of traditional civil law countries, therefore, personality rights are mainly adjusted through tort law and the subject system. However, as the commercial utilisation of personality rights develops in practice, the positive utilisation of personality rights is also developing. In this case, personality rights have both the effect of negative defence and the function of positive utilisation. That entails a positive right confirmation model to standardise the right of personality. The commercial use of personality rights, an important embodiment of the exercise of personality rights, needs to be confirmed and adjusted by separate provisions of personality rights, rather than only through contract. In particular, it should be noted that in the case of the unauthorised commercial use of personality rights, it may be necessary to consider the amount of the proposed reasonable royalty and the amount of profit by the actor to determine the actor's liability for compensation.[30] All this is beyond contract law.

Second, there are a large number of special rules for the commercialisation of personality rights. If the commercialisation of personality rights involves property losses, the standard of reasonable royalty or profit return can be considered. According to the laws of most countries, the economic value of personality rights can be inherited.[31] This shows that the commercialisation of personality rights does involve some special rules. Apart from property damage compensation, the commercialisation of personality rights also involves the protection of personal dignity; that is, the law should establish relevant rules to prevent the excessive commercialisation of personality rights.[32] For example, for the contract for licensed use of personality rights, it can be considered to grant the obligee the right to terminate the contract for licensed use in special cases. However, that is not stipulated in the contract law that only provides for the general rules for contract termination.

Third, it is difficult for contract law to adjust the commercial utilisation of personality rights as this law can't make detailed rules for the commercial utilisation of personality rights. The contract law contains provisions on the general property transaction, which are applicable to all kinds of transaction relations. However, it can't make special provisions on the contract for the licensed use of personality rights. It should also be noted that it is difficult to include the contract for the licensed commercial use of personality rights in the named contract in the civil code being compiled or to make detailed provisions on it. Therefore, the commercial utilisation of personality rights can only be stipulated in the personality rights law.

Fourth, not all rules related to the contract need to be stipulated in the contract law, outside which special transaction rules should be made. In the property law of China, for example, the contract for the transfer of the right to land for contractual management and the contract for the transfer of the right to construction land use are all related to contracts, but it does not mean that they need to be stipulated in the contract law. A look at China's legislation shows that the rules for the commercial utilisation of the right to human dignity are also specifically made outside the contract law. In terms of the right to portrait, it is stipulated in the General Principles of the Civil Law that citizens enjoy the right to portrait and the portrait of citizens shall not be used for profit without their consent. This is actually the stipulation of the utilisation of the right to portrait. It can be seen that it also embodies China's existing legislative experience to separately provide for rules for the commercial utilisation of the right to personality beyond the contract law.

1.4.3 The Tort Liability Law Can't Protect Personality Rights

A review of the legislative experience from comparative law shows that from the 18th to 19th centuries, the personality right was mainly protected by tort law as it didn't become an independent right. The civil codes of some civil law countries all adopted the negative protection of personal rights such as the right to life, reputation and name and clarified the scope of listed rights and interests to be protected in the tort law although they had made provisions on these rights. In the Civil Code of Germany, the right to name is stipulated only in Article 12 in a positive way, and other personal interests are mainly protected through tort rules. For example, the Civil Code of Germany stipulates in Paragraph 1 of Article 823 the protection of several personality rights and interests such as the right to life, body, health and freedom. Moreover, it strictly restricts the liability for property damage that infringes on personality rights and interests; that is, the provisions on the liability for property damage are applicable only in the case of serious infringement on personality rights and interests and without other remedies.[33]

When stipulating the rights and interests protected by the tort law, the Tort Liability Law of China lists in Article 2 the various specific personality rights of civil subjects. Some scholars argue that the tort liability law can fully protect personality rights in the future, and there is no need to establish personality rights as an independent part of the civil code. The author believes that this view is not appropriate as the future tort liability law in the civil code stipulating the tort liability for infringing on the personality right can't comprehensively protect the personality right. On the one hand, the tort law, also a kind of relief law, focuses on the negative protection of personality rights and can't confirm personality rights in a positive way. Article 2 of the Tort Liability Law of China confirms personality rights to some degree as it stipulates a wide range of specific personality rights enjoyed by civil subjects, including the right to privacy. However, this article can't really confirm personality rights enjoyed by the obligee in a positive way because these personality rights are stipulated from the perspective of right protection, and it is impossible to stipulate their connotation and effectiveness. The specific provisions of the tort liability, for example, can protect the right to privacy, but they can't confirm the right to privacy enjoyed by the obligee, nor can they contain its specific content. On the other hand, it is difficult for the tort law to conform to the development of the personality rights system. As personality rights develop, the type and content of personality rights are becoming increasingly diversified. The specific personality rights enjoyed by natural persons and legal persons and their contents cannot be confirmed by the tort liability law but must be specified in the law of personality rights. Such complex types of rights make it hard and impossible for the tort liability law as a kind of relief law to stipulate them.

It should also be noted that the forms and consequences of the tort liability for infringement on personality rights have a certain particularity. For example, in Article 22 of the Tort Liability Law of China, the liability for mental damage is mainly applicable to the infringement on personal rights and interests, as well as personality rights. For another example, apology and reputation restoration are the main forms of responsibility for infringing on personality rights. The specific provisions of the tort liability in the civil code can contain the comprehensive forms of liability for infringement on civil rights and interests, but it is difficult for them to specify the forms of liability for infringement on personality rights. When the specific provisions of tort liability in the civil code can't be significantly different from those of the current tort liability law, it is even more necessary to provide for in detail various forms of liability for infringement on personality rights in the specific provisions of personality rights in the civil code. Moreover, rights protected by the tort law contain not only the personality right but also the real right (including ownership, usufructuary right and security interest), intellectual property and so on. However, the real right can no longer be specified in other laws, such as the real right law, because it is protected by the tort law. Similarly, intellectual property law cannot be compiled separately because intellectual property is protected by tort law. If all the specific rules of civil rights are contained in the specific provisions of tort liability, the adjustment of the tort liability law will be all-inclusive. This will disrupt the system of the specific provisions of tort liability and make the design and arrangement of rules very difficult.

1.5 The Separate Compilation of the Law of Personality Rights Aims to Directly Respond to Trial Practice

In responding to the increasing number of trials of personality rights in practice, the Supreme People's Court has issued a large number of judicial interpretations, which lays a practical foundation for the independent compilation of personality rights. However, adjudication rules are still in short supply for personality rights. Since the establishment of the system of personal rights in the General Principles of the Civil Law, the cases related to personality rights have been rapidly increasing every year, many of which involve reputation, portrait, privacy, name, personal credit, personal freedom and so on. In *China Judgments Online*, 124,400 civil judgment documents can be found using only "reputation" as the keyword. Although they don't have large subject matter, these cases, related to the basic rights of citizens, will cause significant repercussions in society due to great social attention if they are not handled well. For example, the "Case of infringing the reputation of the five heroes who sacrificed in the Battle of Langya Mountain" and the "Case of insulting Qiu Shaoyun, a hero who died in the War to Resist US Aggression and Aid Korea" in recent years have aroused widespread concern in society. One of the important reasons for the separate compilation of personality rights is that it may provide enough space for the rules of personality right judgment and lay a clear basis for the court to judge personality rights disputes.

As mentioned above, in terms of the general development trend, the right of personality is developing from negative protection through tort law to positive confirmation through the rules of personality rights. The enumeration of personality rights for their protection helps not only confirm the right of personality of citizens and legal persons and safeguard human dignity but also provides a clear judgment basis for judges. On the one hand, judges are allowed great discretion to protect the right of personality only through tort law. For example, although the infringement elements of different personality rights are different, there is no specific stipulation on how to judge whether they constitute infringement. If the case is entirely at the discretion of the judge, the judge will be given too much discretion. Therefore, the rules for the restriction on personality rights and for the conflict of rights should be solved through legislation. Bias will arise if the judge has complete discretion. As tort liability law contains very simple norms without the confirmation of the content, type and constituent elements of various personality rights, it is entirely at the discretion of the judge whether personality rights are infringed, which will inevitably lead to different judgments of the same case. This problem is reflected in the above judicial practice, where the concept of public figures was created to restrict their personality rights. Excessive discretion will also lead to different judgments of the same case due to inconsistent judgment standards and damage the unity of justice. Therefore, only the positive confirmation of rights can help develop clear and specific rules for the protection of personality rights so as to unify the rules for judgment and stabilise the law. On the other hand, it is not proper for China to protect the right of personality through precedents,[34] as China is a typical written-law-oriented country, where constitutional laws such as legislative law stipulate that the basic civil system should be established by legislation. Obviously, the right of personality, one of the most basic civil systems, is not suitable to be confirmed by precedent. Otherwise, the application of law may not be unified and even contradict itself. For example, because of imperfect provisions on the right of personality, some judges created some new rights (such as the right to kiss,[35] the right to sacrifice,[36] etc.) through precedents for some new cases of infringement on the right of personality, which has caused a lot of disputes. It should also be noted that legal precedents of scattered cases themselves cannot form a systematic personality right system as they can only be made for specific cases.

According to comparative law, the protection of the right of personality completely through tort law is closely related to the judicialisation of the constitutions in Western countries, where judges protect the right of personality by invoking the provisions of personality rights often enumerated in the constitution. This gives rise to the so-called judicialisation of the constitution.[37] But this approach is difficult to implement in our country as in accordance with the provisions of the current constitution, it is the Standing Committee of the National People's Congress, not the judge, that has the right to interpret the constitution. In this regard, it is stipulated in Article 4 of the Provisions on the Reference of Laws, Regulations and Other Normative Legal Documents in Judicial Documents issued by the Supreme People's Court that laws, legal interpretations, or judicial interpretations shall be referred to for civil judicial documents and that applicable administrative regulations, local regulations, autonomous regulations and separate regulations can be directly cited. As this article does not include the constitution in what can be cited in civil judgment documents, judges cannot directly invoke the constitution to judge civil cases. As a result, the constitution of China can't be directly used as the judgment basis for judges to deal with disputes over personality rights. This also requires us to improve the law of personality rights, especially the provisions on general personality rights. Only in this way can the principles of respecting and protecting human rights and safeguarding human dignity, established in the constitution, be transformed into the system of personality rights in civil law so as to provide a clear basis for judges to rule disputes over personality rights. In other words, personal dignity in the constitution must be specified by the civil code. Only the general provisions, concepts and rules in the civil code can serve as the basis for judgment, effectively regulate civil activities and address civil disputes.

1.6 The Separate Compilation of Personality Rights is Feasible

1.6.1 The Separate Compilation of Personality Rights is Derived from the Same Legislative Experience of the General Principles of the Civil Law

The Communist Party of China (CPC) and the government attached importance to the protection of political and property rights of individuals after the founding of the new China. However, affected by feudal traditions and extreme left thoughts, they once ignored the respect and protection of personality rights and human dignity, so the Cultural Revolution witnessed serious, unprecedented violations of personality rights and trampling on human dignity. Based on reflection on the atrocities of the Cultural Revolution, the General Principles of the Civil Law adopted in 1986 specifies personal rights and personality rights enjoyed by citizens in a special chapter of civil rights. This presented a milestone event on the road to human rights protection in China. The General Principles of the Civil Law stipulates the right of personality in parallel with the real right and creditor's right, which reflects that the first should be compiled independently from the other two. A separate section allocated to make more systematic and centralised provisions on the right of personality in the General Principles of the Civil Law has been proven to be a successful and advanced legislative experience. The separate formulation of the law of personality rights in the civil code embodies the inheritance and summary of the successful experience in the legislation of the General Principles of the Civil Law and reflects the continuity and stability of legislation. That is why we should compile the law of personality rights independently in the civil code. It should also be noted that this legislative style is actually a practice in China's legislation. In the Draft Civil Code in 2002, for example, the right of personality was compiled independently. This legislative experience should continue.

1.6.2 There is a Lot of Legislative Experience for Reference in the Separate Confirmation of Personality Rights in the Civil Code

Although China has not yet enacted an independent law of personality rights, the relevant legislation contains a large number of rules for personality rights protection. This can also provide a useful reference for the design of rules for personality rights in China's civil code. On the one hand, there are many provisions on the right of personality in China's current legislation. In terms of the protection of personal information, for example, the Law of Network Security specially stipulates network information security in Chapter 4, in which a large number of obligations of network operators are listed to protect personal information. Another example is the Decision on Strengthening the Protection of Network Information made in 2012 by the Standing Committee of the National People's Congress that also specifically stipulates the obligations of network information service providers and other subjects to protect personal information. Many of these rules can serve as an important reference for the design of rules for personal information protection in the inclusion of personality rights in China's civil code. On the other hand, the legislature also issued legislative interpretations on the protection of personality rights. In terms of the protection of the right to name, the Standing Committee of the National People's Congress issued the Interpretation of Paragraph 1 of Article 99 of the General Principles of the Civil Law of the People's Republic of China and of Article 22 of the Marriage Law of the People's Republic of China in 2014, which stipulate the rules for naming and exercising the right to name. This has laid a solid foundation for refining the rules for personality rights and the right to name in China's civil code.

1.6.3 There Is Sufficient Basis of Judicial Practice for the Separate Compilation of Personality Rights in the Civil Code

From the perspective of judicial interpretation, the Supreme People's Court has made a lot of replies and judicial interpretations to strengthen the protection of personality rights. For example, since its reply to the famous case of the Lotus Lady as early as 1988,[38] the Supreme People's Court has made a large number of letters and replies on the protection of personality rights.[39] It has also issued many judicial interpretations on the right to personality, including the Interpretation on Several Issues Concerning the Trial of Cases on the Right to Reputation in 1998, the Interpretation on Several Issues concerning the Determination of Liability for Mental Damage in Civil Tort in 2001 and the Interpretation on Several Issues Concerning the Applicable Law in the Trial of Cases on Compensation for Personal Damage in 2003. These highly targeted specific rules of judicial interpretation, which are also tested by practice to accommodate China's personality rights protection, can provide a useful reference for the provisions of personality rights in the civil code.

Apart from the above rules, the judicial practice has also provided vivid materials for the normative design of personality rights since China initiated reform and opening up in 1978. China's current legislation, for example, contains no provisions on public figures, but judicial practice has developed rules for them. In the reputation dispute case of *Fan Zhiyi v. Wenhui Xinmin United Press Group*,[40] Shanghai Jing'an District People's Court ruled that Fan Zhiyi lost the case and used the term "public figure" for the first time in the judgment, meaning that even if the plaintiff believes what the controversial report says of his suspected gambling by naming him is detrimental to his reputation, the plaintiff, as a public figure, should tolerate and understand the slight damage that may be caused by the media exercising legitimate public opinion.[41] In the case of *Yang Lijuan v. Infzm*, the court created in the second instance the "voluntary public figure" to identify Yang Lijuan and her mother as public figures, thus denying the infringement by Infzm.[42] Relevant judicial practice has established a lot of landmark rules for the protection of personality rights. For example, in the case of *Liu Xiang v. Life Style* for portrait right infringement,[43] the court established relevant rules for the commercial utilisation of personality rights. In the case of "disclosing the owner's address," the court clearly noted that where the citizen lives is personal information and is personal information that he or she is unwilling to disclose.[44] This establishes rules for the protection of residential privacy.

Besides, in recent years, China has made significant progress in the theoretical research in the law of personality rights, which provides theoretical support for the legislation and independent compilation of personality rights. It is important that we should systematically sum up China's existing experience in legislation and administration of justice as well as the theoretical research results of the law of personality rights and take them as the basis for the design of specific rules of personality rights in the civil code, so as to make the rules of personality rights more scientific and rational.

1.7 Conclusions

Promoting people's legal status is the most important development trend of modern civil law. The personality rights system is the latest legal field with the most distinctive characteristics of the times in civil law. The civil code being compiled in China should be fully based on the national conditions of modern China, learn from the experiences of comparative law, and leverage the advantage of backwardness of codification in modern China. It is expected to surpass the classical civil code in the comprehensive protection of personality rights through institutional innovation to become a model of civil code in the 21st century and fully highlight the value of humanistic care. This is not only the historical mission of the civil code of China but also China's contribution to the world's development of law.

Notes

1 Originally published in Law Review, 2017, issue 6.
2 Zhang Zhicheng: On the Jurisprudential Basis and Dual Structure of Science and Technology Law, Science Technology and Law, 2005, issue 3.
3 A. Michael Froomkin: Cyberspace and Privacy: A New Legal Paradigm? The Death of Privacy? 52 Stanford Literary Review, 2000, issue 1461.
4 Xu Ming: On the Privacy Crisis in the Era of Big Data and Response to it in the Tort Law, China Legal Science, 2017, issue 1.
5 "Numerous mechanical devices threaten to make good the prediction that 'what is whispered in the closet shall be proclaimed from the housetops'," Ellen Alderman and Caroline Kennedy, The Right to Privacy, Knopf, 1995, p. 323.

6 Xie Yuanyang: On the Value of Personal Information from the Perspective of Information Theory—Also a Review of the Mode of Privacy Protection, Tsinghua University Law Journal, 2015, issue 3.
7 Liu Yuan: The Future at the Crossroads: Research on Gene Patents, Science and Technology Management Research, 2015, issue 4.
8 Facial Technology: Keeping a Straight Face, The Economist, September 9–15, 2017, pp. 67–69.
9 Facial Technology: Keeping a Straight Face, The Economist, September 9–15, 2017, p. 67.
10 Tu Zipei: On Big Data, Zhongxin Publishing House, 2014, p. 337.
11 Wang Yichen: How Does Big Data Make Money, Writer's Digest, 13th edition, July 25, 2017.
12 Two Thirds of Consumers' Personal Information has been Leaked, Beijing Times, March 15, 2015.
13 Ma Shujuan: Apps' Cross-Border Access to Personal Information has Become the Main Source of Online Fraud, Legal Weekly, July 25, 2017.
14 Gai Qi: Weibo Era and Nude Loan: Reflections on the Symptoms of Media Culture in the Context of Mobile Internet, Exploration and Free Views, 2017, issue 2.
15 Fan Weiguo: Legal Governance of Internet Rumors: British Experience and the Path Taken by China, Academic Exchanges, 2015, issue 2.
16 Yang Fang: On the Theory and Review of the Right to Self-determination of Personal Information—Also on the Protected Object of the Personal Information Protection Law, Journal of Comparative Law, 2015, issue 6.
17 Shangguan Piliang: On Personal Dignity in the Constitution, Jiangsu Social Sciences, 2008, issue 2.
18 Zhang Lian, Han Xuzhi: On the Private Law Attribute of the Right to Personal Information in the Era of Big Data, Legal Forum, 2016, issue 3.
19 Roger Nerson, *La Protection de la Vie Privée en Droit Positif Français*, *Revue Internationale de Droit Comparé*, 1971, issue 4, pp. 740.
20 Wang Yegang: Discussion on the Legal Protection Mode of the Economic Journal of Comparative Law, 2014, issue 1.
21 Jean-Christophe Saint-Pau (dir.), *Droits de la Personnalité*, LexisNexis, 2013, p. 37.
22 Gao Shengping: On the Development of Personality Rights from the Perspective of Comparative Law—Taking the Right to Privacy in the United States as an Example, Studies in Law and Business, 2012, issue 1.
23 Wang Zejian: Legal Thinking and Examples of Civil Law, China University of Political Science and Law Press, 2001, p. 225.
24 Montesquieu: *De l'Esprit des Lois* (Volume II), translated by Zhang Yanshen, The Commercial Press, 1994, p. 190.
25 Chen Huabin: Issues on the Formulation of Civil Code of China, Science of Law—Journal of Northwest University of Political Science and Law, 2003, issue 5.
26 Sun Peng: Research on the Codification of Civil Law, Modern Law Science, 2001, issue 2.
27 Li Hongling: On Several Issues of the Right to Credit, Political Science and Law, 2006, issue 4.
28 Wang Yegang: Reflection on the Assignability of Economic Value in Personality Rights, Social Sciences in Guangdong, 2014, issue 2.
29 Gert Brüggemeier, Aurelia Colombi Ciacchi, Patrick O'Callaghan: Personality Rights in European Tort Law, Cambridge University Press, 2010, p. 572.
30 Zhu Yan: The Claim Basis of Profit Deprivation—Also on Article 20 of the *Tort Liability Law of the People's Republic of China*, Studies in Law and Business, 2011, issue 3.
31 Gert Brüggemeier, Aurelia Colombi Ciacchi, Patrick O'Callaghan: Personality Rights in European Tort Law, Cambridge University Press, 2010, p. 572.

32 Yao Hui: Several Issues on the Commercial Utilization of Personality Rights, Legal Forum, 2011, issue 6.

33 Gert Brüggemeier, Aurelia Colombi Ciacchi, Patrick O'Callaghan: Personality Rights in European Tort Law, Cambridge University Press, 2010, p. 8.

34 According to comparative law, some countries protect personality rights through precedents. In France, for example, the court has gradually incorporated personality rights and interests into the civil code and developed a huge case system of personality rights through the interpretation of "damage" in the general clause of fault liability in Article 1382 of the civil code. In Germany, the court has developed general personality rights through the interpretation of Article 1 on human dignity and Article 2 on the free development of personality of the Federal Basic Law. Since then, German law has established a system for the protection of personality rights through a series of landmark precedents such as the protection of the personality interests of the deceased.

35 *Tao Liping v. WU Xi Dispute over Compensation for Personal Injury in the Road Traffic Accident*, Judgment No. 832, Guanghan Minchuzi, Guanghan People's Court of Sichuan Province (2001).

36 *Cui Yan v. Cui Shufang's Infringement on the Right to Sacrifice*, No. 08923 (July 18, 2007), Feng minchuzi, Fengtai District People's Court of Beijing (2007), Selected Cases of the People's Court, Vol. 1, 2009, People's Court Press, 2009.

37 Franz Werro: Tort Law at the Beginning of the New Millennium, A Tribute to John G. Fleming's Legacy, 49 American Journal of Comparative Law 154.

38 Letter issued by the Supreme People's Court on the Reputation Right Protection of the Deceased by Law, No. 52, Min tazi [1988].

39 For example, in terms of the right to reputation only, the Supreme People's Court has issued a large quantity of letters and replies, such as the Answers to Several Questions on the Trial of the Right to Reputation Case in 1993, the Letter on the Dispute over the Right to Reputation among Xijing Hospital Affiliated to the Fourth Medical University of the Chinese People's Liberation Army, Fan Daiming and Yang Linhai in 1995, and the Reply that the Organ Liable for Compensation Should Eliminate the Impact and Restore the Reputation of the Victim in 1999, and the Reply to the Request for Instructions from Higher People's Court in Guangxi Province on the Reputation Infringement Case among Huang Shiguan and Huang Dexin v. Guangxi Legal Newspaper and Fan Baozhong in 2000.

40 Civil Judgment by Shanghai Jing'an District People's Court, No. 1776, Jingminyi (min) chuzi (2012).

41 See the first instance judgment of *Fan Zhiyi v Wenhui Xinmin United Press Group for Infringement on Reputation*, Shanghai Jing'an District People's Court (2002) Jingminyi (min) chuzi No. 1776.

42 See Judgment No. 3871, Guangzhou Zhongfaminyizhongzi by Guangzhou Intermediate People's Court of Guangdong Province (2008).

43 Judgment No. 8144, Yizhongminzhongzi, Beijing No. 1 Intermediate People's Court (2005).

44 See the civil judgment by Bao'an District People's Court of Shenzhen City, Guangdong Province (2010), No. 1034, Shen baofaminyichuzi.

2 Discussion on the Positive Rights Confirmation Mode of Personality Rights[1]

Also on the Relationship between the Law of Personality Rights and Tort Liability Law

By Wang Liming

One of the characteristics of the 21st century is valuing the protection of rights and privacy. The law of personality rights and tort liability law, intended to confirm and protect rights, have an increasingly prominent status and role as a new growth point of modern civil law. There are fierce disputes over how to deal with the relationship between the two laws in the process of formulating China's civil code. Whether the personality rights law should be compiled separately is a problem that must be solved prior to the formulation of the civil code. However, even if the personality right law is compiled as a separate part of the civil code, the relationship between the two laws still needs to be dealt with properly. It is related to the legislative style of the civil code, how to stipulate the personality right law and how to deal with the relationship between the two laws. This paper intends to provide insight into the relationship between the two laws from the perspective of the positive confirmation mode of personality rights.

2.1 The Change of Personality Rights from Negative Protection to Positive Confirmation is an Important Development Trend in Civil Law

The positive confirmation mode of personality rights means listing and confirming in legislation the personality interests that are universally recognised so as to protect personality rights. In contrast to this is the negative protection model, in which the law does not specify the specific form of personality rights, but the judge invokes the relevant provisions of tort law to provide relief for personality rights after the infringement of personality rights.

The early law mainly adopted the mode of negative protection. In the beginning, personal rights and interests such as the right to life, health and reputation were protected by tort law. Private crime in Roman law included infringement on personality and the human body. In Roman law, there was also a suit of infringement and humiliation; that is, insulting others in language could be punished as a private crime against personality.[2] This model has had a far-reaching impact on the legislation of Civil Law System countries.

DOI: 10.4324/9781003300168-2

In the 18th and 19th centuries, the right of personality was protected mainly through tort law as it had not yet developed an independent right. Although provisions were made on personality rights such as the right to life, reputation and name in the tort law, the civil codes of some civil law countries adopted a negative protection mode. This model can be further divided into the following two types: one is the French model, in which the right of personality was protected through the general provisions of tort law. In France's civil code, influenced by Roman law, tort was listed as a non-consensual debt in Volume III, Methods of Obtaining Property. The concepts of tort and quasi-tort replaced private crime and quasi-private crime in Roman law and the rights and interests such as the right to body and health were included in the tort law for protection. Article 1382, as set forth in the civil code of France, stipulated that any person who causes damage to another person due to his action shall be liable for compensation to that person. Although it didn't enumerate personality rights, this provision constituted a general provision on tort damage compensation. It could be widely applied to all kinds of violations, including infringement on personality rights and had a significant impact on later tort legislation. As Taribo, the drafter of France's civil code, said, "This article includes all types of damage and requires compensation for the damage."[3] As this article regulated violations of property rights and interests as well as infringement of personal rights and interests, theoretically, violations of personality rights could be regulated by this article.[4] This practice of France's civil code was followed by that of Belgium, Spain, Italy and other countries.[5] The second is the German model, in which German law did not protect rights and legal interests through the general provisions of tort law but defined rights and interests protected by tort law through enumeration. In Germany in the 19th century, when private law scholars focused on freedom of contract, property rights and property damage, civil law had not provided comprehensive relief for the protection of personality rights. In a German case in 1908, for example, the imperial court declared that civil law had yet to know what personality rights were.[6] In the civil code of Germany, the right to name was directly stipulated in Article 12 only and other personal interests were mainly protected through tort rules. Paragraph 1 of Article 823, as set forth in the civil code of Germany, for example, stipulated the protection of several personal rights and interests such as life, body, health and freedom. In addition, the civil code of Germany strictly restricted property compensation liability for infringement on personal rights and interests. In other words, this provision for property liability could be applied only in the case of serious infringement on personal rights and interests and without other remedies.[7] It can be seen that German law protected personality rights and interests mainly through the rules in tort law. However, the difference between the German model and the French model is that the German model gave a very limited list of specific personality rights and provided more specific guidance to judges.

These two models were drawn on by the laws of other countries in the European continent. The civil code of Austria, for example, stipulated the infringement on privacy (Article 1328), personal freedom (Article 1329) and reputation (Article 1330) in the tort law. In particular, Article 1328A on the protection of the rights in the private field was extended to cover physical health, honour, portrait and the personal interests of the deceased. The recent Draft Common Frame of Reference (DCFR) also protects the right of personality mainly through tort law. Overall, DCFR mainly regulates property relations, including contracting and other legal acts, contractual and non-contractual rights and obligations and related property rights, without specifications on the right of personality. DCFR, however, stipulates the infringement on personal dignity, freedom and privacy in the part of liability outside the contract (Article 6-2: 204).

From the beginning of the 20th century, the two world wars promoted the development of the human rights movement. In particular, the fascist atrocities during the Second World War prompted people to deeply reflect on the protection of human dignity and launch large-scale movements for human rights protection. This also showed that the legal protection of human dignity was valued as never before. In terms of legal technology, more and more countries began to move from the traditional negative protection mode to the positive confirmation mode. This was specifically seen in the following aspects: on the one hand, the expanded protection of human dignity in tort law promoted the development of personality rights. The right of personality, as a basic right in the constitution, mainly resists infringement by state power. The state has an obligation to regulate the right of personality in private law in order to prevent it from being infringed upon by the state or a third party.[8] Due to the prevalence of the concept of innate human rights and natural rights in Europe,[9] constitutionalised human dignity could be directly invoked in judgments. The constitutions of many countries confirmed the basic rights of citizens, such as the right to life, personal freedom, body and health, which are also an integral part of the personality right of civil law. In this process, personality rights were confirmed in private law. German courts, for example, agreed that rights recognised in the constitution could be applied to private law relations. As was stipulated in Articles 1 and 2 of the basic law formulated by Germany after the Second World War, human dignity shall not be infringed, the obligation of all state powers (organs) is to respect and protect human dignity and anyone has the right to freely develop his personality without infringing on the rights of others or violating the provisions of constitutional or public order and good customs. Based on these provisions, the general personality right was established in judicial decisions, which is called the framework right in the civil code of Germany.[10] On the other hand, the legislation of some countries began to develop from the negative protection of personality rights to the positive confirmation of rights. This transformation was largely influenced by international conventions on the protection of human rights. Nearly all European countries, for example, have acceded to the European Convention on Human Rights, which stipulates many personality rights and develops them through courts in each country and the European Court of Human Rights. Of course, European constitutions and the International Convention on Human Rights have built a relatively perfect system of personality rights protection, which will also reduce, to a certain extent, the provisions on personality rights in the civil code.

The development of personality rights is realised through the positive confirmation of rights by legislation from negative protection. In civil law countries, the 1950 European Declaration of Human Rights greatly promoted the reform of domestic laws in European countries.[11] The civil code of France, for example, protected the personality rights of individuals by the general provisions of tort law and the legal system of personality rights was developed through precedents. On July 17, 1970, France enacted a law by adding to the civil code of France, Article 9, that everyone has the right to respect his private life. In accordance with the court's jurisprudence, private life included address, portrait, voice, health status, emotional life, private communication and so on. However, the court's disclosure of the property information of public figures was not considered to infringe on their private life. On July 29, 1994, the civil code of France saw an addition to Article 16 that the law must guarantee the priority of humans by prohibiting infringement on human dignity and ensure that human beings are respected from the beginning of their life. Based on this article, French law stipulated that the paid disposal of human tissues and organs shall be prohibited. Therefore, the right of personality was given a higher position in civil law, which could better protect the beneficiaries. Specifically, when the object of a civil right is also protected by basic rights, said civil right will be more exclusive than other rights.[12] Some civil law countries and regions outside the EU adopt the positive right confirmation model to stipulate the personality rights system. In Quebec, Canada, for example, the 1975 Quebec Charter of Human Rights stipulated some personality rights and the 1994 Civil Code of Quebec also stipulated the system of personality rights in nearly 30 articles, all in Book 1 Persons, including respect for reputation and private life in Chapter 3, protection of the personal interests of the deceased in Chapter 4 and the right to name in Chapter 1 of subsection 3. The code positively affirmed personality rights. For example, Article 3, as set forth in the code, stipulated that everyone has the inalienable right of personality, such as the right to life, the sacred and inviolable right, security, the right to security and integrity and the right to name, reputation and privacy being respected. The right of personal integrity was stipulated in Article 10.

With regard to the protection of personality rights, the so-called pigeonhole model is adopted in Anglo-American law, in which various tort lawsuits are enumerated to protect personality rights. In particular, with a long history, the protection of the right to reputation and portrait in accordance with tort law has developed a complete system.[13]However, in American law, the right to privacy emerged in judicial confirmation. At first, it was just a right to be alone and maintain one's own personality in American law.[14] Later, the concept of the right to privacy continued to expand, covering most personality interests, including the right to reputation and portrait.[15] In the 1960s, American courts, especially the Federal Supreme Court, gradually elevated the right to privacy from a common law right to a constitutional right through judicial precedents, creating the constitutional right to privacy. This right is classified into basic rights enjoyed by citizens and serves as the basis for federal decrees and state unconstitutional review.[16] What was most prominent was that the court interpreted the right to privacy as the right of citizens to resist illegal police searches and refuse self-incrimination in accordance with the fourth and fifth amendments to the constitution.[17] In judicial practice, judges interpreted the constitutional amendment through judicial judgment, thus expanding the protection of the right to privacy. In 1965, for example, in the case of *Griswold v. Connecticut*, the right to privacy was formally established as a general constitutional right independent of the fourth and fifth amendments.[18] It is worth noting that some written laws in the United States also confirmed the protection of the right to privacy.

A look at the development of the two legal systems shows the right of personality experienced a shift from negative judicial protection to positive legislative confirmation. According to comparative law, the transformation of personality rights and interests in many countries started from substantive judicial protection and ended up with legal recognition[19] and a relatively independent legal system of personality rights. The development of personality rights also further expanded the protection of tort law.

2.2 The Transformation from Judicial Confirmation to Legislative Confirmation of Rights Shows the Spirit and Characteristics of Civil Law in the New Century

2.2.1 The Positive Confirmation of Personality Rights in the Civil Code Highlights the Value of Humanistic Care

The 21st century is witnessing the promotion of human dignity and value. As Montesquieu said, in the motherly eyes of civil law, each individual is the whole country.[20] As Japanese jurist Tanaka Kōtarō (たなかこうたろう) once said, the basic concept of private law is the person.[21] China's civil code should also fully reflect the spirit of modern humanistic care. The development of modern science and technology is posing challenges to the humanistic care of civil law. The development of biotechnology, for example, makes it possible to transplant and even clone human tissues and organs, which may become the adjustment object of jus rerum or the law of obligation. All this threatens the status of persons as subjects and human dignity. Therefore, this calls for emphasis that any act that damages human dignity as a basic principle of civil law is invalid in civil law. In the 21st century, when the value and concept of civil law are undergoing profound changes, the humanistic caring spirit of civil law should also be reflected in the implementation of the concept of autonomy in private law.

As far as the law of personality rights is concerned, the humanistic caring spirit of civil law is to strengthen the protection of personality rights and maintain personal dignity and freedom. In traditional civil law, the right of personality could not find its due position. There were simple provisions on the inherent rights of natural persons in the civil subject system or a brief mention of personality rights as a special form of protection objects in tort law. In short, there was no space for the right of personality in the specific provisions of civil law. In terms of the realities in China, the stipulation of the right of personality in the chapter on civil rights in the General Principles of the Civil Law reflected the legislators' care for persons after the Cultural Revolution and showed a strong spirit of humanistic care. This was also a correction of valuing objects over persons in the traditional civil law and would provide valuable experience for the independent compilation of personality rights in China's civil code in the future. For the first time, the General Principles of the Civil Law declared that everyone has the right of personality according to law, including the right to life, health, reputation, portrait, name and the right to claim compensation for mental damage after being injured. After the promulgation of the General Principles of the Civil Law, there were corresponding judicial decisions on the first case of personality rights dispute to appear in China. It was the pioneering provisions on personality rights in the General Principles of the Civil Law that promoted their burgeoning and growth across China today. Since then, people have gradually realised that hanging an iron card on someone, putting a high hat on someone's head, riding on someone's shoulders and shaving only half of the head are violations of the right to personality and are prohibited by law. Since then, academic discourse and public discussion have begun to tell the story of the right of personality. Judging from this, it is no exaggeration for us to call the General Principles of the Civil Law a declaration of civil rights and the protective talisman for personal rights. The promulgation of the General Principles of the Civil Law presents great progress in the cause of human rights protection in China.

The General Principles of the Civil Law provides centralised and operational specific rules and a legal basis for the judicial protection of personality rights, develops an effective mechanism for realising the cause of human rights and highlights the characteristics and spirit of humanistic care of the times in the civil code. The formulation and development of the personality rights law in China not only helps enhance the consciousness of the public to respect and protect personality rights but also strengthens the practical protection of various specific personality rights. It also presents the effective implementation of the article in the 2004 amendment to the constitution that the state respects and protects human rights. For quite a long time, some Chinese scholars have been used to discussing abstract human rights, but they have not reached a consensus on the connotation of human rights for the broad concept of human rights. As such, we should concretise human rights by implementing the protection of human rights through the specific legal system according to the national conditions of China. That is how the constitutional task to respect and protect human rights is realised. Therefore, we should rely on the experience in the legislative and judicial practice of the General Principles of the Civil Law to make provisions on specific personality rights such as the right to life, health, privacy and portrait in the independent personality right law, so as to highlight the value of humanistic care. As Atsushi Omura said, civil law should be made the true law for the living people and those who want to live better.[22]

2.2.2 The Positive Confirmation of Personality Rights in the Civil Code Conforms to the Characteristics of the 21st Century

The centralised provisions on the right of personality in the General Principles of the Civil Law have laid a solid foundation for positioning the right of personality in China's future civil code. China's civil code should reflect the characteristics of the 21st century. If the civil code of France is considered to be typical of an agricultural society in the 19th century and the civil code of Germany is representative of the civil code of an industrial society in the 20th century, China's civil code should become that of the 21st century. So, how does China's civil code reflect the characteristics of the 21st century?

The development of computer and Internet technology has brought humanity into the information explosion era. The Internet has profoundly changed human life and brought great convenience to human communication and information acquisition and dissemination. The Internet shortens the distance between people and consolidates the ties between our life and the Internet. In this context, the traditional civil law rules are bound to face opportunities and challenges in many aspects. First, the development of network technology has generated many types of rights and interests as never before. Personality interests such as voice and unique body movements, for example, are not of prominent importance in traditional technical conditions, but they have increasingly prominent economic value with the help of the Internet and can serve as an object of personality rights. Some scholars even believe that personality interests in the cyberspace environment can become a right.[23] Second, infringement is inclined to occur in cyberspace. The boundless Internet space and infinite audience allow infringing speech to spread all over the world instantly once it is published. Moreover, once the damage is caused, the rapid and extensive dissemination of information makes it difficult to restore the original state. This also requires considering the convenience and broad coverage of the network for personality right relief. Finally, the calculation of damages is special. As the Internet attracts a wide range of audiences that can release information at a low cost, once the infringement is caused, it may lead to serious consequences. In calculating the amount of damages to award, the seriousness of the consequences of the damage and the asymmetry between the cost and consequences of the tort should be considered.

In modern society, the respect and protection of personal rights have become an inevitable development trend of human civilisation. The rapid growth of technologies in modern network communication, computers, bioengineering and other advanced technologies has brought great benefits to humankind while changing the traditional way of production and life and increasing the risk of infringement on the rights of civil subjects. Many high-tech inventions, for example, have posed a great threat to the protection of personal privacy, so some scholars believe that zero privacy has become common.[24] Therefore, the civil codes of some countries specifically provide for the right to privacy.[25] For example, the development of biotechnology and the emergence of in-vitro fertilisation have transformed people's understanding of life. Although the growth of artificial organ manufacturing technology, stem cell research, cloning technology and tissue engineering has helped humankind to finally solve the problem of sourcing organs, the abovementioned science and technology have also posed new challenges to personality rights, such as the dignity of life, body and health. In modern society, as medicine develops, fertilised eggs and frozen embryos can become independent life entities. In some countries, such as Germany, the protection of life begins when the fertilised egg is formed. The German court holds that the fertilised egg, once formed, should be regarded as life for protection as it has the attribute of a life form and can develop into life. Relevant cases have also appeared in China's judicial practice. In the case of the Wuxi frozen embryo, the legal status of frozen embryos was proposed.[26] The presiding judge argued that the embryos left by dead couples were the only carrier of the family blood of both sides, carrying personality interests such as grief sustenance and spiritual and emotional comfort.[27] It calls for the legal response to whether frozen embryos can be protected by personality rights law, whether mental damage compensation can be applied when the embryos are damaged and whether the law of personality rights should allow paid surrogacy.

Since the 1980s, human society has gradually entered the information age, when personal information has gradually become an important social resource. It is increasingly necessary to provide legal protection for personal information. The development of digitisation and databases makes it very easy to collect and process information. As a result, more attention has been paid to the market value of information and there is also an increasing demand for the protection of the right to information and privacy. As a basic human right enjoyed by individuals, personal information has been given more attention by the law. In 1976, a German scholar Christoph Mallmann first advanced the personal right to self-determination (*rechts auf informationelle selbstbestimmung*), which was widely accepted by two legal systems, on the basis of the Steinmüller report.[28] In Europe, the popular view still treats personal information as an independent right.[29] The author, however, believes that personal information, with attributes of both property and person, still falls under personality right in essence and it is difficult to separate it from the right to privacy. The right to personal information should be stipulated as a basic or an important personality right in personality rights law. China has begun to provide protection for personal information in judicial practice.[30] Therefore, it is necessary to stipulate the right to personal information in the law of personality rights to balance the relationship between the utilisation and protection of personal information.

As such, in compiling the future civil code, we must strengthen the legislation of personality rights, confirm rights in a positive way and focus on the right to life and health, reputation, privacy and personal information, as well as the protection of personality interests in the Internet environment. This is also a response to challenges and demands facing civil legislation in modern society and a concrete embodiment of the spirit of the 21st century.

2.3 Positive Right Confirmation Has Irreplaceable Advantages over Negative Right Protection

As mentioned above, the negative protection mode adjusts the relationship among personality rights through rules in tort law, while the positive right confirmation mode confirms in a positive way systematic provisions on the personality rights and interests enjoyed by the subject. The two modes play their respective roles in the development of personality rights. Although it can promote the protection of personality rights by avoiding the excessive expansion of the actor's responsibility and interfering in the freedom of behaviour excessively, negative protection doesn't help establish a systematic legal system of personality rights. The right to privacy, for example, was not recognised in Britain for a long time. As early as 1932, the British scholar Winfield proposed that the British court should treat the infringement of privacy as a rights infringement, but it was not adopted.[31] British common law also established the concept of privacy through the infringement lawsuit on breach of confidence.[32] But, in fact, the protection of this new type of personality right could only rely on the existing causes of infringement due to the lack of legislative basis. Although this could solve problems for the time being, this partial protection could hardly form a scientific and perfect privacy protection system, so this practice was long criticised.[33] Therefore, British law later protected the right to privacy of personal information by enacting a separate law.[34]

Comparatively speaking, establishing a personality right system through positive right confirmation is cost-efficient in the legislation and administration of justice and can also avoid the inconsistency of judges' law-making. More importantly, the positive rights confirmation model can facilitate the quick establishment of a systematic framework of personality rights and provide a clear basis for judges to confirm and protect the new type of personality rights. Specifically, compared with the negative protection model, the positive right confirmation model has the following functions.

First, right confirmation maintains freedom. Freedom is a right exercised to the extent permitted by law. Therefore, the confirmation of a right itself is also a definition of freedom. The core and essence of rights depends on how to define freedom. The recognition of a certain right gives the obligee the freedom of action while delimiting the boundary of others' freedom of action. As far as the protection of personality rights is concerned, it is difficult for the negative protection model to maintain freedom of action as it can't accurately delineate the boundary between the obligee and the third party's freedom of action. Larenz believes that it is very difficult for the German court to determine the content of general personality rights through judicial confirmation, so infringement on general personality rights does not apply to the provisions of the civil law on tort.[35] It can be seen that the negative protection mode doesn't help to fully maintain individual freedom of action. Therefore, it is necessary to define the protection of personality rights through positive right confirmation if individual freedom of action is to be fully maintained.

Second, rights confirmation guides action. The positive confirmation of rights can establish an action model stipulating the action boundary and the legal consequences of violating relevant rules. When specific personality rights are confirmed through legislation, the obligee and the third party can know the boundary of their freedom of action and the rules for rights conflicts. German courts, for example, directly invoke the basic law to create the general personality right and expand the specific personality right, which has been criticised by some authoritative scholars.[36] In their view, such an approach exceeds the competence of the court and exacerbates the uncertainty of the law.[37] Some German scholars believe that general personality rights should not be used as a legal concept because it is universal and uncertain.

Third, positive right confirmation prevents infringement. For example, it is stipulated in Paragraph 1 of Article 99, as set forth in the General Principles of the Civil Law, that citizens enjoy the right of name—the right to decide, use and change their names in accordance with regulations and prohibit others from interfering, stealing and counterfeiting their names. This article stipulates the right of personality from the positive perspective and prohibits infringing actions from the negative perspective, which helps warn the public and prevent infringement. In addition, the positive confirmation of rights can clarify the boundaries of rights and allow judges to identify different types of personality rights. In particular, in the event of conflicts between rights, the positive mode of right confirmation can help judges clarify different rights so as to make correct judgments in accordance with accurate laws. Obviously, the conflict of rights cannot be solved only from the perspective of tort defence and it is extremely important to clearly stipulate the rank of rights in the law.

Fourth, positive rights confirmation prevents rights conflicts. It also helps clarify the exercise and restriction rules of personality rights to prevent conflict between various personality rights and between personality rights and other rights. As a specific civil right, the exercising of personality rights should be limited. The recognised principle of "public figures have no right to privacy," for example, shows that the right to privacy should be limited. Such a restriction on rights is difficult to achieve through negative protection and is not completely suitable for the judges' discretion. In China, the right to privacy is realised through judicial precedents because there is a lack of provisions on the protection and restriction of the right to privacy in the legislation.[38] It is inappropriate for judges to completely determine the rules for the protection of the right to privacy of public figures due to the complexity of the concept of public figures. The judge's complete discretion of the right of personality, which falls under the category of basic civil rights, also violates the principle that basic civil rights should be stipulated by law in accordance with the legislative law.

Fifth, positive rights confirmation restricts discretion. A look at the judicial practice of the negative protection mode finds it doesn't help limit the discretion of judges. In civil law countries, the French model covers the protection of various personality rights through only an abstract and general concept of damage. This can neither distinguish personality rights and interests nor accurately enumerate the type and content of rights, thus leaving huge discretion for judges. In the German model, although specific protected rights and interests are listed, it is difficult for the hollow Article 823 to accommodate the opening and developing system of personality rights and interests. Although the establishment of the general personality rights system can get rid of the shackles of the law, the system also confronts a problem facing the aforementioned French model.[39] The above two negative power confirmation modes have a common disadvantage of giving judges too much discretion. The same problem appears in Anglo-American law. In terms of the right to privacy in the United States, for example, after the concept of the right to privacy was formed in 1896, the federal court and state courts judged about 300 cases of the right to privacy in 1960. However, these cases differed in the content and constituent elements of infringement on the right to privacy, resulting in the instability of the application of the law. For this reason, Professor Prosser sorted out the privacy cases in detail and categorised them into four types of infringement on privacy. In 1960, he redefined the right to privacy and classified it into four types after summarising more than 200 precedents.[40] Nevertheless, he still complained that privacy essentially constituted a collective concept as there was no common ground among the four categories of privacy.[41] In China, the imperfect legislation of personality rights will inevitably give the judge too much discretion. This is reflected in the creation of "public figures" in the above judicial practice to restrict their personality rights. Besides, too much discretion will also lead to different judgments in the same case and inconsistent judgment standards, which will damage the unity of justice. Therefore, only the positive confirmation of rights can develop clear and specific rules for the protection of personality rights to unify the judgment rules and promote the stability of law.

Sixth, positive rights confirmation carries personality rights forward. The right of personality is both inherent and legal. The formation of the awareness of personality rights relies on the clear provisions in legislation and the conceptual enlightenment of the subject of rights. Only when people endowed with rights by law are fully aware of their legal rights and volunteer to exercise and protect these rights can such rights truly become the welfare of citizens. The systematic construction and confirmation of personality rights through independent personality rights law will help announce human dignity to the public and the bright prospect for personality development will guide citizens to have a heartfelt awareness of their personality rights and encourage them to claim their own personality rights and respect the personality rights of others with practical actions. Our goal is to help people form a new awareness and ideological level of personality rights protection. In fact, China has successful experience of this. The promulgation of the property law has played a vital role in promoting public awareness of property rights and protecting property rights.

In addition, positive rights confirmation also conforms with China's current mechanism of constitutional implementation. According to comparative law, the negative protection model is closely related to the judicialisation of the constitution because the judge will invoke the constitution to protect the right of personality enumerated in it. But this approach is difficult to implement in China. In accordance with the current constitution, it is the Standing Committee of the National People's Congress, not the judge, that has the right to interpret the constitution. In this regard, it is stipulated in Article 4 of the Provisions on the Reference of Laws, Regulations and Other Normative Legal Documents in Judicial Documents issued by the Supreme People's Court that civil judicial documents shall quote laws, legal, or judicial interpretations. Administrative regulations, local regulations, autonomous regulations and separate regulations that should be applicable can be directly quoted. This article does not include the constitution in what can be cited in civil judgment documents. Therefore, the constitution cannot be directly invoked by the judge as the basis to deal with personality rights disputes. This requires China to formulate and improve the personality rights law, especially provisions on the general personality rights, so as to provide a clear basis to judge personality rights disputes. In short, personal dignity in the constitution must be concretised through the civil code, in which specific concepts and rules can become the basic rules for judges to regulate civil activities and solve civil disputes.

2.4 Functional Distinctions Between the Law of Personality Rights and Tort Liability Law

Eighteen rights are listed for protection in Article 2 as set forth in the Tort Liability Law of China, of which nearly half are personality rights. That shows that great attention is paid to the protection of personality rights. The eight relief methods stipulated in Article 15 and the compensation for mental damage in Article 22 of this law can be applied to the relief of infringement on personality rights. The Tort Liability Law of China strengthens the protection of personality rights by expanding rights and interest protection and clarifying various forms of liability so as to consolidate the tie between the tort liability law and the law of personality rights. The positive rights confirmation mode is bound to generate the problem of how to coordinate the tie between tort liability law and the law of personality rights. But even so, the distinction between the two laws in legal function can't be ignored.

The relationship between the tort liability law and the law of personality rights is essentially that between rights law and relief law. Actually, the rules of personality rights include confirmation, protection, utilisation and conflict coordination of rights. The tort law cannot fully cover the above rules, although it may also involve them. Therefore, these rules should be stipulated in the personality rights law. As personality rights law has a different legal function than tort law, the latter can't completely replace the former.

First, the confirmation of the type of personality rights should be completed by the personality rights law. The tort law, a relief law, is not designed to confirm rights positively but to prevent and compensate damages. The personality rights law, a law of rights, is designed, like the property law, to confirm the right, that is, to provide a legal basis for the relief through tort law by specifying all kinds of personality rights and their effectiveness. More importantly, because a variety of new personality rights and interests continue to appear with the rapid development of society, specific rules for the protection and utilisation of personality rights need to be clearly stipulated by law. This important task is obviously too heavy for the tort law that is, in essence, a relief law.

Second, the specific content of personality rights should be stipulated by the personality rights law. Each personality right has its own diverse functions. Article

2 of the Tort Liability Law of China provides declarative protection for eight personality rights, but it doesn't and can't further regulate the specific functions of various rights. The right to portrait, for example, has the function of image reproduction, use and transfer. The right to privacy can be further concretised into the right to be alone, the rights to the privacy of one's personal life, freedom of communication, peace of private life, residential privacy and so on.[42] The privacy of personal life can be further classified into physical privacy, personal information privacy, genetic privacy, health privacy, family privacy and so on. Different types of privacy have different contents of rights and different constitutive elements of infringement. Both the general and specific personality rights of citizens and legal persons have rich and complex content. In this sense, only by formulating the personality rights law can we fully confirm the specific personality rights and fully respond to the exercise and protection of private rights.

Third, the rules for the utilisation and exercise of personality rights should be stipulated in the personality rights law. However, in modern society, we have seen the rapid development of the personality rights system and continuous expansion of the type and connotation of personality rights. With the development of Internet technology, for example, the economic utility of personal information is becoming increasingly prominent and there is more infringement on personal information, which also promotes the development of the system of personal information rights. Both the denotation and connotation of personality rights are expanding. The commercial use of personality rights, for example, makes some personality rights no longer just negative defensive rights but a right that can be used in a positive way to some extent.[43] The law should not only list and commend rights but also specify the exercise and effect of such rights. Although the right of personality cannot be transferred in principle, the obligee can authorise others to make use of his personal rights. The right to the use of portrait and right to name of a legal person, for example, can be transferred. In particular, if the personal information right is stipulated in the future personality rights law, the rules for the use of personal information must also be stipulated. It should also be noted that although most personality rights are inherent, such as the right to life and health, some personality rights, such as the right to reputation, can only be obtained through the implementation of some acts. The law should also provide specific rules for exercising and using personality rights, which are obviously not included in tort law.

Fourth, the rules for the conflict between personality rights and other rights should be stipulated by the law of personality rights. The right of personality, when exercised, often conflicts with other rights, including the conflicts between the right to personality and property, between the right to privacy and press freedom and between the right to reputation and public opinion supervision. The right of personality, when exercised, may also conflict with public rights. On top of that, there may be conflicts between specific personality rights, so the rules for addressing conflicts need to be established in the law of personality rights. The rules for the exercise and conflict of rights can't be established in the law of tort. In addition, it is necessary to restrict the right of personality to some extent in law to safeguard the public interest and social order. These restrictions (such as the restriction on the right of personality of public figures, the relationship between the right of personality and freedom of speech, etc.) can hardly be stipulated in the tort law, only in the law of personality rights.

In addition, there are insurmountable technical obstacles in the legislation for the law of tort to absorb the law of personality rights. The passive protection in the form of ex post facto relief through the law of tort can't suffice to fully protect the right of personality. The Tort Liability Law of China, with distinct Chinese characteristics, has its system based not on the infringed object but the central axis of the principle of imputation. The tort liability law is built on the imputation system of fault liability, fault presumption liability and strict liability. Under this system, the general rules of fault liability are put in the general provisions of the tort liability law and the special imputation principles beyond the fault principle, such as strict liability and fault presumption liability, are stipulated in the specific provisions. The right of personality, if put in tort law, is mainly applicable to fault liability. Therefore, it is difficult to include the infringement on personality rights as a special infringement in tort law. In the tort liability law, Paragraph 1 of Article 6 can apply to the infringement of personality rights and it is unnecessary to list the liability for infringement on personality rights in specific provisions. Such enumeration will lead to a system conflict. The infringement of personal rights can't be specifically included in the general provisions of tort law because the general provisions mainly stipulate the constituent elements and defences of tort liability and are not constructed according to the object of infringement. Therefore, the tort law can't fully confirm the protection system of personality rights, although it can provide certain protection for personality rights.

The above analysis shows that although the implementation of the tort liability law strengthens the protection of personality rights, it should not affect the formulation of the law of personality rights. On the contrary, a separate law of personality rights should be compiled to recognise and protect personality rights together with the law of tort.

2.5 Functional Synergies Between the Law of Personality Rights and Tort Liability Law

The separate compilation of the law of personality rights does not mean completely separating it from the law of tort. Positive rights confirmation is the inevitable requirement of the law of personality rights as the law of rights. Of course, the separate compilation of the law of personality rights will not weaken the function of the law of tort. On the contrary, it, if properly designed in the system and content, can complement the law of tort. Intellectual property law, for example, has become a relatively independent legal department since its separation from traditional civil law. However, when infringed upon, the intellectual property right calls for specific judgment rules from the law of tort, which also shows the organic coordination between intellectual property law and tort law. Such experience is also applicable to the legislation of personality rights. In other words, we can confirm the personality right through the separate compilation of the law of personality rights and then protect it through the specific rules in the tort law. In this way, a benign interaction between the two is realised.

What requires further discussion is whether positive rights confirmation will weaken the protection of personality rights in terms of legal application. There is a view that the provisions for personality rights are still incomplete even if the positive confirmation mode is adopted because such provisions do not clearly stipulate the legal consequences of violating the right of personality. Therefore, it is better to include all of them into the law of tort to complete this law and protect personality rights carefully. This view is an important reason against the compilation of the law of personality rights as a separate part of the civil code. The author thinks that this view, although not unreasonable, is not feasible in practice because the law of tort, mainly the law of relief, cannot positively confirm the right of personality or design relief provisions for each personality right and personality interest to form a complete law. Personality rights, complicated and open, cannot be fully realised in the law of tort. The positive confirmation of personality rights through the law of personality rights, however, can provide a basis for the protection of personality rights in the law of tort. This will not weaken but strengthen the protection of personality rights by serving as a rights declaration. It should also be noted that the law of personality rights, as both a judgment norm and a code of conduct, can guide acts. The positive confirmation of personality rights, therefore, not only helps the protection of personality rights but also guides the actions of civil subjects, such as respect for life, the obligation to rescue life, respect for the privacy and freedom of others and so on. Even the common law has also begun to confirm the right of personality through written laws, such as the Privacy Act issued by the United States and the Personal Data Protection Act promulgated by the United Kingdom. In particular, some written laws in the United States also confirm the protection of the right to privacy. The United States Congress has enacted six laws to protect the privacy of personal information. Some states in the United States have also formulated corresponding laws. At present, at least ten states in the United States have defined the protection of privacy in their constitutions to strengthen the protection of privacy.[44]

In particular, it should be noted that positive rights confirmation helps the judicial function of tort law work fully and effectively. On the one hand, the provisions of the law of personality rights and the law of tort can jointly constitute complete legal provisions for the protection of personality rights. Complete legal provisions usually refer to those with both constituent elements and legal effects. Legal norms, as a major premise, should generally include constituent elements and legal effects. Complete provisions, however, cannot be formed only through law or isolated provisions. Actually, the combination of incomplete legal provisions consistent with the factual elements can lead to a judgment conclusion. This model is also a type of syllogism reasoning.[45] In terms of the protection of personality rights, the positive confirmation of personality rights through the law of personality rights and the establishment of relevant protection rules through the law of tort can jointly form the basis of a judgment. The law of personality rights, for example, stipulates the right to portrait and its rules for utilisation. If an actor infringes the right to portrait, the judge can order the infringer to bear tort liability by invoking the relevant rules of the law of personality rights and the tort liability rules of the tort law to form complete provisions. On the other hand, logically, the original right occurs before the relief right caused by the infringement on the original right. In the Anglo-American law system, which advocates relief prior to rights, the judge can create precedents to directly provide relief and doesn't depend on the confirmation of substantive rights in the statutory law. In the civil law system, different from the Anglo-American law system, the judge adjudicates in accordance with the statutory law and only when there is a statutory law first can relief be given. In terms of property law, for example, all kinds of property rights stipulated in the property law, of course, are protected by the law of tort. However, it cannot be considered that provisions related to property rights and those protected by the law of tort must be combined.

It should also be noted that the protection of the real right is not limited to the claim of infringement. The claim of real right, as a function of the real right itself, is more beneficial to the real right protection in some cases; so is the protection of the law of personality rights. The rules for personality rights confirmation and protection should not be stipulated in the tort law. Instead, positive confirmation through the law of personality rights should provide the basis for the protection of the tort law. The positive confirmation of personality rights not only provides an explicit and sufficient basis for judicial judgment to confirm and protect personality rights but also helps the tort law act as a referee. According to statistics, 110,000 cases of personality rights were announced by courts across the country from January 2014 to June 2015 alone,[46] many of which were disputes over new types of personality rights and interests. The rights and interests of tort law are listed for protection in Article 2 of the Tort Liability Law of China in an open way and expressed in the same method as civil rights and interests. However, as new personality interests continue to emerge, the types of personality rights in litigation are becoming increasingly complex in practice. In many cases, it is often hard for the judge to find enough judgment bases due to the generality and abstraction of Article 2 of the Tort Liability Law of China, even if the judge has enough value consensus to protect a new type of personality interest. On the other hand, this vague article also can't guide the behaviours of the civil subject clearly, which has affected the protection of personality rights and the authority of judicial judgment itself. Therefore, it is necessary to coordinate the functions of the law of personality rights and the tort law in order to protect personality rights to the greatest extent.

Specifically, following the confirmation of personality rights, the law of personality rights also needs the cooperation of the tort liability law in the following aspects so as to complement and interact with each other.

First, when a personality right is confirmed, it is necessary for the tort law to determine the remedy for the infringement on said personality right. The law of personality rights should specify the specific connotation, exercise rules and special constituent elements of tort liability of the personality right, while the tort law should stipulate the general constituent elements of infringement on the personality right and the responsibility for the infringement on the personality right. As far as the composition of infringement is concerned, thc provisions of the right of personality help specify the object protected by the tort law. In fact, the tort law stipulates the general provisions of tort due to a fault in Paragraph 1 of Article 6. The general provisions can be integrated with those determined by the law of rights to form complete provisions. In the case of the infringement of the right to name, for example, Article 99, as set forth in the General Principles of the Civil Law and Paragraph 1 of Article 6, as set forth in the Tort Liability Law of China, constitute a complete set of provisions on infringing the right to name.

Second, the law of personality rights can make positive confirmation of the right of personality and list prohibitive provisions from the negative side. Prohibitive provisions, as the mandatory provisions of the law, can determine the level of the civil subject's freedom of action. Prohibitive provisions should not be listed in the tort law but follow the provisions of listed rights. They are legal provisions that order the litigant not to conduct a certain act, which, in nature, are mandatory norms that prohibit the litigant from conducting a certain act.[47] Prohibitive provisions, which are different from right relief rules in tort law, essentially fall under the code of conduct to specify the exercise of rights, so they should not be included in the tort law. In the field of personality rights, prohibitive provisions are usually stipulated by the law of personality rights. When enumerating personality rights, the General Principlcs of the Civil Law also lists some prohibitive norms that can be combined with the provisions of tort liability law to constitute elements of infringement on personality rights. For example, as stipulated in Article 101 set forth in the General Principles of the Civil Law, citizens and legal persons enjoy the right to reputation; citizens' personal dignity is protected by law; the use of insult and slander to damage the reputation of citizens and legal persons is prohibited. The use of insult and slander to damage the reputation of citizens and legal persons constitutes an important element of infringement on the right to reputation. This can be integrated with the general provisions on fault liability in Paragraph 1 of Article 6 set forth in the Tort Liability Law of China to form a set of complete provisions for the protection of the right to reputation.

Third, the rules for the conflict of rights in the law of personality rights can be combined with the provisions of the tort law. In practice, for example, there are often conflicts between the personality right and the right to freedom of speech between the personality right and supervision by public opinion and between the right to portrait and copyright. In this case, which right should be given priority really needs to be dealt with in accordance with the rules for the conflict of rights. The rules for the conflict of rights help determine the duty undertaken by the actor so as to define the constitutive elements of fault in fault tort liability. News reports, for example, may disclose others' privacy and portraits, but they are not generally considered to have infringed personality rights. This actually determines the boundary of the personality right. It can be seen that, in a sense, rules for the conflict of rights are essentially those to delimit the boundaries of personality rights. These rules, falling under norms for personality rights, should be stipulated in the law of personality rights. In the case of a conflict of rights, however, the rules of tort law should be invoked to judge whether the relevant act constitutes infringement and what kind of tort liability should be borne. Rules for the conflict of rights in the law of personality rights can provide the basis for the identification of tort liability.

Fourth, provisions on the commercial utilisation of personality rights in the law of personality rights can complement the rules of property damage compensation in the tort law to form a complete set of legal provisions. The right of personality was initially a negative defensive right, for which the tort law was enough to provide full protection. However, with the development of the personality rights system, especially the commercial utilisation of personality rights, the active use of some personality rights is constantly developing. The commercial utilisation of personality rights in nature results from the expansion of the active function of personality rights being used. Therefore, rules on the commercial utilisation of personality rights, falling under the positive confirmation norms of personality rights, should be stipulated in the law of personality rights. The actor's commercial use of the personality right and interest of others without permission, however, constitutes a tort and the specific liability determination and assumption should be subject to the rules of tort law. In terms of the right to portrait, for example, it is stipulated in Paragraph 2 of Article 99, as set forth in the General Principles of the Civil Law, that legal persons, individual businesses and individual partnerships enjoy the right to name and enterprises as legal persons, individual businesses and individual partnerships have the right to use and transfer their own names according to law. This article actually stipulates the rules for the active use of the right to name. When the right to name is infringed, however, the tort liability of the perpetrator should be judged in accordance with the rules of the tort law. The tort liability law specifies the tort liability for infringing on personal rights in Article 20. It can be seen that China's current legislation has adopted a combination of the positive confirmation of personality rights with the protection through tort law.

Fifth, the law of personality rights can refine the specific tort liability in the case of infringement on personality rights. The Tort Liability Law of China stipulates the ways of bearing tort liability in Articles 15 and 22, which are only applicable to the forms of liabilities of personality rights. The relevant provisions on apology, restoration of reputation and compensation for mental damage are overgeneralised, which is not applicable to specific forms of liability. As such, it is necessary to make detailed provisions on the relevant liabilities in the law of personality rights. In recent years, as misconduct increases in the infringement on the right of personality through the Internet, some countries have made special provisions on the protection of personality rights, such as issuing prohibitions, to prevent the consequences of damage from expanding.[48] Before the final judgment is made, the judge may also make a pre-ruling, ordering the perpetrator to stop publication, prohibiting distribution and circulation, or ordering the whole or part of the publication to be banned.[49] In China, it is necessary to further refine measures for personality rights protection in the personality rights law. German law also often adopts injunctions to regulate infringement on personality rights.[50] The laws of some countries generally grant the victim the right to delete, request the withdrawal of the declaration and so on. This is especially manifested in the infringement on others' reputations by means of speech.[51] In China, it is necessary to further refine measures for personality rights protection in the law of personality rights. In terms of mental damage, for example, Article 22 set forth in the Tort Liability Law of China cannot provide specific rules for the complex identification of compensation for mental damage as it is overgeneralised. The judicial interpretation of mental damage compensation issued by the Supreme People's Court in 2001 can serve as a basis for China to summarise the existing judicial experience and make comprehensive provisions on the tort liability for mental damage compensation for infringement of personality rights.

To sum up, the existence of the negative protection of personality rights in tort law cannot deny the necessity of the law of personality rights as an independent part of civil law. In comparison, the positive rights confirmation model has more obvious advantages in rights confirmation. Actually, both positive confirmation and negative protection involve the recognition and protection of rights. If a right is not positively recognised by the law, it is difficult for tort law to protect it. At the beginning of the specific provisions of the civil code, a separate part is allocated to specify the personality right. This will help refine the system of civil rights, highlight the protection of personality interests, promote the development of human rights and the legal system in China and reflect the achievements made by China's civil law scholars in exploring the improvement of the civil law system under the new social conditions.

Notes

1 Originally published in The Jurist, 2016, Issue 2.
2 Chen Chaobi: Principles of Roman Law, Law Press, 2006, p. 138.
3 Jean Limpens: International Encyclopedia of Comparative Law, Vol. 4, Torts, Chapter 2, Liability for One's Own Act, J.C.B. Mohr (Paul Siebeck, Tübingen), 1975, p. 14.
4 Gert Brüggemeier, Aurelia Colombi Ciacchi, Patrick O'Callaghan: Personality Rights in European Tort Law, Cambridge University Press, 2010, pp. 10–15.
5 Gert Brüggemeier, Aurelia Colombi Ciacchi, Patrick O'Callaghan: Personality Rights in European Tort Law, Cambridge University Press, 2010, p. 8.
6 RG, 07.11.1908, RGZ 69, 401, 403 Nietzsche letters.
7 Gert Brüggemeier, Aurelia Colombi Ciacchi, Patrick O'Callaghan: Personality Rights in European Tort Law, Cambridge University Press, 2010, p. 8.

8 Wang Zejian: On the Law of Personality Rights, Sanmin Book Co. Ltd., 2012, p. 80.
9 Tom Barkhuysen, Siewert D. Lindenbergh (ed.): Constitutionisation of Private Law, Brill, 2005, for the special discussion on the constitutionalization of private law.
10 MünchKomm/Rixecker, Anh. zu § 12, 2012, Rn. 9.
11 Daniel Friedmann, Daphne Barak Erez (ed.): Human Rights in Private Law, Hart Publishing, 2002, for the thematic discussion in this regard.
12 Jean-Christophe Saint-Pau (dir.) : Droits de la Personnalité, LexisNexis, 2013, pp. 432–434.
13 Gert Brüggemeier, Aurelia Colombi Ciacchi, Patrick O'Callaghan: Personality Rights in European Tort Law, Cambridge University Press, 2010, p. 8.
14 Arita L. Allen: Privacy Law: Cases and Materials, West Academic Publishing, 2016, pp. 14–15.
15 William L. Prosser: Privacy, California Law Review, 1960, issue 3, p. 383.
16 Richard G. Turkington and Anita L. Allen: Privacy, West Group, 2002, p. 24.
17 Richard G. Turkington and Anita L. Allen, Privacy, West Group, 2002, p. 24.
18 *Griswold v. Connecticut* U.S. Supreme Court 381 U.S. 479 (1965).
19 Gert Brüggemeier, Aurelia Colombi Ciacchi, Patrick O'Callaghan: Personality Rights in European Tort Law, Cambridge University Press, 2010, p. 3.
20 Montesquieu: On the Spirit of Law (Volume II), translated by Zhang Yanshen, The Commercial Press, 1997, p. 190.
21 ほしの えいいち: People in Private Law, translated by Wang Chuang, China Legal Publishing House, 2004, p. 20.
22 See Atsushi Omura: Studies in Japanese Civil Law from Three Dimensions, translated by Qu Tao et al., China Legal Publishing House, 2015, p. 36.
23 Gert Brüggemeier, Aurelia Colombi Ciacchi, Patrick O'Callaghan: Personality Rights in European Tort Law, Cambridge University Press, 2010, p. 575.
24 A. Michael Froomkin, Cyberspace and Privacy: A New Legal Paradigm? The Death of Privacy? Stanford Law Review, 2000, issue 5.
25 See Article 9 of the Civil Code of France and Article 26 of the Civil Code of Portugal. In addition, some EU countries directly protect the right to privacy in decisions in accordance with Paragraph 1, Article 8 of the European Convention on Human Rights.
26 A young couple in Yixing, Jiangsu Province, who tried to bear a baby through in-vitro fertilization in Nanjing Gulou Hospital left four frozen embryos after they died in a car accident. In order to fight for the embryos for the continuation of the family genes, the parents of both sides confronted the hospital at court and asked the hospital to return the embryos. The second instance of the court ruled that the parents of both sides should jointly dispose of the four frozen embryos. See the civil judgment of Wuxi Intermediate People's Court of Jiangsu Province, (2014) Ximinzhong zi, No. 01235.
27 See Couples as the Only Child of Their Original Families Killed in a Car Accident, Parents Compete for Embryos with the Hospital, Chutian Metropolis Daily, September 18, 2014.
28 Vgl. Mallmann, Christoph, Datenschutz in Verwaltungsinformationssystemen, München, 1976, S. 54 f.
29 James B. Rule and Graham Greenleaf (ed): Global Privacy Protection, Edward Elgar Publishing, 2008, p. 58.
30 See Civil Ruling on Retrial Review and Trial Supervision of Zhu Yingguang's Privacy Dispute with Lianyungang Branch of China United Network Communication Co., Ltd. and FU Hong, Jiangsu Higher People's Court (2015) Sushenerminshen zi, No. 01014.
31 Wang Zejian: The Law of Personality Rights, Sanmin Book Co. Ltd, 2012, p. 225.
32 David Price and Korieh Duodu: Defamation, Law, Procedure and Practice, Sweet & Maxwell, 2004, p. 472.

33 Angus Charles Johnston, Basil Markensinis and Simon Deakin: Markesinis and Deakin's Tort Law, 2008, p. 860.

34 In the UK, personal information is also included in privacy protection. In 1998, the UK promulgated the Data Protection Act, which, although called data protection, is protected as privacy. The law defines storable data, data processing and disclosure and stipulates the personal right to information and materials

35 Larenz, Lehrbuch des Schuldrechts, Bd. II. 1962, S. 366.

36 Larenz, NJW, 1955, 521.

37 Wang Zejian: Protection of Personality Rights and Compensation for Non Property Damage, in Research on Civil Law Theories and Precedents, 1992, p. 31.

38 This rule was first established in the case of Fan Zhiyi v. Wenhui Xinmin United Press Group for Infringement on Reputation. See the first instance judgment of Fan Zhiyi v. Wenhui Xinmin United Press Group for Infringement on Reputation, Shanghai Jing'an District People's Court (2002) Jing Min Yi (Min) Chu Zi No. 1776.

39 Palandt, Kommentar zum Bürgerlichen Gesetzbuch, 15. Aufl., 1956, S. 674.

40 William L. Prosser, Privacy, 48, California Law Review, 1960, issue 3.

41 William L. Prosser, The Law of Torts, West Publishing Co., 1964, p. 843.

42 Patrick O'Callaghan: Refining Privacy in Tort Law, Springer, 2013, pp. 32–34.

43 Huw Beverley-Smith: The Commercial Appropriation of Personality, Cambridge University Press, 2002, p. 173.

44 California, Florida, Louisiana, Alaska, Arizona, Hawaii, Illinois, Montana, South Carolina, Washington.

45 Wang Zejian: Civil Law Thinking, Peking University Press, 2009, p. 158.

46 Wang Zhu: Reflections on the Constitutionality of Civil Code Compilation, China University of Political Science and Law Press, 2015, p. 360.

47 Wang Yi: On the Normative Allocation of Property Law, China Legal Science, 2007, issue 6.

48 It is stipulated in Paragraph 2, Article 9 as set forth in the Civil Code of France that without prejudice to the compensation for the damage suffered, the judge may prescribe the adoption of any measures such as custody and seizure of disputed property or other measures suitable for preventing or stopping the obstruction of the privacy of private life and in case of emergency, such measures may be ordered in accordance with the emergent hearing.

49 Koziol et al.: The Protection of Personality Rights Against Violations by Mass Media, translated by Yu Jianan et al., China Legal Publishing House, 2013, p. 170.

50 BGHZ, 138, 311, 318.

51 Koziol et al.: The Protection of Personality Rights Against Violations by Mass Media, translated by Yu Jianan et al., China Legal Publishing House, 2013, p. 284.

3 Legislation of Personality Rights in China

System, Boundary and Protection

By Zhang Xinbao

3.1 Sorting out the Personality Rights System: Starting with China's Current Legal Documents

In terms of the laws, regulations and judicial interpretations that have been promulgated in China, legal sources related to the right of personality mainly include the following:

1 (a) The General Principles of the Civil Law of the People's Republic of China (hereinafter referred to as the General Principles of the Civil Law) 1986 contains a special section on personality rights in Chapter 5, Civil Rights. Provisions on the right of personality were first seen in the General Principles of the Civil Law. Four main civil rights are stipulated in Chapter 5 Civil Rights: Section 1 is about property ownership and property rights related to property ownership; Section 2 is about creditor's rights; Section 3 is about intellectual property rights; Section 4 is about personal rights. Although Section 4 mentioned above is titled "personal rights," in fact, there are no provisions on the right to identity, but only stipulations on the right of personality,[1] including the right to life and health, name, portrait, reputation, honour and to marital autonomy. Such legislation represents a new model for the legislation of personality rights in the world and greatly enhances the importance of personality rights as independent civil rights. Therefore, it is highly praised by the legal community at home and abroad and hailed as China's declaration of human rights and civil rights.[2]

2 (b) The Tort Liability Law of the People's Republic of China (hereinafter referred to as the Tort Liability Law) specifies in Article 2, through generalisation and enumeration, civil rights and interests protected by it, including many specific personality rights and interests. Article 2 on the protection of personality rights is characteristics of (i) enumerating the main types of personality rights, including the right to life, health, name, reputation, honour, portrait and privacy. In particular, what deserves more attention is privacy; it should be considered as one of the personality rights so that it can remove the restrictions of the right to reputation and become an independent personality right. (ii) Lack of provisions on personal freedom and the right to body,

DOI: 10.4324/9781003300168-3

or enumerated provisions on personality interests in its so-called civil rights and interests. (iii) The use of "and other personal and property rights and interests" as the bottom clause. This helps to recognise and protect rights and interests, including personality rights and interests that have not been listed yet in new laws or judicial interpretations in the future.

3 (c) Several judicial interpretations issued by the Supreme People's Court have improved the provisions on personality rights in China. The incomprehensive provisions on personality rights in the General Principles of the Civil Law contain limited types of personality rights, unclear provisions on the right to body and lack provisions on the right to privacy and personal freedom. The Supreme People's Court, therefore, issued relevant judicial interpretations to supplement the deficiencies of the General Principles of the Civil Law. The Opinions on Several Issues Concerning the Implementation of the General Principles of the Civil Law of the People's Republic of China issued by the Supreme People's Court in 1988 first involved privacy and defined the act of exposing and publicising the privacy of natural persons as an infringement on the right to reputation. Interpretation on Several Issues on the Determination of Compensation Liability for Mental Damage in Civil Tort issued by the Supreme People's Court in 2001 undoubtedly played an important role in improving China's personality rights system. This interpretation specifies the right to body, the right to personal freedom, the right to personality dignity and the protection of privacy interests and protects the personality interests of the dead and specific commemorative items with symbolic personality significance.

4 (d) Some separate laws and regulations also contain provisions on personality rights. The Consumer Protection Law of the People's Republic of China (hereinafter referred to as the Consumer Protection Law), for example, stipulates in Article 14 that consumers' personal dignity shall be respected, and in Article 25 that consumers' personal freedom shall not be infringed. The Juvenile Protection Law of the People's Republic of China (hereinafter referred to as the Juvenile Protection Law) stipulates in Article 30 that the personal privacy of juveniles shall not be disclosed.

It is the relevant provisions set forth in these laws and judicial interpretations that jointly constitute the personality rights system in China. Table 3.1 shows the general situation of the protection of personality rights in the laws issued by China.

According to Table 3.1, we can draw the following conclusions: (i) Both personality rights and some specific personality interests are protected by law in China; (ii) physical personality rights such as the right to life and health are always put in the core position of personality rights protected by law; (iii) the rights to name, portrait and reputation, which are characteristic of human identification interests and spiritual interests (both related to dignity), have always been important specific types of personality rights protected by Chinese law; (iv) the Tort Liability Law reserves space for the expansion of personality right protection through the wording "and other personal and property rights and interests."

Table 3.1 Personality Rights Stipulated in Laws and Judicial Interpretations of China

Personality rights	*General Principles of the Civil Law*	*Tort Liability Law*	*Relevant judicial interpretations*	*Legal effect*	*Remarks*
The right to life	Existent	Existent	Existent	Valid	
The right to health	Existent	Existent	Existent	Valid	
The right to body	None	None	Existent	Valid	
The right to name	Existent	Existent	Existent	Valid	
The right to portrait	Existent	Existent	Existent	Valid	
The right to reputation	Existent	Existent	Existent	Valid	
The right to honor	Existent	Existent	Existent	Valid	
The right to privacy	None	Existent	Stipulated as personal interests	Valid	It is stipulated in Article 30 in the Juvenile Protection Law
The right to personal freedom	None	None	Existent	It can be interpreted as "other personal rights and interests" in Paragraph 2 of Article 2 in the Tort Liability Law, which is valid	It is stipulated in Article 25 in the Consumer Protection Law
The right to personal interests of the deceased (name, portrait, reputation, honour)	None	None	Existent	It can be interpreted as "other personal rights and interests" in Paragraph 2 of Article 2 in the Tort Liability Law, which is valid	
The right to the remains, bones and and so on of the deceased	None	None	Existent	It can be interpreted as "other personal rights and interests" in Paragraph 2 of Article 2 in the Tort Liability Law, which is valid	
The right to commemorative items of specific personalities	None	None	Existent	Uncertain	
"And other personal and property rights and interests"	None	Existent	None	Valid	It is contained in Article 14 in the Consumer Protection Law

3.2 Delimitation of the Boundary of Personality Rights: An Exclusion Method

3.2.1 Social Rights

Social rights, a constitutional concept, means the rights to social life enjoyed by all people guaranteed by the state's active intervention in the economy and society.[3] Traditionally, social rights allow the state to bear positive obligations, that is, to provide specific economic and social benefits.[4] In accordance with the provisions of the Constitution of the People's Republic of China, social rights usually include the rights to work, rest, survival and education. Some scholars think that fundamental rights in the constitution can be divided into "fundamental rights applicable to private law relations, such as the rights to freedom…equality and fundamental rights inapplicable to private law relations…can be divided into: (1) Right of claim with social nature."[5] The reason for this classification is that fundamental rights inapplicable to private law relations mainly take the state as the subject of obligations, the implementation of which requires certain public power of the state. Such a heavy task can't be burdened alone by individuals and private organisations cooperating and providing assistance. In other words, although civil rights are derived from the fundamental rights in the constitution, from which the corresponding basis can or may be found, not all the fundamental rights herein can be transformed into specific civil rights.

The right to education, for instance, is a social right stipulated in the constitution, but it has not evolved into a civil right in almost all countries in the world. The case of Qi Yuling once caused a sensation in China's judicial practice,[6] and the Supreme People's Court issued a special reply, ruling that the impostor and relevant institutions shall bear tort liability for infringement on the plaintiff Qi Yuling's right to education. In December 2008, it issued a judicial interpretation to abolish the above reply. The reason is that the right to education is not a civil right but a basic right stipulated in the constitution. The court had no right to interpret it and apply it to civil disputes. The right to education, therefore, cannot be included in the personality right in civil law.

3.2.2 The So-Called Right to Chastity

The literal interpretation of chastity refers to steadfast moral integrity. In ancient times, it also referred to the integrity of women who didn't lose their virginity and remained loyal to the same man. In the hybrid stage of primitive society, people had no awareness of chastity. Later, as society developed and the marriage and family system improved, the awareness of chastity gradually emerged and was generally acknowledged. Finally, it was considered an obligation by which women should abide. Chastity was even more precious than life for most women. The initial legislative provisions on chastity were those on measures to punish the crime of rape for the violation of women's right to chastity. Relief provided by civil means to women whose right to chastity was violated began with the marriage lawsuit in Prussia and Saxony in the 19th century. Subsequently, the Civil Code of Germany abolished the marriage lawsuit and stipulated in Article 825 and Paragraph 2 of Article 847 that women can claim compensation for damages in accordance with tort law when their right to chastity is illegally infringed.[7] This provision established the recognition and protection of the right to chastity in modern civil law.

Should the right to chastity be established as an independent personality right in the law of China? The answer is no from the author. Worldwide, the right to chastity is dead or dying, which is caused by the requirement for substantive equality between men and women. In modern European countries, neither legislation nor judicature protects the right to chastity as an independent personality right. The Civil Code of Austria, for example, recognised the right to chastity, which was declared unconstitutional because this provision is completely in violation of the provision of equality between men and women in the constitution. The original provisions on the right to chastity in the Civil Code of Germany were also replaced in 2002 by those on the right to make decisions on sexual freedom. Actually, the right to chastity, as a product of medieval law, was basically built on the inequality between men and women. If the civil law stipulates women's right to chastity, the inevitable logic is: (i) Women are inferior in a society composed of men and women; (ii) since they have the right to chastity, women also have the responsibility to safeguard it; (iii) sexually assaulted women will be considered to have lost their virginity and even be discriminated against (personality reduction, etc.). Considering this, the author argues that the right to chastity should not be included in the law of personality rights of China. In this regard, some scholars think that chastity has a new meaning today, that is, people's sexual interests and its rights' subjects include both women and men. Sexual autonomy proposed on the basis of this specifically means natural persons maintain their good conduct of sexual purity and pursue their sexual interests according to their own will.[8] In other words, sexual autonomy is designed to ensure the free dominance of natural persons over their sexuality.[9] The recognition and protection of sexual interests through sexual autonomy may be feasible, but the specific meaning and protection methods of sexual autonomy need further studies.

3.2.3 The Right to Honor and the Right to Credit

It is stipulated in Articles 102 and 120 of the General Principles of the Civil Law that citizens and legal persons enjoy the right to honour. However, there have always been disputes in the theoretical community of civil law over whether the right to honour is a civil right. Some agree that the right to honour is a civil right and some disagree with this view[10]: Advocates of the first view think the right to honour falls under a personality right or right to identity or falls under both.[11] The author disagrees with this view for four reasons: (i) according to comparative law research, the civil codes of most countries or regions do not list honour or the right to honour as a civil right independent of the right to reputation; (ii) honour, different from reputation, can't or needn't be enjoyed by everyone. It should not be protected as civil rights with universal significance as it is a special personality or spiritual interest without universal significance; (iii) there is no unified understanding of its nature and methods of infringement even among the scholars who affirm the right to honour in China; (iv) in practice, it is difficult to specially adjust the civil law to non-standard honorary titles and awards of various types and rank. Actually, the author believes that honour is essentially a special form of reputation and a social evaluation of someone recognised in a certain way. The relief provided by law to honour or the right to honour that is infringed is no different from that of reputation. In addition, awarding someone an honorary title is basically an administrative act, for which a certain general civil right cannot be created according to the civil law theory. The right to honour, therefore, should not become an independent personality right but can be protected with the help of the right to reputation.

As for the right to credit, the author believes that as a part of reputation, credit needn't be protected as a separate right since the law has confirmed the right to reputation. The reasons are as follows: (i) there is no essential difference between credit and reputation. Scholars affirming credit right as an independent personality right hold that credit refers to the social evaluation and trust obtained by natural persons, legal persons and other organisations on their financial strength and willingness to honour agreements.[12] Scholars who hold this view have repeatedly stressed that credit is not evaluated from the aspects of morality, ethics, conduct, virtue and social status but from comprehensive financial strength.[13] Even so, this cannot constitute a sufficient reason for the independence of credit from reputation as the evaluation of financial strength is also a kind of social evaluation within reputation. Some scholars think that credit also has something that isn't contained in reputation and that those who do not have the intention of insulting or degrading personality cannot be governed by the law of reputation.[14] Maybe this sentence tells us in turn that in real life there is infringement on the credit of the subject without insulting or degrading his or her personality. This cannot be included in reputation, so the right to credit needs to be independent. If so, is there really infringement on the subject's credit without insulting or degrading his or her personality? This scholar explains that illegal acts that infringe on the right to credit include derogation, misleading and other acts that exert improper influence on the subject's financial strength. Typical acts that infringe on the right to credit include advocating untrue facts, alluding to and attacking the credit of others and so on.[15] The scholar also put forward that the damage of infringing on the right to credit means such an act affects society, leading to the damage of the public trust in the financial strength of the specific subject and to the reduction of social and financial evaluation.[16] So far, the author still hasn't found infringement on the credit of the subject without insulting or degrading his or her personality. In fact, infringement on credit, a kind of personal interest, inevitably means that the personal interest of the subject is infringed. The damage consequence of credit as a kind of social evaluation is also reflected by the reduction of social evaluation, which does not go beyond reputation. (ii) From the perspective of legal practice, the General Principles of the Civil Law, the Tort Liability Law and relevant judicial interpretations do not stipulate the right to credit, and the judicial practice has included the protection of credit interests in the right to reputation for a long time. Therefore, the author believes that we should continue to put credit in reputation in judicial practice unless there are sufficient theories and evidence to show that credit does have something that reputation cannot include or there are a large number of personality interests that must be protected with the help of the independent right to credit in real life.

3.3 Personality Rights Protected in Civil Law: Special Jurisprudence and Legislative Development

Nowadays, there are mainly four representative legislative models of personality rights in countries around the world, of which the General Principles of the Civil Law is unique. It contains a section of personal rights in the chapter on civil rights and gives equal priority to personality right, real right, intellectual property right and creditor's right. This is what is called the Chinese model.

Although the Civil Code of Germany does not make detailed provisions on personality rights, that does not hinder the judicial protection of personality rights because the Basic Law of Germany contains more comprehensive provisions on them. Besides, Germany has a special constitutional court that focuses on the trial of human rights and personality rights. In contrast, there is no constitutional court that can directly supervise and guarantee the implementation of the constitution in China although the constitution also stipulates the basic rights of citizens. In addition, the constitution is interpreted through legislation in China, that is, by the National People's Congress and its Standing Committee, and no other organ or individual has the right to interpret the constitution. In judicial practice, therefore, it is impossible for judges to apply the constitution to specific cases through interpretation. This is precisely illustrated by the repeal of the reply made by the Supreme People's Court to the case of Qi Yuling.

Actually, in the field of constitution, the theory of third-person effect of basic rights has long been embraced by some scholars; that is, basic rights that originally go against state power also produce an effect among equal civil subjects to regulate the relationship between individuals. The theory includes the theory of direct third-person effect of basic rights and the theory of indirect third-person effect of basic rights. The former means that the legal relationship between individuals can directly be judged through the provisions on basic rights or on the right to claim. The latter means that basic rights cannot be directly used to adjust the legal relationship between individuals, provisions of basic rights can only be formulated through the applicable general clause (*Generalklauseln*) in civil law, and provisions of basic constitutional rights cannot be directly cited as the basis for civil judgments.[17] In terms of the current situation in China, there is no system or path that allows direct application of constitutional provisions to specific cases. Besides, as the amendment of the constitution is a very sensitive topic, China will face many difficulties in realising constitutional judicialisation by amending the constitution. Therefore, it will be difficult to transform the constitutional application in China for a long time. It can be seen that the effective way to meet China's realities is to adopt the theory of indirect third-person effect of basic rights and rely on the provisions of the constitution as the basis to transform basic rights into civil rights. The personality right in China is a kind of civil right based on basic rights provided for in the constitution. It presents the concretisation of the provisions of the constitution. Although the Tort Liability Law enumerates many specific personality rights in Paragraph 2 of Article 2, it is still of great significance to formulate a separate law of personality rights in China. On the one hand, the provisions of the Tort Liability Law are only a simple list of these specific personality rights. On the other hand, the law also contains the general provision through the wording of "and other personal and property rights and interests" in Article 2. As such, it is necessary to formulate a law of personality rights to specify the connotation and denotation of various specific personality rights, define the relationship between different types of rights and make rules for interest measurement in case of conflict between rights. Only in this way can China build a perfect personality right system to truly realise the protection of personality rights of the civil subject.

Three ideas on the specific model of personality right legislation have been advanced by Chinese scholars: (i) formulate a separate law of personality rights by following the guideline of the General Principles of the Civil Law; (ii) act on the Civil Code of Switzerland to stipulate the personality rights of the civil subject in the part of civil subjects in the general provisions; (iii) stipulate personality rights in the tort law by drawing lessons from the Civil Code of Germany.[18] At present, the first idea has gradually been mainstreamed. Special provisions on personality rights, for example, are made in the Scholars' Proposal for the Civil Code (Draft) of the People's Republic of China presided over by Professor Wang Liming; the Proposal for the Draft Civil Code of China in the charge of Professor Liang Huixing; the Draft of the Green Civil Code presided over by Professor Xu Guodong; and the Civil Law (Draft) of the People's Republic of China drafted by the legal working committee of the Standing Committee of the National People's Congress.[19] The author believes that the legislative method adopted to stipulate personality rights doesn't basically involve value but legislative technology. What matters in the civil law system is not where personality rights are put but what is stipulated and how it is stipulated. Therefore, it is acceptable to formulate a law of personality rights or expand personality rights when revising the General Principles of the Civil Law in the future. It should be noted that whichever scheme is adopted, the following needs to be achieved: (i) highlight the basic value orientation of the protection of personality equality, freedom and dignity of natural persons; (ii) focus on the confirmation of various specific personality rights and define rights and their nature, content and boundary; (iii) confirm the right to claim personality rights as an absolute right in the aspect of right relief; (iv) give an appropriate position to personality interests that should be protected; (v) make the bottom clause (general clause) reserve space for the development of personality right protection. Also, attention should be paid to the coordination of the law of personality rights and the Tort Liability Law in legislation.

Notes

1 Liang Huixing: Problems Facing the Civil Law and Economic Law of China, Law Press, 1991, pp. 59–67.

2 Liang Huixing: General Introduction to the Civil Law, Law Press, 1996, p. 71; Yang Lixin: The Emergence, Development and Prospect of the Law of Personality Rights – from the General Principles of the Civil Law to the Judicial Interpretation of Compensation for Mental Damage, accessed on X, website: http://article,chinalawinlo.COM/articledetail, ASP?ArticleID=35270,2011—11—15.

3 Han Dayuan et al.: Special Research on Constitutional Law, China Renmin University Press, 2008, p. 397.

4 Zhang Xiang: Norm Construction of Basic Rights, Higher Education Press, 2008, p. 40.

5 Zhang Hong: Basic Rights and Private Law, Law Press, 2010, pp. 65, 72-77.

6 See the Case of Qi Yuling v. Chen Xiaoqi et al. over Infringement on Citizens' Basic Right to Education Protected by the Constitution by Infringing the Right to Name, published in the Bulletin of the Supreme People's Court of the People's Republic of China, 2001, issue 5.

7 Yang Lixin: On the Law of Personal Rights, People's Court Press, 2002, pp. 721–722, 880–881.

8 Ma Qiang: On the Right to Chastity, Science of Law, 2002, issue 5; Guo Weihua: On the Definition of Sexual Autonomy and its Private Law Protection, Studies in Law and Business, 2005, issue 1.

9 Ma Junju: Lectures on Personality and the Theory of Personality Rights, Law Press, 2009, p. 276

10 Zhang Xinbao: Legal Protection of the Right to Reputation, People's Publishing House, 2004, p. 43.

11 Yang Lixin: On the Law of Personal Rights, People's Court Press, 2002, pp. 721–722, 880–881.

12 Yang Lixin: Report on the Legislation of the Law of Personality Rights, Intellectual Property Press, 2005, pp. 21–76, 392, 395.

13 Wang Liming: Research on the Law of Personality Rights, China Renmin University Press, 2005, p. 538.

14 Yang Lixin: the Law of Personality Rights, People's Court Press, 2009, pp. 33–35, 348, 354.

15 Yang Lixin: Report on the Legislation of the Law of Personality Rights, Intellectual Property Press, 2005, pp. 21–76, 392, 395.

16 Yang Lixin: the Law of Personality Rights, People's Court Press, 2009, pp. 33–35, 348, 354.

17 Zhang Hong: Basic Rights and Private Law, Law Press, 2010, pp. 65, 72-77.

18 Yang Lixin: the Law of Personality Rights, People's Court Press, 2009, pp. 33–35, 348, 354.

19 Yang Lixin: Report on the Legislation of the Law of Personality Rights, Intellectual Property Press, 2005, pp. 21–76, 392, 395.

4 Rational Thinking on the Major Controversy over the Inclusion of the Law of Personality Rights in the Civil Code[1]

By Yang Lixin

It has been nearly 30 years since the General Principles of the Civil Law of the People's Republic of China was adopted on April 12, 1986, and took effect on January 1, 1987. It stipulated China's personality rights system for the first time. Over the past 30 years, China has witnessed personality rights protection and the theoretical research into the law of personality rights developing rapidly. In implementing the decision made by the Central Committee of the Communist Party of China (CPC) to strengthen the rule of law, it is of great significance to further strengthen the legislation of the law of personality rights and improve the protection of personality rights in the civil code compilation. Therefore, a heated theoretical debate is going on over how to compile a law of personality rights in the civil code in the academic circle of civil law. Some scholars even think that the separate compilation of the law of personality rights will lead to political risks,[2] which has had a great impact on society. In this regard, if explanations are not made clear, the public will believe the bias, thinking that the separate compilation of the law of personality rights may trigger a colour revolution. This alarmist statement has a significant impact on the compilation of the civil code. In this paper, therefore, I will give explanations to clarify these problems, point out the mistakes of the above-mentioned conclusion and give my views on solving these problems.

4.1 The Focus and Background of the Major Debate over the Legislation of Personality Rights in China

4.1.1 The Focus of the Major Debate on the Legislation of Personality Rights in China

There was a debate on the personality rights legislation before the Fourth Plenary Session of the 18th CPC Central Committee made the decision to strengthen the rule of law and compile the civil code. After the compilation of the civil code started, the debate became more intense over how to compile the law of personality rights in the civil code. The focus of the debate is whether the law of personality rights is compiled as a separate part of the civil code, placed in the part on natural persons in the General Provisions, or in the Tort Liability Law. There are

DOI: 10.4324/9781003300168-4

also opinions on putting personality rights in the constitution. Among the advocates of different opinions, Professor Wang Liming and I are the most unswerving champions for the compilation of personality rights as a separate part of the civil code. In this regard, scholars with different academic opinions advanced different views against our opinions. These opinions were originally discussed within the academic and legislative fields, but since September 2015, the debate has changed in nature. Some scholars oppose the separate compilation of the law of personality rights by pointing out that it will lead to political risks. This has triggered a major debate on the political risks of the personality rights legislation, which is also the focus of what is to be discussed.

4.1.2 The Background of the Major Debate on the Legislation of Personality Rights in China

The debate on how to formulate the law of personality rights in the civil code of China has occurred against the following background.

First, the General Principles of the Civil Law strengthened the legislation of personality rights.

On April 12, 1986, the General Principles of the Civil Law was adopted by China's legislature and officially took effect on January 1, 1987. Although it contains only 156 articles, the General Principles of the Civil Law summarises the basic contents of civil law and meets the urgent need for the civil law system in China's social development. What is particularly important in the General Principles of the Civil Law is provisions on personality rights. Although titled "personal rights," these provisions are actually on personality rights.[3] Personal rights include personality rights and identity rights. Identity rights are stipulated in the Marriage Law, and personality rights, including the rights to life and health, name, portrait, reputation, honour, marital autonomy and so on. are stipulated in this section in the General Principles of the Civil Law. This is a particularly important stipulation of historical significance and practical value.

The reason why eight articles are allocated to stipulate personality rights separately in the General Principles of the Civil Law (which has 156 articles in total) is that a large number of historical tragedies seriously infringed the right of personality in the ten-year turmoil before the reform and opening up. After the reform and opening up, civil law scholars, like other people who suffered serious violations of personality rights in the Cultural Revolution, drew a lesson from the bitter experience and decided to formulate a law to strengthen the protection of personality rights. Therefore, they made comprehensive provisions on personality rights, including nearly all important personality rights in the General Principles of the Civil Law.[4]

A review of what happened in the past shows that the General Principles of the Civil Law strengthened personality rights legislation for the same reasons as in Europe and other countries that initiated a legislative movement to strengthen the protection of personality rights after World War II. In the Second World War, fascists trampled on the personality rights of people in other countries, resulting in serious consequences. Countries all over the world, therefore, generally consolidated the legislation and protection of personality rights. Not only did the victorious countries pay attention to the legislation of personality rights, but even the defeated countries drew lessons to strengthen the legislation of personality rights. Principled provisions on the protection of personal dignity and human dignity were added to the then Basic Law of Federal Germany and the constitution of Japan.[5] That was both the legislative measure taken after drawing on the bitter experience and the reflection by the defeated country on the historical tragedy. China has strengthened the legislation of personality rights since the reform and opening up, and other countries in the world have strengthened the legislation of personality rights since World War II. Comparing the practice of the two parties, we will find that they did so for the same reason—correcting historical mistakes and strengthening the protection of personality rights.

Second, China strengthened the protection of personality rights in judicature. Since the General Principles of the Civil Law was implemented on January 1, 1987, judicial organs across the country have made great efforts to strengthen the protection of personality rights in accordance with the provisions hereof. From then on, the Chinese people's awareness of personality rights suddenly increased, and then a large number of cases were brought to the court to seek the protection of personality rights. I personally experienced this turbulent trend and was deeply impressed with it. The first litigation climax facing the court was the fever of suing reporters. A large number of lawsuits against the media's infringement on personality rights were brought to the courts, and the victims claimed they were safeguarding their right to reputation. The second climax was the fever of suing writers for violating personality rights in literary works to claim the protection of rights. Relying on accumulated judicial experience in the practice of personality rights protection, the court helped form two judicial interpretations by the Supreme People's Court on the protection of the right to reputation. Later, the Supreme People's Court issued the judicial interpretation on spiritual damage compensation in 2001, making a comprehensive summary on the protection of spiritual personality rights. Thus, the protection of personality rights, especially the protection of spiritual personality rights, was raised to a height never seen before.[6] In terms of the major debate on the legislation of personality rights, the Supreme People's Court embraces the separate compilation of personality rights because the courts across the country have accumulated a great deal of judicial experience in practice in protecting the personality right. These established cases was consistently mentioned as judicial experience can enrich civil legislation if they are written in law. The separate legislation of personality rights will provide more space for the legislation of personality rights. The Supreme People's Court has issued two judicial interpretations only for the protection of the right to reputation, which shows the wealth of judicial experience. If the judicial experience in the protection of various personality rights is written into the civil code, there will be a full-grown and practical law of personality rights with Chinese characteristics.

Third, the continuous development of the theory of personality right law in China. When the General Principles of the Civil Law stipulated the right of personality, China had not made sufficient theoretical preparation for the right of personality in the civil law. It was after the legislation of personality rights that the theory of the personality rights law of China was gradually improved in practice and has developed to what it is now. After 1987, the earliest theoretical discussion was about the protection of the personality rights of the deceased.[7] Later, many articles and monographs on the research into personality rights gradually appeared with the development of personality rights protection. In 1993, *On the New Theory of Personality Right Law*, co-authored by Professor Wang Liming and me, was first published[8] as the earliest monograph on the theory of personality rights, and then *Personality Rights and News Infringement* was published.[9] Then, the *Studies into the Law of Personality Rights* by Wang Liming,[10] the monograph, *On the Law of Personality Rights*,[11] and the textbook, *On the Law of Personality Rights*, by me[12] were published, followed by *On the Personality Right Law* by Yao Hui[13] and *On the General Theory of Personality Rights* by Zhang Hong.[14] So far, a relatively rich theoretical system of personality rights law has formed in China, which highlights the characteristics of the personality rights law in mainland China. That is equal to Professor Wang Zejian's monograph *On the Law of Personality Rights*[15] in theoretical value. China's personality rights law outperforms that of other countries and regions in the world in theoretical development and research depth.

Thanks to 30 years of practice, China has accumulated rich legislative and judicial experience in personality rights law and developed a relatively perfect theoretical foundation. Today, China has solid theoretical and practical foundations for compiling personality rights law in the civil code. But then different opinions came.

4.1.3 The Development of the Major Debate over the Legislation of the Law of Personality Rights in China

The debate on the legislation of the personality rights law in China evolved from the debate on academic views, legislative technology and political risks.

Initially, the debate on the legislation of personality rights law was purely a dispute of academic views. Scholars all realised the importance of the legislation of personality rights, but there were divergences on the way of expressing them in legislation. Subsequently, this debate developed into that of legislative technology, focusing on how the experience, theory and achievement in China's personality rights protection could be better reflected in the civil code to show the characteristics of China's personality rights law. Overall, the main views include: (i) The personality rights law should be compiled as a separate part of the civil code of China and placed in the first part of specific provisions[16]; (ii) the personality rights law should be put in the part of natural persons as the subject of rights in the General Rules of the Civil Law because the personality right is the right enjoyed by the natural person[17]; (iii) the personality rights law should be compiled in the Tort Liability Law in accordance with the legislative style of the Civil Code of Germany; (iv) the law of personality rights should be compiled in the constitution to give a higher position to the right of personality.[18] These propositions were all debates on the legislative technology of the personality rights law. The focus of the debate was on which part of the civil code it was better to put the personality right law. The reason why Wang Liming and I first proposed the separate compilation of the personality rights law is that the personality right is also a civil right. Why should it be written in the General Provisions rather than in the specific provisions of the civil law like other civil rights? Our proposition to this question is similar in logic to Professor Xu Guodong's humanistic proposition of legislation[19] in the civil law.

As reform and opening up deepens, the independent status of China's personality rights law in civil law has been strengthened in theoretical research and legislation. First, the state organised the publication of the unified textbook, *On the Law of Personality Rights*, for the ninth, five-year plan and proposed that the law of personality rights should be published as a separate civil law discipline among them. Then *On the Law of Personality Rights*,[20] co-authored by Wang Liming, Yao Hui and me, was published by the Law Press as a textbook. Second, in 2001, the Standing Committee of the National People's Congress decided to speed up the formulation of the civil code by setting up a leading group to draft the civil code. In the discussion, both the personality rights law and the Tort Liability Law were proposed to be compiled as a separate part of the civil code, and experts were entrusted with drafting the specific laws of the civil code. Wang Liming and I were assigned the drafting of the expert proposal for the Tort Liability Law and the law of personality rights. The two proposals were completed in early 2002 and submitted to the Standing Committee of the National People's Congress in the name of the Research Center of Civil and Commercial Jurisprudence of Renmin University of China. The two drafts were discussed by the legal working committee of the Standing Committee of the National People's Congress at the conference centre of the National People's Congress in April 2002. Third, in December 2002, the Standing Committee of the National People's Congress discussed the Civil Law of the People's Republic of China (Draft), of which the law of personality rights was separately compiled in the fourth part. Obviously, the legislature intended to compile the personality rights law separately. After the discussion, separate legislation of personality rights was chosen in the compilation of the civil code. The legislation of the Property Law and the Tort Liability Law was completed, and most of the civil code was completed.

Going forward, the law of personality rights should be formulated. Different opinions on the legislation of the personality rights law in the academic circle of civil law prevented the legislature from continuing the work on this, and it turned to the revision of the Inheritance Law. I was entrusted by Wang Shengming, then deputy director of the legal working committee, to design the specific contents of the personality rights law and enrich it on the basis of the personality rights law in the Civil Law of the People's Republic of China (Draft) to make it more convincing. I did so as required.

After the compilation of the civil code started in 2015, in line with the central government's decision to strengthen the rule of law, the dispute about the academic viewpoint and legislative technology in the legislation of the personality rights law evolved into one about political risks. Some scholars opposed the independent compilation of the personality rights law in the discussion on the excuse of risks caused by political issues such as human rights and colour revolutions. That was how the dispute developed.

The debate over the political risk in the legislation of personality rights law was mainly reflected in the ongoing legislation of the General Rules of the Civil Law.

An inevitable problem to be solved in the legislation of the General Rules of the Civil Law is whether the right of personality should be stipulated. If it is stipulated in the General Rules of the Civil Law, there is no need to formulate the law of personality rights alone. If it is not stipulated herein, the law of personality rights or provisions on the right of personality must be specially formulated in the future. Wang Liming, therefore, advocated in an article that the General Rules of the Civil Law should not stipulate the right of personality.[21] This view is embraced by me and some other scholars. Other scholars, of course, wrote about the academic discussion to express their view against a separate personality rights law in the civil code.

In September 2015, there was a dispute over political risk from the legislation of the personality rights law. A heated debate was going on among scholars at the first expert seminar on the General Rules of the Civil Law (Draft) held by the legal working committee of the National People's Congress from September 14 to 16, 2015. First of all, they debated two problems: what is the basis for the argument that a separate compilation of the law of personality rights will raise China's human rights protection to an unprecedented level, and will the Civil Code of China stipulate provisions of personality rights for the first time in the history of world civil law? Secondly, the controversial issues began to escalate, with scholars holding that there would be a huge political risk after the independent compilation of the personality rights law. Worldwide, the personality rights law was first compiled separately in the civil code in Ukraine, and this triggered two colour revolutions. That was why some scholars were opposed to the independent compilation of the personality rights law. Thirdly, some assented to the independent compilation of the personality rights law because they thought the Tort Liability Law couldn't protect the personality rights well. They didn't hesitate to completely derogate the Tort Liability Law to support the separate compilation of the personality rights law. At this seminar on legislation, many scholars believed that the academic issues of civil law legislation should not be led to the political field. In particular, the exaggerated political risk should not be used to suppress different academic opinions because this is not a normal attitude to academic discussion.

The issues discussed at the legislative seminar should be solved only at the meeting, but the discussion on the political risk from the separate compilation of the personality rights law was introduced to the Academic Circles university and then posted on the Internet to further expand the impact of this opinion. Some people even noted that it was either deception or ignorance that the protection of human rights could be raised to an unprecedented position as long as personality rights were compiled separately in the civil code and that the separate compilation of the personality rights law might be one of the important reasons for the colour revolutions. Such an attitude toward the discussion of the legislation of personality rights law led the dispute from academic views and legislative technology to political risks caused by the legislation of personality rights law. This view should call for a response.

4.2 The Focus of the Debate Over the Academic Viewpoint and the Legislative Technology in the Legislation of the Personality Rights Law

4.2.1 It is a Basic Consensus in the Academic Circle that the Legislation of Personality Rights Should Be Strengthened in the Civil Code of China

So far, nobody opposes strengthening the legislation of personality rights in the legislative, judicial, or academic community and the whole of society in China. This is a consensus based on China's General Principles of the Civil Law and the legislative and judicial experience in personality rights over the past 30 years. In the 21st century, the development of personality rights should be an important symbol of civil law because there is still room for further development in the personality rights law alone despite the considerable maturity of civil law theory and the perfection of civil legislation. As society progresses and science and technology develop, there will be more personality interests that need the protection of the law of personality rights, so it is necessary to specify personality interests as personality rights. Today, no one opposes strengthening the protection of personality rights in the civil code. This is a gratifying gospel to the Chinese people and society.

4.2.2 The Focus of the Debate on the Academic View in the Legislation of Personality Rights in China

The academic view on the legislation of personality rights focuses on whether the personality rights law should be compiled separately. The focus of the debate includes the following issues.

4.2.2.1 Opposition to the Separate Compilation of Personality Rights Due to the Essential Relationship between the Personality Right and Personality, and the Query about This View

Scholars against the independent compilation of personality rights law believe that the life, body, health, freedom, name, portrait, reputation and privacy, as the object of the personality rights of natural persons, are the carriers of personality. The personality rights and personality, therefore, are always inseparable and co-existent. This is the legal basis for stipulating personality rights in the chapter of natural persons.

This opinion contains both something right and wrong. It is correct that the right of personality is inseparable from personality. Personality, however, should be correctly interpreted as the capacity of civil rights and not the object of the right of personality. The object of the personality right is the personality interest, not abstract personality; that is, it is not the capacity of civil rights. Although it is indeed inseparable from personality, the personality right is not completely inseparable from the object of personality rights, that is, specific personality interests. Some personality interests are always inseparable from personality, such as human life, health and body, while some personality interests will be separated from personality to a certain extent. In this regard, the right to portrait is most typical. The object of the right to portrait, which is the image of a natural person's face, is a specific personality interest. The portrait, however, once formed, becomes the reproduction of the facial image of a natural person. It always depends on a material carrier and can even be circulated in separation from the personality itself.[22] The fluidity of portrait makes the infringement of the right to portrait so frequent and convenient, so portrait becomes the object of frequent infringement on spiritual personality rights. It is the same with the right to name. One of the important reasons why the Civil Code of Germany attaches special importance to the right to name and its protection is that the right to name and personality are integrated. Name, however, can be separated from the subject and used by others, so the right to name is also likely to be infringed by others. So is the right to privacy. These personality rights are different from the rights to the body, health and life. The body is inseparable from life and health. Without life, there will be no health; the body will become remains, and the personality will not exist. After the death of a natural person, however, many of his personality interests still exist and still need to be protected. As such, the personality elements protected by personality rights such as the rights to name, portrait and privacy can be partially separated from personality itself. This problem was found in the research on the theory of personality rights. In America, for instance, there is the right to personality commercialisation or publicity. In China, the rules for compensating the loss of property interests arising from the damage of personal rights and interests are stipulated in Article 20 of the Tort Liability Law. The problem is that some scholars made contradictory expressions. On the one hand, they firmly recognise the inseparable essential relationship between personality rights and personality. On the other hand, they believe that the loss of Wang Junxia's property interests should be compensated for infringement on her portrait, agreeing with the view that the judgment recognised the property value of the right of personality and solved the calculation of the amount of property loss. The rules established in the judgment, in this case, have been upgraded to legal provisions by the legislature and written in Article 20 of the current Tort Liability Law. How this contradictory expression was born is puzzling. It is a logical error that scholars should not make. It should also be noted that the judgment of the case of Wang Junxia is not the only basis for the formation of Article 20 of the Tort Liability Law, but only one of the pieces of experience. What has the same legal principle reflected in this Article 20 as the judicial experience accumulated in numerous cases such as the Wang Junxia case, and the theoretical research results of the right to publicity in China includes the recognition of the property value of the right of personality in German law, the right to commercialisation and the right to publicity in American law and the right to business image in Japanese law?[23] In legislation, it is a necessary method to learn foreign legal principles and rely on China's theoretical research results and judicial experience. In the reform and amendment of the law in the late Qing dynasty, the legislature paid attention to the most common laws in the world, developed the most accurate legal principles, sought the laws most suitable for the conditions of the Chinese people and expected to improve the laws involving the most interests.[24] This is a classic theory for legislative reference, so there is no need to have a servile attitude to foreign things.

It seems to be a conclusion that the law of personality rights cannot be compiled independently, so it should be contained in the part of natural persons. The right of personality, however, is enjoyed by both natural persons and legal persons. Legal persons, for example, enjoy the rights to name and reputation, which are stipulated in the General Principles of the Civil Law. This practice is a success. It is impracticable to stipulate the right of personality only in the part on natural persons, not in the part of legal persons. It must also be stipulated in the part of legal persons separately. This will inevitably lead to overlapping legislation of the law of personality rights in the civil code.

4.2.2.2 Opposition to the Separate Compilation of Personality Rights Due to the Essential Difference between the Personality Rights and Other Civil Rights, and the Query about This View

The view against the separate compilation of personality rights is based on the essential difference between personality rights and other civil rights. The object of personality rights is the life, body, health, freedom, name, portrait, privacy and other personality interests existing in natural persons themselves. Personality rights, therefore, exist in the subject itself, not in the relationship between persons. The right of personality, together with the capacity for rights, conduct, birth and death, is what is owned by the subject. Therefore, there is no legal relationship on the so-called right of personality in civil law. Only when the personality right is infringed is the relationship between the subject of personality rights and the actor is involved. The personality right, therefore, cannot stand side by side with the part of real right, creditor's right, relatives and inheritance as specific provisions of the civil code.

This view is also incorrect. Civil rights, including the right of personality, must be accompanied by civil obligations, so the right of personality involves the legal relationship. How can we say that there is no legal relationship involved in personality rights? The right subject of personality rights (a specific natural person or legal person) and the obligation subject of personality rights (anyone other than the natural person or legal person) constitute the absolute legal relationship on personality rights. The right subject has an absolute right to control his own personality interests, and any other person has the legal obligation not to infringe the personality rights of the right subject. As Professor Wang Zejian said, the person with personality rights can directly enjoy his personal interests (dominant) and prohibit infringement from others. In this regard, the personality right is similar to real right in absolute exclusivity, so it is an absolute dominant right.[25] The legal relationship involved in personality rights is an absolute legal relationship. When the personality right is infringed, it constitutes an infringement involving a relative legal relationship as a creditor's right does. The absolute legal relationship is different from the relative legal relationship, but they both exist objectively. Therefore, although the right of personality, also a kind of civil right, is different from other civil rights, there is no essential difference between them. In particular, the so-called view that the personality right doesn't involve a legal relationship is wrong.

4.2.2.3 Opposition to the Separate Compilation of Personality Rights Because the Right of Personality Cannot Be Obtained or Disposed of According to the Will and Act of the Obligee, and Are not Applicable to the Provisions of Legal Act, Agency, Prescription, Date and Period in the General Rules of the Civil Law and the Query about This View

Some scholars also believe that the right of personality is naturally obtained when a natural person is born and naturally disappears when he dies. Its acquisition is not subject to people's will and behaviour. In principle, it cannot be disposed of, transferred, donated, offset, or abandoned. The legal act, agency, prescription, date and period set forth in the General Rules of the Civil Law, therefore, are applicable to all civil rights to some extent but the right of personality. The right of personality, therefore, cannot be stipulated in specific provisions in parallel with real right, creditor's right, relatives and inheritance. This practice separates the essential relationship between the right of personality and personality, confuses the right of personality and other civil rights and destroys the logical relationship within the civil code.

This viewpoint sounds reasonable, but it is actually wrong. The reason is that although the personality right, as an inherent right, is not obtained through human acts, this does not mean that the object of personality rights, that is, personality interests, cannot be applied to the civil law system, such as legal acts. Many personality interests—objects of personality rights—can be disposed of, transferred, donated, or even abandoned through legal acts. The transfer of the right to use the portrait, for instance, is allowed by law. It is legal for a legal person to dispose of their own right to name and transfer part or even all of it. A natural person even has the right to dispose of, transfer, or donate his own body parts, namely organs, tissue and his own remains. Donating one's own organs or tissue to others is a commendable noble act of feasibility. If there are no applicable rules to stipulate these right subjects in disposing of their personal interests or conducting other legal acts, how can they realise their wishes? The agency system is applicable to a person with personality rights disposing of part of his personal interests. Minors who dispose of their body parts must be represented by legal agents. Even adults who dispose of their personal interests can also apply the principal–agent system. Therefore, it makes no sense to say that the right of personality is not a right of domination but a right of confirmation. The right of personality, of course, has the attribute of the right of domination. Some personality rights, of course, do not apply to the legal act and other systems. However, as long as the exercise of some personality rights applies to the legal act, agency and other systems, we cannot draw the wrong conclusion that all civil rights but the right of personality are applicable to the legal act, agency, prescription, date and period set forth in the General Rules of the Civil Law to some extent. It can be seen that the basis for opposing the independent compilation of the law of personality rights is not logically tenable. In particular, the argument that the separate compilation of the personality rights law violates the logical relationship between the general rules and specific provisions of the civil code cannot be justified.

4.2.2.4 The View That the Right of Personality Must Be Stipulated in the Part of individuals as corporate bodies Do not Enjoy This Right and the Query about This View

Some scholars believe that the right of personality is enjoyed by natural persons, not by legal persons. It is not enjoyed by all civil subjects. This statement is also incorrect.

It should be said that the personality right enjoyed by natural persons is complete because it is necessary to comprehensively protect the personality interest that natural persons have. The legal person, however, is also a civil subject that has a stipulated personality. Although the personality of a legal person differs from that of a natural person, the General Principles of the Civil Law also recognises that the right of personality is enjoyed by a legal person, and their rights to reputation and name must be protected in accordance with the law. According to Professor Wang Zejian, a legal person can be the subject of personality rights, but it is restricted by law and the nature of personality rights. The restriction by law is mostly seen in the property rights enjoyed by legal persons, and there is no provision to restrict the personality rights of legal persons in the current law. The restriction by the nature of personality rights means that a legal person shall not enjoy the personality rights exclusively owned by a natural person, such as life, body, health, freedom and portrait. A legal person may enjoy those that do not belong exclusively to natural persons, such as name, reputation (goodwill), credit, privacy (trade secrets, etc.).[26] Recently, in a typical case of the protection of the right to reputation of legal persons, the Shanghai court ruled that the infringer should compensate 1.5 million RMB/CNY losses to the enterprise legal person suffering infringement on the right to reputation.[27] It is very persuasive that this typical case has registered the highest amount of compensation in the case of infringement of the right to reputation so far.[28] The right to reputation of enterprise legal persons must be protected. It is logically untenable that one of the reasons for the opposition of the independent compilation of personality rights is that a legal person has no personality right, such as the right to reputation.

4.2.2.5 Summary

The above academic views against the separate compilation of the law of personality rights have logical and factual defects, so they are not sufficient to demonstrate their views. On the contrary, Wang Liming and Liu Shiguo's arguments on the separate compilation of the personality rights law are more sufficient and persuasive. According to Wang Liming, there are obvious differences between personality rights and the subject system. The specific provisions of the personality rights are incompatible with the abstractness of the General Rules of the Civil Law, which cannot fully cover the developing personality rights. The placement of the personality right in the General Rules will take a toll on the full protection and utilisation of the personality right.[29] Liu Shiguo believes that personal dignity is the basis for the independent compilation of personality rights.[30] These opinions are correct. It can be seen that those who oppose the independent compilation of the personality rights law cannot overturn the academic basis of those who advocate the independent compilation of the personality rights law.

In fact, these issues are normal academic disputes in the academic circle of civil law. Different academic opinions can be expressed, but reasonable views are most persuasive only when they are expressed in a euphemistic way. After all, there will be a standard to judge academic right and wrong eventually. It is inadvisable to righteously declare that other people's opinions are wrong and only their own are correct. It is even more inappropriate to be unjustified but fierce. Beneficial, normal, academic debate that can promote progress in academic research, legislation and judicature should continue.

4.3 Focus of the Dispute about the Legislative Technology of China's Personality Rights Law

The debate over legislative technology—how to stipulate the personality rights law in the civil code—is actually the embodiment of the dispute over academic views in legislation. In terms of legislative technology, the focuses of the arguments are as follows.

4.3.1 Personality Rights Should Be Stipulated in the Part on Natural Persons in the General Rules of the Civil Code

Some scholars advocate that personality rights should be stipulated in the section on natural persons in civil subjects in the General Rules of the Civil Code. This opinion is based on the fact that only natural persons enjoy the right of personality, while legal persons have no right of personality. Other bases are mentioned above. The biggest problem facing this legislative proposition is that if the personality right is stipulated in the part of natural persons in the General Provisions, there is no way to stipulate the personality right of legal persons; if it is stipulated in this part, the personality right of a legal person must be stipulated again in the provisions of legal persons. This overlapping practice is not in line with the principle of simplicity in legislation. It is not as good as the method of stipulating the right of personality in the General Principles of the Civil Law.

4.3.2 Personality Rights Should Be Stipulated in the Tort Liability Law

Some scholars proposed stipulating the right of personality in the Tort Liability Law.[31] This opinion is outdated because it is the legislative model of the Civil Code of Germany in 1896. The Civil Code of Germany stipulates only a few types of personality rights, including the rights to life, body, health and freedom in Article 823, the right to credit in Article 824, sexual autonomy in Article 825 and the right to name in Article 12. It should be noted that the Civil Code of Germany was produced before World War II when the legislation and protection of personality rights were far less important than after World War II. In that condition, it was understandable to protect the right of personality with tort law. Today in the 21st century, however, it is unrealistic to do so. It should be emphasised that China's Tort Liability Law aims to protect rights and provide relief for the damage of rights rather than an enabling law. The Tort Liability Law can't specify the system, types, and specific content of personality rights. The Civil Code of Germany, in fact, is also a right relief law as it does not grant persons the right of personality but stipulates relief rules for the infringement of rights. In modern society, it is very difficult to stipulate the right of personality in the Tort Liability Law. Compared with the Civil Code of Germany, China's Tort Liability Law is much better as many more specific personality rights, for instance, are listed in Paragraph 2 of Article 2 of the Tort Liability Law. Therefore, China's personality rights legislation should be considered to have been improved. The personality rights law, mainly provisions of right granting, should specify the types and specific content of both abstract and specific personality rights. In short, the inclusion of personality rights in the Tort Liability Law should not be adopted.

4.3.3 Personality Rights Should Be Stipulated in the Constitution

Long ago, some proposed stipulating personality rights in the constitution so that they could be given a higher status and better protected. But if it is stipulated in the constitution, the personality right will become a public right rather than a private right. The change of the nature of personality rights will transform the obligation subject of personality rights from the unspecified individual to the state because rights stipulated in the constitution are public rights, the subject of which is citizens and must be protected by the state, the subject of obligations. To stipulate the personality right, a kind of private right, in civil law is to protect it by means of civil law. If the right of personality is not stipulated in civil law but in the constitution as the legal basis for the protection of personality rights, the court will not be able to apply the norms of the constitution to make civil judgments. The reply by the Supreme People's Court to the case of infringement on the right to education by means of infringing the right to name[32] was widely criticised and has been revoked for violation of the above rules. I don't agree that if constitutional rights have the nature of private rights, constitutional norms can be applied to make civil judgments and Germany's judicial model of invoking the constitution to protect general personality rights is the best explanation. This approach, however, will bring great challenges to China because the mainstream view is that constitutional norms cannot be applied to civil judgments. Therefore, it is not advisable to compile the law of personality rights in the constitution.

4.3.4 Personality rights should be stipulated in the part of civil rights in the General Rules of the Civil Law

Another way to solve the legislation of personality rights is to stipulate them in the part on civil rights and objects in the General Rules of the Civil Law.[33] This is actually a legislative model copying the General Principles of the Civil Law. This will be explained later.

4.3.5 The law of Personality Rights Should Be Compiled Separately in the Civil Code

Although personality rights, as a kind of civil right, are different from other civil rights, they are of the same nature. Therefore, the law of personality rights should be compiled in the first part of the specific provisions to fully reflect the humanism of the civil code. Both Wang Liming and I believe that the above practice is the perfect legislative choice for the personality rights law. This practice can best complete the system of personality rights and enrich specific personality rights so as to better respect people's status and personality and lay a solid foundation for the protection of personality rights in the Tort Liability Law. Unfortunately, no consensus has been reached, although more and more scholars agree with this opinion.

4.4 Main Viewpoints on the Dispute over Political Risks Arising from the Separate Compilation of China's Personality Rights Law

There are four main viewpoints on the dispute over political risks arising from the separate compilation of the personality rights law in the civil code.

4.4.1 Can the Separate Compilation of the Personality Rights Law in the Civil Code Improve the Protection of Human Rights in China?

One of the main bases for the view that the separate compilation of the personality rights law in the civil code will lead to political risks is that the civil code will raise the protection of human rights to an unprecedented height. The relationship between the civil code and human rights protection didn't receive enough attention in the past. Input two keywords of "civil code" and "human rights protection" in Baidu, and a slogan "the civil code should raise the protection of human rights to an unprecedented height" (hereinafter referred to as the slogan) will appear. This is the basic basis for advocating the independent compilation of personality rights law, and it is this proposition that may cause political risks. Wang Liming denied that he had said so. What he actually said was that the civil code should raise the protection of people to an unprecedented height. Although the protection of human rights is different from the protection of people in the nature of law (public law and private law) and in political sensitivity, there is no essential difference between the two statements, which are both what China's law aims to achieve.

I think the following analysis needs special comments.

First, I think this slogan will cause ideological confusion and ambiguity. Although it cannot be said that the civil code has nothing to do with human rights, when did the textbook of civil law say that the purpose and function of civil law are to protect human rights? It should be clearly noted that the right of personality is an important part of human rights, and so the civil code is related to human rights. It is self-evident logic that the strengthened protection of personality rights in the civil code is bound to improve the protection of human rights. This, however, does not mean that human rights are the object protected by civil law or that the function of civil law is to protect human rights. Civil law indirectly improves the protection of human rights through the protection of personality rights. If the civil code makes greater efforts in the separate compilation of the personality rights law, it can indeed improve the protection of human rights. The judgment will not lead to political risks that the civil code will raise the protection of human rights to an unprecedented height. It is stipulated in Paragraph 3 of Article 33 set forth in China's constitution that the state respects and safeguards human rights. The responsibility of all legal departments is respecting and safeguarding human rights, and civil law is no exception. There is nothing wrong with this opinion, and Professor Wang Liming does not have to avoid the query.

Second, it is not tenable that the slogan that the civil code should raise the protection of human rights to an unprecedented height implies the terrible situation of human rights protection in China currently. "Unprecedented height" is based on a considerable height. The latter is the premise of that former. If it is really terrible in China, human rights protection should be raised to a higher level or a not very terrible height. Such speculation shows a mistake in logical reasoning. The correct understanding of the slogan is that China's current human rights protection has reached quite a high level. If the civil code further strengthens the protection of personality rights, China's human rights protection can be raised to a level as never before. This is fully in line with the requirements of China's constitution to respect and protect human rights and with the realities of human rights protection, and the slogan doesn't deny the current situation of human rights protection in China at all.

Third, is the right of personality part of human rights? Resolution 32/120, the Resolution on the New Concepts of Human Rights issued by the United Nations in 1977, expressly stipulates 12 categories of basic human rights but doesn't stipulate specific personality rights. But this is not the basis for denying that the right of personality is part of human rights. Human rights, broadly defined, refer to the rights that a person should enjoy. Therefore, it contains all rights related to persons. One of the basic policies of the state is to strengthen the protection of human rights. All that involves the decision made by the 14th plenary session of the CPC Central Committee on strengthening the rule of law to strengthen the protection of people, personality rights and human rights. Therefore, it is a correct proposition to strengthen the protection of personality rights and further improve human rights protection in China through the compilation of the civil code. This proposition will not cause ideological confusion or political risks and will not violate the United Nations resolution.

4.4.2 Can the Separate Compilation of the Personality Rights Law Trigger the Political Risk of a Color Revolution

That the separate compilation of personality rights in the civil code may trigger a colour revolution is a political reason for some people opposing the separate compilation of the personality rights law.

> They explained, "Now we advocate learning from the Civil Code of Ukraine, which has been in effect for more than ten years. Has Ukraine become richer and stronger? Actually, the situation in Ukraine is just the opposite. The Color Revolutions took place in Ukraine in 2004 and again in 2013. The country has been trapped in social unrest, economic collapse, disorder and national division for a long time. It is puzzling whether the inclusion of personality rights in the Civil Code of Ukraine has anything to do with, or is one of the reasons for the long-term unrest in Ukraine? It is not difficult to see that the long-term turmoil caused by the two Color Revolutions has something to do with the Civil Code of Ukraine, especially the law of personality rights." "The law of personality rights, although not considered to be the main culprit, is at least one of the important culprits."

This particularly important issue—whether the separate compilation of the law of personality rights in the civil code will trigger the political risk of a colour revolution—calls for careful analysis and discussion for a correct conclusion.

4.4.2.1 The transformation of the social system of Ukraine took place in 1991

Ukraine was once one of the 15 republics of the former Soviet Union and became independent after the disintegration of the Soviet Union in 1991. It is an independent and democratic republic rather than a socialist country, where the political principle of the separation of powers is adopted. The Color Revolution, also known as the Flower Revolution, was a series of regime change movements named by color and were carried out in a peaceful way in the Commonwealth of Independent States (CIS) countries in Central Asia and Eastern Europe at the end of the 20th century to resist the controlling regime of their country. So far, colour revolutions have achieved success in several countries such as Georgia, Ukraine and Kyrgyzstan, resulting in the overthrow of the original regime and the establishment of democratically elected governments.[34] However, the fundamental change of Ukraine's political system took place in 1991, when the new civil code had not been formulated, let alone the independent compilation of the law of personality rights. The subsequent Color Revolutions in 2004 and 2013 were intended to seek a change to its existing political system.

4.4.2.2 Non-Property Rights Are Stipulated in Part 2 Non-Property Rights of Natural Persons of the Civil Code of Ukraine

Part 2 of the Civil Code of Ukraine, titled Non-Property Rights of Natural Persons, consists of 3 chapters and 46 articles. Chapter 20 is about general provisions on the non-property rights of natural persons. Articles 270 to 280 are about the type, essence, exercise, restrictions and protection of non-property rights of natural persons, as well as relief for the infringed natural person's non-property rights, proving false information, prohibiting the dissemination of information in violation of a natural person's non-property rights, failing to perform the legal consequences of the court's judgment on the protection of a natural person's non-property rights, and the right of the infringed to claim compensation. Chapter 21 is about the naturally existent right of natural persons. Articles 281 to 293 stipulate the right to life, the right to eliminate threats to life and health, the rights to physical health protection and medical assistance, the right to health information, the rights to confidential health information, hospitalisation, freedom, personal immunity and family, the rights to obtain guardianship or custody and a safe environment, and the right to donate body tissue and organs. Chapter 22 is about provisions on the social life of natural persons. Articles 294 to 315 stipulate the right to name; the right to change and use name; the right to dignity and reputation; the right of the deceased to be respected; the right to inviolability of goodwill; the rights to personality, personal privacy, confidentiality, information and private documents; the rights to dispose of private documents and know the contents of private documents transferred to the library archives; the right to privacy of communication; the right to the protection of the interests of natural persons photographed, televised, or videotaped; the right to the protection of the interests of the performers of photography and other artistic products; the right to literary, artistic, scientific and technological creation; the rights to residence and inviolability of residence; the right to free choice of occupation; and the rights to freedom of movement, association and assembly.[35]

A look at Part 2 of the Civil Code of Ukraine reveals that both the title and specific content involve more than the rights of personality. First, the above title clearly shows that it does not stipulate only personality rights but the non-property rights of natural persons. Second, the specific provisions of this part are not all about personality rights, but also include identity rights such as the right to family in Article 291; the right to obtain guardianship or custody in Article 292; as well as political rights, that is, public rights, such as the right to literary, artistic, scientific and technological creation in Article 309; the right to residence in Article 310; the right to free choice of an occupation in Article 313; the right to freedom of association in Article 314; and the right to freedom of assembly stipulated in Article 315. These rights, especially the right to free choice of occupation and the right to freedom of association and assembly, do not fall under the right of personality for their nature, at least in China's legislative environment.

4.4.2.3 The Independent Compilation of the Personality Rights Law Has Nothing to Do With a Colour Revolution

Following the introduction of the rights stipulated in Part 2 of the Civil Code of Ukraine, the following should be emphasised.

First, if there are provisions on personality rights of the Civil Code of Ukraine related to its two Color Revolutions, serving as one of the important reasons for the Color Revolution, they are the provisions of the rights to freedom of association and assembly stipulated in Articles 314–315. This is exactly what some scholars think. These two rights, however, are not personality rights at all. They are not stipulated in any proposed draft of the civil code, general principles of civil law, or of the law of personality rights drafted by Chinese scholars, including us. According to this logical inference, there should be no political risk of a colour revolution if there is no personality rights law that stipulates these two rights.

Second, more importantly, it is stipulated in Article 35 of China's constitution that the citizens of the People's Republic of China have the freedom of speech, press, assembly, association, procession and demonstration. This is what has long been stipulated in the constitution with the highest legal guarantee and has a higher effect than the civil code. If this logical inference is tenable, China's constitution has also led to the political risk of a colour revolution, but this is obviously not the case.

Third, if the separate compilation of the personality rights law will lead to a political risk of a colour revolution, the compilation of it in any part of the civil law will trigger risks. This is not a political issue but a technical issue in legislation. If it is considered to be one of the important reasons for the political risk of a colour revolution, the consequences are the same whether the personality rights law is compiled separately, or in the General Provisions, specific provisions of civil law, or Tort Liability Law. If the separate compilation of the personality rights law will lead to political risk, why will provisions of personality rights put in the section on natural persons in the General Provisions of the Civil Law not cause political risk? This opinion makes no logical sense at all.

Fourth, in Central Asia, Eastern Europe and other countries where a colour revolution took place, the law of personality rights is not compiled separately.

If the independent compilation of the personality rights law in the Civil Code of Ukraine is to blame for the two Color Revolutions, why did colour revolutions take place in other Central Asian and Eastern European countries, such as Georgia, Kyrgyzstan and Egypt, where personality rights laws are not compiled separately? These facts show that the separate compilation of the personality rights law has nothing to do with colour revolutions. This statement is farfetched, even if it is not a sheer fabrication out of nothing.

These facts are sufficient to draw a conclusion that there is no logical and factual basis for the subjective view that the independent compilation of the law of personality rights in the civil code is one of the important reasons for a colour revolution. As has been said before, one of the outstanding features of the General Principles of the Civil Law of China is that there is a special section of personality rights to strengthen their protection. We have seen in practice over the past 30 years that the strengthening of personality rights protection in legislation and judicature has greatly promoted social and economic development, improved human status, human rights protection and human dignity, and strengthened people's awareness of these rights. This displays that it is correct for the General Principles of the Civil Law to strengthen the legislation and protection of personality rights. Civil law is human-centred and a law for people. As long as we continue to move toward the protection of personality rights initiated by the General Principles of the Civil Law, China will see the continuous development of society as well as the improvement of human rights protection and people's lives.

4.4.3 Were Massive Violations of Personality Rights in the Field of Public Law and Public Power the Reason for Negating the Separate Compilation of the Law of Personality Rights?

Some scholars think because massive violations of personality rights mostly occurred in the field of public law and public power has nothing to do with personality rights, it is unnecessary for the personality rights law to be compiled independently. This is also a reason for denying the independent compilation of personality rights law. Indeed, it is correct that massive violations of personality rights occurred in the field of public law or public power. The Cultural Revolution in China, the Great Purge in the former Soviet Union and the actions of the Stasi secret police in former East Germany, for example, all took place in the field of public law and public power. However, it should be noted that the rights infringed by these public power acts are personality rights. In the Great Purge in the former Soviet Union, innocent people were hung on the gallows, which violated their right to life and trampled their human dignity. The strengthening of the legislation and protection of personality rights in the civil code can prevent the infringement by public power on people's private rights. The independent compilation of the law of personality rights is a measure taken to combat illegal public power acts. The wisdom of the mainland Chinese leaders lies in correcting the tragedy of the Cultural Revolution in time, formulating the General Principles of the Civil Law, and strengthening the legislation and protection of personality rights. It is under the leadership of these wise leaders that the Chinese people have their current status and dignity. This deserves our gratitude. The purpose of strengthening the legislation of personality rights and even the independent compilation of personality rights law is to prevent us from returning to an era when public power massively infringed on private rights, especially personality rights.

4.4.4 Does the Separate Compilation of Personality Rights Law Mean Derogating and Dismembering China's Tort Liability Law

According to some scholars (those scholars who advocate the separate compilation of personality rights) at present, they strongly emphasise the nature and importance of Tort Liability Law as a law of civil rights protection and suggest the separate compilation of Tort Liability Law in the civil law. This suggestion was adopted by the legislature. Today, with the purpose of compiling a separate law of personality rights, these advocators say that the Tort Liability Law is not enough to protect personality rights and don't hesitate to belittle the current Tort Liability Law. This practice shows a self-denying of their past position.

That the Tort Liability Law is not enough to protect personality rights. We did strongly emphasise the separate compilation of the Tort Liability Law. On December 26, 2009, the legislature passed the law and gave birth to the Tort Liability Law. This has always been the source of our pride.

But the "self-denying" statement is not true. So far, neither Wang Liming nor I have derogated China's Tort Liability Law. I have always been proud of the Tort Liability Law of China. After the Tort Liability Law was adopted, I initiated the establishment of the East Asian Society for Tort Liability Law and the World Society for Tort Liability Law, and introduced to foreign countries the legislative experience and theoretical research results of China's Tort Liability Law, allowing more people understand China's Tort Liability Law. The basis for criticising those who derogate China's Tort Liability Law is that Wang Liming mentioned in his paper on the legislation of the personality rights law that the incomplete provisions of personality rights in the Tort Liability Law couldn't fully protect personality rights.[36] This is an objective fact. But there is no derogation of the Tort Liability Law.

The direct provisions of the Tort Liability Law on the protection of the right of personality are mainly as follows: first, Paragraph 2 of Article 2 stipulates only seven rights, including the right to life, health, name, reputation, portrait, privacy and marital autonomy, but doesn't stipulate the right of personality such as the right to body, image, credit and sexual autonomy. It cannot be said that the personality rights listed here are complete. Second, the provisions on fault liability in Paragraph 1 of Article 6 are the general provisions of tort fault liability, including infringement on spiritual personality rights, and are the basis of claims for compensation for damage to spiritual personality rights. They are, of course, also the basis of claims for general violations of the right to life, the right to health, the right to body and other rights, but the damage compensation for infringement on the right to material personality is also applicable to the principle of presumption of fault and the principle of no-fault liability. These provisions are very clear, but they need to be explained because they are not self-explanatory enough to those who are unfamiliar with the law. Third, the provisions of Article 22 are about spiritual damage compensation. The damage compensation for infringement of spiritual personality rights is mainly spiritual damage compensation. Fourth, the rules for compensating property losses caused by infringement on personality rights and interests stipulated in Article 20 are actually the provisions on the right to publicity. The above provisions are clear and relatively perfect. These, however, are general relief provisions on the protection of personality rights rather than legal norms granting rights. Due to its function and nature, the Tort Liability Law cannot stipulate what personality rights each civil subject enjoys, what specific personality rights are and what specific rights should be protected. In this regard, it has the same defect as the tort law in the Civil Code of Germany. Wang Liming's opinion, therefore, shouldn't be considered to be wrong. He did not derogate from or division the Tort Liability Law but just expressed an objective fact. Although the Tort Liability Law is an outcome of our own painstaking efforts, we cannot evade its shortcomings. Shortcomings exist indeed. Only by facing up to the shortcomings in legislation can we improve these deficiencies. It is an exaggeration to consider the criticism of the shortcomings in legislation as belittling and dismembering the law. The attitude to the criticism shows the lack of due tolerance of jurists. Wang Liming and I have never intended to or said anything to derogate from or dismember the Tort Liability Law. Today, we still believe that although it is not the best among the world's tort liability laws, China's Tort Liability Law is very good. In terms of rights granting, the Tort Liability Law is really powerless to provide for personality rights for its legal nature. If there is a separate law of personality rights, it will be better to publicise personality rights and help apply the Tort Liability Law correctly. This idea contains nothing wrong.

4.5 In What Way Is It More Reliable to Stipulate Personality Rights in the Compilation of the Civil Code?

In the current situation, it is particularly worth studying how to stipulate personality rights in the compilation of the civil code. In this regard, I will make the following analysis.

4.5.1 Difficulties in Realising the Separate Compilation of the Personality Rights Law in the Civil Code

As has been said before, China has been committed to the independent compilation of the law of personality rights in the civil code. Specifically, there have been state-compiled textbooks of personality rights law. More importantly, the Standing Committee of the National People's Congress group for drafting the civil code decided to prepare the draft proposal of the personality rights law and stipulated personality rights in Part 4 of the Civil Law (Draft) in 2002. That shows the clear position of the legislature. However, as far as the current situation is concerned, great difficulties have occurred in the independent compilation of the law of personality rights in the civil code. They are in the following four aspects.

First, the statement that the independent compilation of the personality rights law can lead to political risks may have influences. This statement may have had an impact. Although we have repeatedly stressed that the independent compilation of the law of personality rights will not trigger political risks, it is unknown whether this statement will imperceptibly inform the decision-making of legislators. It may affect the judgment of many people. At present, some people believe there will be political risks. This is the main obstacle to the independent compilation of the law of personality rights. This statement, although absurd, may harm the independent compilation of the law of personality rights and blight the legislative process.

Second, no consensus has been reached on the separate compilation of the personality rights law in the academic community of civil law. At the beginning of drafting the civil code, I stressed that the scholars should try to unify their thoughts regardless of their own academic views to ensure the progress of legislation and strive to write the civil code better because the legislation of the civil code is totally different from the academic discussion of civil law. On the contrary, every scholar is trying to express his views in the legislation, and there is no way to reach a consensus. The lack of a unified opinion in the academic circle of civil law makes it difficult for legislators to make a choice. Actually, scholars don't have a great influence on the legislation. The unified opinion advanced by the academic circles of civil law is not necessarily adopted, let alone non-uniform opinions.

Third, scholars who advocate the separate compilation of the personality rights law also think that the compilation of the personality rights law is a technical problem, and other methods can be selected to stipulate this law. There can be compromise in academic disputes, and it is necessary to compromise in order to unify the understanding of the legislation. However, the impact of a certain statement of political risks is limited. Although there is pressure from the statement of political risks, it is not daunting. Moreover, people have their own fair evaluation, and we should withstand the test.

Fourth, it is not clear whether legislators have decided to compile the personality rights law separately in the civil code. When the Civil Law (Draft) was formulated in 2002, the legislature was positive and firm in this regard. Therefore, Part 4, the law of personality rights, was born. The General Rules of the Civil Law (Draft) discussed this time does not contain the personality rights law in the part on natural persons, and from this, we can also see the definite legislative intention. Although it has not expressed its position on this, the legislature seems not as firm as when drafting the Civil Law (Draft) in 2002.

4.5.2 Two Choices in Compiling the Personality Rights Law in the Civil Code

Actually, the scholars may never reach a consensus on how to formulate the personality rights law. The legislature should weigh it up to make a quick decision on how to compile the personality rights law in the civil code. Here, the best scheme is the compilation of the personality rights law as a separate part of the civil law, and the alternative scheme is to stipulate personality rights in the chapter on civil rights and objects in the General Rules of the Civil Law.

4.5.2.1 The Best Solution Is to Compile the Personality Rights Law as a Separate Part of the Civil Law

Despite the above difficulties in the independent compilation of the law of personality rights, it is not impossible to realise it. In particular, recently, many older generations of civil jurists support the independent compilation of the law of personality rights in the civil code, which has had a significant impact. At the fifth (2015) Cross-Strait Forum of Civil and Commercial Law Frontier on Civil Code Compilation and the Development of System Establishment held on November 14, 2015, Professor Jiang Ping and Professor Wei Zhenying were brave to speak out about the feasibility and possibility of the independent compilation of the personality rights law in the civil code. At the beginning of this century, the drafting group of the civil code made it clear that the law of personality rights should be compiled as a separate part of the civil code, which was reflected in the Civil Code (Draft) in 2002. That is how Professor Jiang Ping especially advocates that the independent compilation of personality rights law in the civil code should be put into practice. Difficulties arising from legislation can be overcome, and the independent compilation of the personality rights law in the civil code can be realised. Hearing the above opinions of the older generation of civil law experts at the meeting, I, as a participant, was moved to tears by their firm position.

Therefore, the best solution is to compile the personality rights law separately in Part 2 instead of Part 4 of the Civil Law, so as to highlight the status of people and the important position of personality rights in the civil rights system and show the outstanding characteristics of the civil code in the 21st century. There have been several proposal drafts of the personality rights law in China. Drawing on the main opinions of the proposal drafts, we can enrich Part 4 on the personality rights law in the Civil Law (Draft) in 2002 to compile a personality rights law with Chinese characteristics and the spirit of the 21st century.

4.5.2.2 The Alternative Scheme Is to Stipulate Personality Rights in the Chapter on Civil Rights and Objects of the General Rules of the Civil Law

In addition to the separate compilation of the personality rights law, there are three other alternatives: first, the law of personality rights is put in the part on natural persons. But the biggest disadvantage of this approach is that the legal person's personality rights cannot be stipulated, which will lead to overlapping in the legislation. Second, personality rights are stipulated in the Tort Liability Law. This will affect the nature and function of the Tort Liability Law as it is a relief law rather than a rights law. Obviously, it is not a good idea. Third, the law of personality rights is put in the part on civil rights and objects. This may be the second-best choice except for the separate compilation of the personality rights law.

In the current General Rules of the Civil Law (Draft) (indoor draft) drafted by the civil law office of the legal working committee, the part on civil rights and objects is not written in the text but put in the appendix with the chapter on civil rights in the 2002 Civil Law (Draft). One choice is to stipulate civil rights in civil law. The other is to put it in the special part on civil rights and their objects according to the draft proposal by the China Law Society. Which one will be chosen has not been decided. I think it is better to choose the latter.

It is better to stipulate personality rights in the part on civil rights and their objects. The specific methods are as follows: in the first section, personality interests are simply stipulated as the object of personality rights, and the types, content and rules of personality rights are stipulated in detail. In the second section, the real right is simply stipulated, but the object of the real right, that is, the concept and type of property are focused upon. The third section stipulates the creditor's right, especially unjust enrichment as well as debts of spontaneous agency and unilateral promise that cannot be stipulated if the general provisions of debt law are not separately stipulated. The fourth section stipulates intellectual property rights. In particular, an interface with the civil code should be left for the separate law of intellectual property rights. In the fifth section, the right to identity and the right to inheritance and their objects are moderately stipulated. In this way, the part on personality rights can be expanded to more than 30 articles, including the rights to life, health, body, name, portrait, reputation, privacy and personal freedom. Many scholars advocate that the right to honour should not be stipulated but as a special provision in the right to reputation. I agree with this opinion.

The above-mentioned practice shows the commitment to the legislative tradition and model of the General Principles of the Civil Law. The experience learned since the General Principles of the Civil Law was implemented 30 years ago tells us that this approach is advantageous and should be continued. It should be the second-best scheme as this approach contains new legislative innovation based on the General Principles of the Civil Law and can avoid disputes among scholars.

4.5.3 Problems Needing Attention in the Inclusion of the Personality Rights Law in the Civil Code

First, the law of personality rights must be concise no matter which part of the civil code it is put.[37] It is inappropriate for the Expert Proposal for the Law of Personality Rights in the Civil Code of the People's Republic of China (Draft for Comments) proposed by the China Civil Law Society to contain 105 articles as it includes in many rules of tort law. In my opinion, it is advisable to stipulate about 40 articles on the law of personality rights in the Civil Code. The concise, specific provisions of personality rights can be accepted by most scholars and the legislature.

Second, the personality rights law is a law of rights, not of relief. It should stipulate personality rights enjoyed by the civil subject and those that should be protected and restricted. If the way is stipulated to remedy the damage to the right of personality, it will become the provisions of tort law. Since I began writing the draft law of personality rights in 2001, one of the basic principles I have adhered to is to distinguish the law of rights and the law of relief. Only in this way can we draw a clear distinction between the personality rights law and the tort law.

Third, it should be particularly made clear that both natural persons and legal persons enjoy the right of personality. The above-mentioned judgment by a Shanghai court on protecting the right to reputation of an enterprise legal person was well done. It was a great blow to an enterprise legal person and serious infringement on its right to reputation that a newspaper posted slander and insult on several pages, which was reprinted on the newspaper's website, on the enterprise out of thin air. We have seen from experience learned since the General Principles of the Civil Law was implemented 30 years ago that it is correct for the General Principles of the Civil Law to stipulate that legal persons also enjoy the right of personality, and this practice must continue.

Notes

1 This paper is the phased achievement in the major project of the National Social Science Fund in 2014 (the third batch) titled "Research on Improving the Legal System of Socialism with Chinese Characteristics with the constitution as the core" (project approval No.14ZDC008).
2 Liang Huixing: The Most Heated Debate and My Attitude to the Compilation of the Civil Code of China— Lecture at the Law School of Sichuan University, lcgal publicity network, accessed on November 27, 2015, website: http://www.chinalaw124.com/lilunyanjiu/20151024/12866.html. The following citations of this article without indicating the source are all quoted from this article.
3 In this regard, Professor Liang Huixing's opinion that the personal right stipulated in the General Principles of the Civil Law is the right to personality is wrong. Obviously, he ignores the scope of the connotation of personal rights.
4 See Yang Lixin: On the Law of Personal Rights, People's Court Press, 2002, p. 6.
5 See Article 1 of the Basic Law of Germany, "Human dignity shall not be infringed. It is the obligation of all state powers to respect and protect human dignity." Article 13 of the Constitution of Japan stipulates that the personality of all citizens shall be respected.
6 The three judicial interpretations made by the Supreme People's Court are the Answers to Some Issues Concerning the Trial of Cases on the Right to Reputation (August 7, 1993), the Interpretation on Several Issues Concerning the Trial of Cases on the Right to Reputation (July 14, 1998), and the Interpretation on Several Issues Concerning the Determination of Compensation Liability for Mental Damage in Civil Tort (March 8, 2001).
7 A typical case is the case of the Lotus Lady. For the details of the case, see Yang Lixin: On the Law of Personal Rights, People's Court Press, 2002, pp. 337–338.
8 Wang Liming and Yang Lixin: On the New Theory of Personality Right Law, Jilin People's Press, 1993.
9 Wang Liming (ed.): Personality Rights and News Infringement, China Fangzheng Press, 1998 and 2010.
10 Wang Liming: Studies into the Law of Personality Rights, China Renmin University Press, 2005 edition.

11 Yang Lixin: On the Law of Personality Rights, Higher Education Press, 2005.
12 My two books of the same name are *On the Law of Personality Rights*, the Law Press, 2011 and *On the Law of Personality Rights*, the Law Press, 2015.
13 Yao Hui: On the Personality Right Law, China Renmin University Press, 2011.
14 Zhang Hong: On the General Theory of Personality Rights, Peking University Press, 2012.
15 Wang Zejian: On the Law of Personality Rights, Sanmin Book Co. Ltd., 2012.
16 Wang Liming: On the Inadvisability of the System of Personality Rights Comprehensively Stipulated in the General Principles of the Civil Law—Also on the Independent Compilation of Personality Rights, Contemporary Law Review, 2015, issue 3.
17 Liang Huixing (ed.): Proposed Draft of the Civil Code of China, Law Press, 2003 edition, p. 9.
18 Yin Tian: On the Right of Personality and Its Due Status in the Civil Code of China, People's Court Daily, 3rd edition, July 11, 2003.
19 Xu Guodong: On Two Ideas for Drafting the Civil Code: New Humanism vs. Materialism, Volume 21 Civil and Commercial Law Review.
20 Wang Liming, Yang Lixin, and Yao Hui: On the Law of Personality Rights, Law Press, 1997.
21 Wang Liming: On the Inadvisability of the System of Personality Rights Comprehensively Stipulated in the General Principles of the Civil Law—Also on the Independent Compilation of Personality Rights, Contemporary Law Review, 2015, issue 3.
22 Yang Lixin: Infringement of the Right to Portrait and the Civil Liability to Be Burden, Chinese Journal of Law, 1994, issue 1.
23 Yang Lixin: On the Law of Personality Rights, Law Press, 2011, pp. 324–328.
24 Yu Liansan and Liu Ruozeng: Memorials to the Emperor for the Completion of the First Three Drafts of Civil Law, Compilation of the History of the Formulation of the Civil Law of the Republic of China, published by the "Ministry of Justice and Administration", Taipei, 1976, p. 256.
25 Wang Zejian: On the Law of Personality Rights, Sanmin Book Co. Ltd., 2012, p. 52.
26 Wang Zejian: On the Law of Personality Rights, Sanmin Book Co. Ltd., 2012, p. 52.
27 For details of the case, see Yan Gengbin: Insulting Comments by the News Media Constitute an Infringement of the Right to Reputation, People's Judicature, 2015, No. 16, p. 4.
28 Yang Lixin: Judgment on the Limit of Liability for Infringement of the Right to Reputation of the Enterprise Legal Person, People's Judicature, 2015, issue 16; Typical Judgment on Protecting the Right to Reputation of Enterprise Legal Person According to Law, Enterprise and Law, 2015, issue 4, p. 11.
29 Wang Liming: On the Inadvisability of the System of Personality Rights Comprehensively Stipulated in the General Principles of the Civil Law—Also on the Independent Compilation of Personality Rights, Contemporary Law Review, 2015, issue 3.
30 This view was put forward by Professor Liu Shiguo in the theme report of the 2015 annual meeting of the China Civil Law Society on October 25, 2015.
31 This is Professor Yin Tian's new view. See Liu Xuwei and Gao Jianmin: What Kind of Personality Right Law should be Formulated in the Civil Code—Highlights of the 2015 Annual Meeting of China Civil Law Society, Enterprise and Law, No. 6, 2015.
32 That is, the Reply by the Supreme People's Court to Whether Civil Liability Should Be Borne for Infringing the Basic Right of Citizens to Education Protected by the Constitution by Means of Infringing the Right to Name has been declared invalid.
33 Liu Xuwei and Gao Jianmin: What Kind of Personality Right Law should be Formulated in the Civil Code—Sidelights of the 2015 Annual Meeting of China Civil Law Society, Enterprise and Law, No. 6, 2015.

34 Baidu Encyclopedia: Color Revolution, accessed on October 29, 2015, website: http://baike.baidu.com/view/27567.htm.

35 I have comprehensively introduced Part 2 of the Civil Code of Ukraine "non-property rights of natural persons" for two reasons. First, this law is relatively unfamiliar to Chinese readers. Second, I intend to demonstrate that this part is not entirely about personality rights, and is not an example of the independent compilation of the personality rights law.

36 Wang Liming: On the General Principles of the Civil Law Should Not Comprehensively Stipulate the System of Personality Rights—Also on the Independent Compilation of Personality Rights, Contemporary Law Review, 2015, issue 3.

37 This text was submitted to the 2015 annual meeting of the China Civil Law Society for discussion and was not published publicly.

5 Different Views on the Legislative Decision Making Opinions of Denying the Personality Right Law of the Civil Code[1]

By Yang Lixin

We have entered a key period in the inclusion of personality rights in the civil code and are attracting attention from people from all walks of life. It is understandable that scholars have different opinions on some problems, as that is common in the academic community. However, when the legislature has made the decision to compile the law of personality rights in the civil code, it may not be just a simple academic debate to completely deny this legislative decision and the value of the personality rights law. In terms of the legislative environment, it is of little significance to continue to debate whether personality rights should be stipulated in the specific provisions of the civil code. The scholars should focus on improving the overall design and articles of the draft law of personality rights, and after two years of effort, create a commendable law of personality rights in the civil code so as to maximise its legal benefits and better protect people's personality rights. Relying on the review of the development of China's personality rights legislation, the author tries to clarify some specious disputes in the compilation of the law of personality rights so as to advance the inclusion of the law of personality rights in the civil code.

5.1 The Legislation of Personality Rights in China's Civil Law and the Occurrence, Development and Conclusion of Its Debate

The debate over the inclusion of personality rights law in China's Civil Law has been going on for a long time in academic circles. There has long been a legislative conclusion to many of these controversial issues, but some people are unwilling to accept it.

DOI: 10.4324/9781003300168-5

5.1.1 The Legislation of Personality Rights in China's Civil Law and the Occurrence and Development of the Debate

5.1.1.1 The Legislation of Personality Rights by China's Legislature and the Basis for the Debate

The right of personality was not officially compiled in China's civil law from 1949 to 1986. In real life, there was civil law protection for some personality rights, mainly judicial relief for personal damage against the right to life and health, but the protection of other personality rights was out of the question.

The General Principles of the Civil Law passed by the legislature on April 12, 1986, specifies in Section 4 of Chapter 5 personal rights that are mainly about the right of personality, excluding the right to identity. Since then, there have been legal norms of personality rights in China's civil legislation to protect people's personality rights. That is due to the historical experience of the past 30 years in China.

Since the General Principles of the Civil Law took effect on January 1, 1987, in judicial practice, the judiciary has creatively applied the stipulated legal norms of personality rights across the board in accordance with the law. This helps accumulate a large number of typical cases and generate abundant judicial interpretations on personality rights for the protection of people's personality rights.[2] The experience from typical cases and judicial interpretation is the basis for the theory of personality rights law with Chinese characteristics. That has allowed China's judicial practice to no longer only protect personality rights, such as the right to life and the right to health, but enriched China's legislative and judicial protection of personality rights. Accordingly, that has greatly improved the dignity and legal status of the people and promoted the rapid development of society.

This period could be divided into two stages: 1949–1986 and 1987–1998. The former stage saw no legislation for personality rights in China, and the latter stage witnessed the legislation and continuous development of personality rights in judicial practice. In both stages, there was no obvious debate in the academic circle of civil law and judicial circle in China on whether the right of personality should be stipulated.[3] They all believed that the inclusion of the law of personality rights in China's General Principles of the Civil Law was an initiative and a distinctive feature of China's civil law and brought China into a new historical period in the protection of personality rights. In addition, due to the short length of the General Principles of the Civil Law, the chapter on civil rights was considered to be the mini-version of specific provisions of the civil law and the epitome of specific provisions of the future civil law. This chapter contains the basic contents of the real right, creditor's right, intellectual property right, personality right and identity right.

There were no different views on the legislation of personality rights in civil law in academic circles.

5.1.1.2 The Debate on the Legislation of Personality Rights in Civil Legislation

The debate on the legislation of personality rights in China's civil legislation occurred from 1999 to 2000.

When the formulation of the unified Contract Law was completed, the legislature decided to compile a civil code for China. Immediately, it established a leading group for the compilation of the civil code to make a plan for drafting the civil code. As required, the experts should first draft their share of the proposals for the legislation, then submit them to the legal working committee of the legislature for reference and determine the draft legislation.

A major problem to be solved was what should be stipulated in the civil code, that is, how many parts the civil code should be divided into. The experts had no controversies on the general rules as well as the parts on property rights, contract, marriage and family and inheritance of the civil code, but on whether the parts on the tort liability and personality rights should be separately compiled. Most people advocated stipulating the parts on tort liability and personality rights separately by following the experience in the legislation of the General Principles of the Civil Law. The small number of scholars opposed to this opinion, believing that China's civil code should draw lessons from the Civil Code of Germany, consisting of five parts, wanted to stipulate the right of personality in the general provisions and the tort liability in the debt law. Finally, subject to the opinions of the majority of scholars, the legislature decided that the general provisions, the law of real rights, contract, personality rights, marriage and family, inheritance and tort liability, as well as the applicable law of foreign-related civil relations should be compiled respectively and that civil law experts should draft their share of proposals for the separate parts of the civil code. The proposals for the law of personality rights and tort liability were drafted by the Research Centre of Civil and Commercial Jurisprudence of Renmin University of China. The proposals for other parts were drafted by experts from different units.

At the beginning of 2001, Wang Liming and I began to preside over the drafting of the proposals for the law of personality rights and the Tort Liability Law. The first draft was completed by me and then collectively discussed and revised repeatedly. By the Spring Festival in 2002, we had completed the proposals for the two draft laws and submitted them to the legal working committee of the National People's Congress. At the two-day seminar held at the conference centre of the National People's Congress in April 2002, the legal working committee organised dozens of civil law experts to discuss the draft proposals for the separate parts of personality rights and tort liability of the civil law. All of them thought highly of the draft proposals while pointing out the main problems that needed to be improved in the legislation.

Then, the legal working committee began to draft the formal civil code, and the meeting of the Standing Committee of the National People's Congress deliberated the Civil Law of the People's Republic of China (Draft) in December 2002 for the first time, in which the fourth part stipulated the right of personality and the eighth part, the tort liability.

The draft civil code produced at this time was not mature enough as it was drafted in a hurry but was not destroyed. For example, the marriage law and adoption law were directly numbered as Part 6 and Part 7. Therefore, there were nine, not eight, parts in total.

After the draft civil code was produced by the Standing Committee of the National People's Congress, this time, the legislature decided to continue to formulate the separate laws of the civil law. In 2003, the Property Law of the People's Republic of China (Draft) was first formed on the basis of Part 2, the property right of the Civil Law (Draft), and was adopted in March 2007 after being reviewed eight times (first reviewed in December 2002). Subsequently, the Tort Liability Law of the People's Republic of China (Draft) was formed on the basis of Part 3, the tort liability of the Civil Law (Draft), and was first reviewed in December 2002 and adopted in December 2009. After the completion of the Tort Liability Law, there was hesitation on whether to formulate the law of personality rights or Law on the Laws Applicable to Foreign-Related Civil Relations first. Finally, the legislature decided to review the Laws Applicable to Foreign-Related Civil Relations first and completed the legislation in April 2011.

There was also a hesitation about whether to formulate the law of personality rights or revise the Inheritance Law first. Later, the legislature decided to revise the Inheritance Law first but temporarily stopped in 2011 after working for one year. Finally, it decided to amend the Consumer Protection Law first and completed the revision in October 2013. So far, except for the law of personality rights, all the parts determined in the Civil Law (Draft) deliberated by the legislature in 2002 have been formulated, published and implemented separately, forming a loose civil code in China. This indicates that the socialist legal system with Chinese characteristics has been formed.[4]

In this period, whether the civil code should stipulate a separate part on personality rights was the starting point of the debate for a long time. However, most experts had a unified opinion, and the legislature had a clear attitude but didn't complete the legislation.

5.1.1.3 The Latest Development of the Debate on Whether the Law of Personality Rights Should Be Compiled in the Civil Code

In 2014, the central government decided to start compiling the civil code, and the debate restarted on whether the personality rights law should be independent of the civil code. The legislature decided to compile the civil code in two phases.[5] First, it decided to formulate the General Rules of the Civil Law and then formulate the separate parts of the civil law, such as the real right, contract, tort liability, marriage and family, and inheritance. The debate on whether the civil code should stipulate personality rights has restarted ever since and developed to what it is now today.

So far, the debate has had four important moments.

First, during the formulation of the General Rules of the Civil Law in the first stage, there were serious controversies on whether the right of personality should be stipulated in the general provisions or the specific provisions of civil law. The debate reached its peak at the expert seminar on the General Rules of the Civil Law held by the legal working committee of the Standing Committee of the National People's Congress in September 2015. At the seminar, some scholars thought that the separate compilation of the law of personality rights would lead to the political risk of a colour revolution,[6] while other scholars immediately criticised it as nonsense of politicising the formulation of the civil code. This also triggered several major debates among scholars. Subsequently, a comprehensive debate went on between two sides on whether political risks would be caused by the separate compilation of the law of personality rights in the civil code.[7]

Second, the report by the 19th National Congress of the CPC Central Committee proposing protecting people's personal rights, property rights and personality rights once again triggered a debate among the academic circles of civil law.[8] One side believed that the thought of compiling the law of personality rights should be unified to strengthen the legislation of personality rights in the civil code and implement the guideline of the 19th National Congress.[9] The other side proposed that there was no need to stipulate the right of personality in the civil code but the need to make declarative because the right of personality was a constitutional issue and was none of the business of civil law scholars who are not politicians.[10] This debate was very intense.

Third, after some units made comments on the Law of Personality Rights in the Civil Code (Indoor Draft) drafted by the legal working committee in November 2017, the independent compilation of personality rights became the focus of debate over the compilation of the civil code and formed a hot spot online.[11] Scholars of both parties kept publishing articles to express their diametrically opposite views.[12]

Fourth, the ongoing discussion represents a peak of the debate. After the legal working committee of the Standing Committee of the National People's Congress proposed that the exposure draft of each part of the civil code be reviewed on a larger scale, including the exposure draft for the law of personality rights, scholars who denied the legislative decision-making of personality rights were furious. They directly negated the work of the legal working committee and the China Law Society and totally repudiated the indoor draft and exposure draft, calling the drafts a copycat which follow the model of Personality Rights in the Civil Code of Ukraine, and describing the intent of those scholars who support the separate part on personality rights is to flimflam and adulterate.[13] Scholars who advocated for the exposure draft of the law of personality rights have also fully expressed their opinions.[14] The debate is ongoing.

5.2 The Conclusion Drawn from Reviewing the History of the Legislation and Debate on China's Personality Right Law

In particular, by reviewing and combining the origin and development of about 70 years of debates over personality rights stipulated in the General Principles of the Civil Law in 1986 and the inclusion of the law of personality rights in the civil code in 1999, we can draw the following conclusions.

5.2.1 In the Social Development of China, the Existence and Lack of Personality Right Laws in Civil Legislation May Bring Very Different Consequences

We can take the years 1986 and 1987 as the dividing line of time. Before 1986, when there was no legislation of personality rights in China, the protection of personality rights could not be considered to be completely absent, but it was not perfect or comprehensive, and only a few personality rights were practically protected by law.[15] Since 1987, the General Principles of the Civil Law has greatly promoted social progress, although there are not many types of personality rights recognised in it. It is obvious that before 1986, except cases of personal damage compensation as judicial relief to protect the right to life and health, there wasn't a single case of defamation, of infringement on the right to portrait, or of infringement on the right to name in terms of the protection of other personality rights in judicial practice. This shows that although the personality right has certain pre-existing and defensive attributes, the protection of a specific personality right not confirmed by law is basically impossible. Therefore, it is neither probative nor persuasive to take the defensive and pre-existing nature of personality rights as evidence to deny the legislative decision-making of personality rights. This can be proved by only one example. Since there had been no right to privacy in the General Principles of the Civil Law for 30 years, judicial organs had to determine tort liability in regards to infringements on the right to reputation to protect the right to privacy in an indirect way in 1988 if the infringement on privacy damaged the right to reputation.[16] In 2002, the Supreme People's Court recognised the defect of indirect protection of the right to privacy, so the judicial interpretation stipulated that direct protection should be adopted. However, only the interests of privacy rather than the right to privacy were protected because there was no provision on the right to privacy in legislation.[17] It was not until December 2009 that the Tort Liability Law stipulated the direct protection of the right to privacy. This shows that it is extremely difficult to protect the right of personality without legislative confirmation but through defence and prevention. Scholars who advocate that the law of personality rights is the law of rights protection rather than the law of rights confirmation cannot be unaware of this experience and lesson. It is not a realistic approach to research, insisting that they do not know that.

5.2.2 *Since 1986, China's Legislature Has Fully Affirmed the Importance of Personality Rights Legislation and Strengthened the Civil Legislation of Personality Rights*

In 1986, unprecedented provisions on the right of personality were made in the General Principles of the Civil Law. Since 1999, a fierce debate has been going on over whether personality rights should be stipulated in the civil code separately. In such a situation, the legislature still clearly adheres to the consistent position in formulating the law of personality rights in the civil code: (a) in 2000, the leading group for formulating the civil code under the Standing Committee of the National People's Congress decided that the Research Centre of Civil and Commercial Jurisprudence of Renmin University of China would be responsible for the draft proposal for the separate law of personality rights and tort liability; (b) in April 2002, the legal working committee of the National People's Congress held a special meeting to discuss the draft proposal for the separate laws of personality rights and tort liability in the civil code, and determined the legislative guideline of the two laws; (c) the Civil Law (Draft) produced by the Standing Committee of the National People's Congress in December 2002 contained personality rights in Part 4, including a total of 24 articles; (d) in November 2017 and 2018, the legal working committee of the Standing Committee of the National People's Congress launched the indoor draft and exposure draft of personality rights in the civil code for internal comments. Some people believed that the Civil Law (Draft) of the People's Republic of China produced by the Standing Committee of the National People's Congress in 2002 had been repealed. That is not true because the review of the Civil Law (Draft) was taken as the first review of the Property Law, Tort Liability Law and Laws Applicable to Foreign-Related Civil Relations by the Standing Committee of the National People's Congress in 2002. For example, the review of the Civil Law (Draft) in 2002 was taken as the first review of the Property Law, which was reviewed eight times, and the Tort Liability Law, reviewed four times. This shows that the Civil Law (Draft) was not repealed but was the basis for formulating various separate laws of the civil law. The legislation of the civil law is consistent, including the consistent position of stipulating the part on personality rights in the civil code. In this sense, China's legislature has always advocated the formulation of the law of personality rights since 1986. Therefore, this is completely irrelevant to the approach to the inclusion of personality rights in the Civil Code of Ukraine enacted in 2003. This can better prove that China's legislature has always attached importance to the legislation of personality rights.

5.2.3 *Is the Civil Code to Be Compiled This Time the Continuation of the Civil Law (Draft) Reviewed in December 2002?*

Disadvantageous evidence shows that the review of the Civil Law (Draft) in 2002 was not taken as the first review of the General Rules of the Civil Law formulated this time, a practice in contrast to that in the compilation of the Property Law, Tort Liability Law and Laws Applicable to Foreign-Related Civil Relations. The author believes that the compilation of the civil code is seemingly new legislative work this time, but, in essence, it is still a continuation of the previous legislative work. The reasons are as follows. First, both are legislation of the civil code carried out by the same legislature. Second, the separate parts of property rights, Tort Liability Law and Laws Applicable to Foreign-Related Civil Relations in the Civil Law (Draft) in 2002 are the legislative basis of the Property Law, Tort Liability Law and Laws Applicable to Foreign-Related Civil Relations. The separate parts of contract, marriage and family, as well as inheritance, which were included in the Civil Law (Draft), were added to the Civil Law (Draft) in 2002. Third, the Draft of the Separate Laws of the Civil Code (Exposure Draft), in essence, is still the continuation and development of the Civil Law (Draft). Fourth, most of the draft General Rules of the Civil Law is based on the Civil Law (Draft). Therefore, it is attempting to say that the legislation of the civil code this time is the continuation of the civil code in 2002 because they are different in form but intrinsically related. Even if the compilation of the General Rules of the Civil Law (Draft) this time is restarted as a new legislative task deployed by the central government, rather than the direct continuation of the civil code in 2002, this doesn't suffice to deny the connectivity between the General Rules of Civil Law and the Civil Law (Draft) of 2002. That is because the General Rules of the Civil Law and the Civil Law (Draft) have gone through the indoor draft, exposure draft and the four deliberative drafts all the way, and the provisions hereof are borrowed from the Civil Law (Draft) of 2002. Besides, the legal working committee of the Standing Committee of the National People's Congress proposed that the Law of Personality Rights in the Civil Code of the People's Republic of China (Exposure Draft) should be reviewed together with each separate law of the civil code. Although it is a new task, the Exposure Draft is also consistent with Part 4 on personality rights of the Civil Law (Draft) in 2002 in form and content.

5.2.4 China's Government Agencies Adhere to Democratic Centralism[18]

The core of democratic centralism means the minority is subordinate to the majority and the individual obeys the organisation, and it is the same with the legislature. In terms of the academic discussion in legislation, it is understandable for scholars to adhere to their own academic position and express their own academic opinions, and they should be encouraged to speak frankly. When the legislature has determined the legislative plan and is implementing it, however, the minority should be subordinate to the majority, and the individual should obey the organisation. The individuals can reserve their different opinions. Since 1999, the legislature has twice decided to establish personality rights in the civil code, which is an unambiguous position of legislation. Under such circumstances, imposing their will on the legislature is not in line with democratic centralism.

5.2.5 *In the Final Analysis, the Question of whether Personality Rights Should Be Separately Stipulated in the Civil Code Involves Legislative Technology*

The personality rights legislation indeed involves a political foundation and academic position. For instance, in terms of the political foundation, the law itself is an integral part of the superstructure and needs to be subject to socio-economic development. The academic position involves the choice to adopt a traditional civil law system or make innovations to meet the developments of the new era in the formulation of personality rights law. However, the right of personality must be stipulated in the civil code, which is a consensus. The focus of the debate is whether it is put in the general provisions, or in the part on tort liability, or compiled as a separate part. It is very clear that the irreconcilable debate over the legislative technology is never beneficial to scientific legislation. It is more important to concentrate more on studying the design of the draft law to make the provisions more scientific and on stipulating more comprehensive personality rights to better protect them as the time for legislation is very precious.

5.2.6 *Experts from the Legislative and Judicial Organs and Civil Law Scholars Have Made Great Contributions to the Formulation of the Law of Personality Rights or Separate Inclusion of Personality Rights in the Civil Law*

In the legislature, in addition to Peng Zhen, chairman of the Standing Committee of the National People's Congress, Wang Hanbin, Gu Angran, Qiao Xiaoyang, Hu Kangsheng, Wang Shengming, Wei Yaorong and other leaders of the legal working committee and the civil law office, who actually participated in the legislation, promoted the legislation of personality rights with resolution. In the highest judicial organs, Ma Yuan, Fei Zongyi, Tang Dehua and Du Wanhua have made outstanding contributions to the legislation of personality rights. In the community of civil law, Professors Tong Rou, Wang Jiafu, Jiang Ping, Wei Zhenying and Wang Liming are the most influential scholars who advocated for the legislation of personality rights in the civil code. Without their persistence, there would be no personality rights law in China's civil legislation, and the protection of personality rights in China would not be what it is today. Actually, it is unfair for some people to credit the idea of the independent compilation of personality rights to Professor Wang Liming because this will erase what so many experts and scholars have done for it. After all, only a majority of scholars insist on denying the legislation of personality rights.

The above conclusion drawn from reviewing the debate on China's personality rights legislation and legislative thought is based on facts in the historical development of China's personality rights legislation.

5.3 The Inclusion of Personality Rights in the Civil Code is the Correct Choice Made by China's Legislature

5.3.1 The Essential Reasons for the Legislature Insisting on the Establishment of Personality Rights in the Civil Code

There are a variety of theoretical explanations and practical basis for the necessity to compile the personality rights in the civil code by the legislature of China. I can simplify the elaboration with the following three most essential reasons.

First, the legislature has inherited the legislative experience of personality rights stipulated in the General Principles of the Civil Law.

The General Principles of the Civil Law stipulates the law of personality rights, which represents a pioneering undertaking in formulating the law of personality rights in China's civil law, and lays a legislative foundation for protecting people's personality rights. In this sense, this practice has contributed greatly to the social development of China. In the decades before 1986, the right to personality was not well protected. Accordingly, the turmoil known as the Cultural Revolution lasted for a decade when the right to personality was seriously trampled upon. Learning from history, the legislature formulated the General Principles of the Civil Law. Since then, China has witnessed continuous social progress, as well as the improvement of personality rights legislation and of people's status as masters of the country amid reform and opening up. In the new era, it is necessary to formulate a civil code leading the development of the times. The General Principles of the Civil Law is such a law. The legislative experience in stipulating personality rights in the General Principles of the Civil Law must go on so as to enhance the dignity of our people, protect their personality rights and ensure their status as masters of the country. Therefore, it is very logical and necessary to compile personality rights in the specific provisions of the civil code. In other words, in Chapter 5 Civil Rights of the General Principles of the Civil Law, in fact, the framework basis for personality rights has been established, determining the status of specific provisions of the civil code such as real right, creditor's right (including contract and tort liability) and the rights to personality and identity (marriage and family). Moreover, in the chapter on civil rights, the General Rules of the Civil Law, which had just been formulated, comprehensively stipulates the personality right and the right to identity, real right, creditor's right, the rights to intellectual property, inheritance and equity, expanding the macro-framework of the specific provisions of the civil code. This is also what the General Principles of the Civil Law has done. It is attempting to say that in the compilation of the civil code, China's legislature has always advocated the establishment of personality rights in specific provisions of the civil code. This approach must continue.

Second, China's judicial organs have refined the practical experience in the application of law to the recognition and protection of personality rights.[19] Since the General Principles of the Civil Law was implemented on January 1, 1987, China's judicial organs have accumulated experience in the protection of personality rights by providing a large number of fresh and precious cases for the construction of China's legal system of personality rights with distinctive Chinese characteristics. This can be shown in the following list: (i) protection of the personality interests of the deceased; (ii) confirmation and protection of the right to privacy; (iii) specific provisions for the judicial protection of the right to reputation; (iv) recognition and protection of the right to personal freedom; (v) the recognition and protection of general personality rights; (vi) compensation and relief for mental damage to personality interests caused by infringement on specific commemorative objects of symbolic personality significance; (vii) compensation and relief for spiritual damage to the rights to life, body and health and so on. Such judicial experience is beneficial to both China and other countries in the world in the protection of personality rights. These judicial lessons with distinctive Chinese characteristics need to be further refined to become solid legal norms in the law of personality rights in the civil code. These provisions cannot be contained in the General Rules of the Civil Law due to their capacity and the nature of the provisions. As it is intended to protect civil rights, the law of tort liability can't accommodate personality rights, which should be confirmed to exercise positive functions. Therefore, personality rights can only be stipulated in the specific provisions of civil law to connect with the types of civil rights stipulated in the General Rules of the Civil Law. The specific provisions of civil law can provide enough legislative space to accommodate such rich rules. This is also the essential reason why personality rights must be stipulated in China's civil code.[20]

Third, the protection of personal dignity and personality rights should meet the need for China's development in the new era since the reform and opening up. It can be said that the legislation for the protection of personality rights in China was absent from 1949 to 1986. Since 1987, China has witnessed the rise and rapid development of the legislation and protection of personality rights. From now on, with the progress of building socialism with Chinese characteristics and the advent of the new era of reform and opening up, the personality rights legislation and protection in China should meet higher requirements and develop better with more distinctive Chinese characteristics. In the new era of reform and opening up, the development must accommodate people's desire to be masters of the country, meet their need to enjoy better personal dignity and solve the contradiction between people's growing needs for a better life and unbalanced and insufficient development.[21] This is how the normal movement of the contradiction advances social development. People's growing needs for a better life include their needs for their own status and rights. Strengthening the legislation of personality rights is one of the ways to relieve the unbalanced and insufficient development. The essential social contradiction is one that acts as the fundamental restrictive force among the countless contradictions of the social organism, that is, the contradiction between productive forces and production relations, and between the economic foundation and superstructure, which exist in all societies. The contradictory movement between productive forces and production relations, two aspects of the social production mode, proceeds according to the law that production relations must be suitable for the development of productive forces. Strengthening the legislation and protection of personality rights can improve the imbalance and insufficiency of civil legislation, especially personality right legislation, in the basic social contradictions, and make society develop more harmoniously. Therefore, personality rights should be stipulated in China's civil code to meet the people's needs for a better life and ensure their needs for the perfection of personality rights and personal dignity.

The author believes that three reasons alone are enough to explain the necessity for the inclusion of personality rights in China's civil code. This is the summary, inheritance and development of China's own experience in legislative, judicial and social practice. The authentic Chinese experience with Chinese characteristics has nothing to do with the Civil Code of Ukraine or the civil law legislation of the traditional civil law system. We should solve China's civil law legislation, especially the legislation of personality rights, according to China's own experience and theory regardless of the practice of foreign civil codes.

5.3.2 The Simplest Demonstration of the Correctness of Legislative Decision-Making on the Inclusion of Personality Rights in the Civil Code

In fact, the reason for the legislative decision made by the legislature on the inclusion of personality rights in the civil code can also be reflected in a simple argument through three interrogative sentences, that is, has China made progress or regressed, has the personal dignity of our people increased or decreased, and has our people's status as masters of the country been raised or lowered since 1949, especially since the stipulation of personality rights in the General Principles of the Civil Law in 1986? The answers to these questions are all yes. Well, China should and must continue to stipulate personality rights in the civil code and further improve them! Can there be any other conclusion drawn or path to go? Not at all!

China's legislature has always adhered to three pieces of valuable experience in legislation: the leadership of the party, the mass line and the combination of theory and practice in legislation. In the legislative decision-making process of compiling personality rights in the civil code, the legislature drew on the above basic experience and made the correct decision. The German experience, the French experience and even the Ukrainian experience, as well as the theories of so many foreign scholars, including the opinions of Chinese scholars in Taiwan, are all references and examples for China's legislation but are by no means necessary. The reason is that we are formulating the civil code of the People's Republic of China, not foreign and overseas civil codes. Some scholars wrote much in their articles to demonstrate that the exposure draft of personality rights in the civil code proposed by the legal working committee is a misunderstanding of the opinions of the Party Central Committee or even a violation of the mass line. They blamed the legal working committee for not sticking to the mass line or attaching equal importance to theory and practice in legislation, for violating the legislative tradition of foreign civil codes, acting as the shadow of the Civil Code of Ukraine and abandoning three pieces of valuable experience above. In this way, they deny the legitimacy and correctness of the legislative decision made by the legal working committee of drafting personality rights in the civil code. All this is a completely groundless assumption.

5.4 A Brief Analysis of Parts of the Reasons for Denying the Legislative Decision-Making on the Inclusion of Personality Rights in the Civil Code

Those who deny the legislative decision-making of the inclusion of personality rights in the civil code gave many reasons that were logically chaotic and imprecise in argumentation. There should have been no need to make more responses. However, most of them are specious theories and will mislead others if not explained. Therefore, after sorting them out, I have selected some representative statements for brief analysis so as to confirm that these cannot suffice to deny the legislative decision on the inclusion of personality rights in the civil code. In the previous section of this paper, some of their statements have been analyzed. In the section 5.3, several others are selected for analysis.

5.4.1 Analysis of the Facts Related to the Legislative Decision-Making of Personality Rights

5.4.1.1 Has the CPC Central Committee Explicitly Denied the Legislation of Personality Rights in the Civil Code?

Some scholars said that the central government clearly denied the legislation of personality rights and blocked all possibilities for the compilation of personality rights.[22] This is a statement that needs to be proven by facts. However, so far, scholars who advocate for this statement have not provided any conclusive evidence to prove that the central government has done so. Anyone who makes the statement should bear the burden of proof. If there is no evidence provided, scholars who claim this statement are considered to be misreading the guideline of the central government and distorting objective facts. The report by the 19th National Congress announced the protection of people's personal rights, property rights and personality rights.[23] This, we believe, is the spirit of the 19th National Congress and the guiding ideology for unifying the legislation of personality rights in the civil code.[24] Some scholars even cited various authorities to prove that such a great historical document as the report by the 19th National Congress was the result of the proponents of separate legislation on personality rights hoodwinking the CPC. The Plan for Legislation and Law Amendment Guided by Socialist Core Values in the Construction of the Rule of Law issued by the CPC Central Committee proposed accelerating the compilation of separate parts of the civil code, shaping the spiritual soul of the civil code with socialist core values and promoting civil subjects to consciously practice socialist core values.[25] In the first national assembly for training in leading political and legal cadres, jointly held by the Organisation Department, the Political and Legal Commission and the Party School of the CPC Central Committee, from May 3 to 7, 2018, the Political and Legal Commission of the CPC Central Committee especially stressed that in responding to valuing the protection of personal rights and property rights over personality rights, we should take legal, technical and management measures to protect citizens' personal information, especially the rights to privacy and reputation.[26] The planning made by the CPC Central Committee and the opinions of the Political and Legal Commission of CPC Central Committee prove that our view is correct. How can they say that strengthening the protection of people's personality rights is the result of being hoodwinked? These statements should not have come from a serious scholar.

5.4.1.2 Has the China Civil Law Society (CCLS) Ever Voted on the Proposed Draft for the Compilation of Personality Rights?

Some scholars said that in a vote on the proposed draft for the compilation of personality rights initiated by the China Civil Law Society (CCLS) in 2015, it was impossible to make a decision because three people agreed and three people disagreed. They also said that the China Civil Law Society planned in vain to submit the draft to the annual meeting of civil law for voting in 2017 because the majority of the executive directors and directors opposed that. This statement also needs to be proved by facts. As far as I know, the above two statements are a distortion of the facts because I have participated in almost all major activities held by the China Civil Law Society as the vice president of this society for more than ten years, and have never seen all that was mentioned happen. The most basic fact is that the proposed draft for the inclusion of personality rights in the civil code provided by the China Civil Law Society to the legal working committee was indeed discussed, but what was discussed was how to amend it, not whether to submit it to the legal working committee because there was no need to vote on it. In particular, in the so-called 3-3 vote, at least six people should vote, but who are these six people? If the leaders of the society above the vice president are qualified to vote, there are more than a dozen, not six, people qualified, and voting among six people will not be effective. If a standing director is qualified, there are dozens of people qualified. Therefore, the voting among six people is false.

5.4.1.3 How and By Whom Should the Word "etc." in the Plan for the Specific Provisions of the Civil Code Be Interpreted?

At the legislative explanation and press conference on the General Rules of the Civil Law, the legislature made it clear that the specific provisions of the civil law include the separate parts of the real right, contract, tort liability, marriage and family, as well as inheritance when talking about the legislative plan for the specific provisions of the civil code.[27] Does the word "etc." mean that specific provisions of personality rights are included in the civil law? Some scholars think it is impossible for specific provisions of personality rights to be included in the civil law. This is a problem between semantics and fact. In terms of word meaning and grammar, the word "etc." means a linguistic sign for endless enumeration in principle. Although some people think so, it is not a common interpretation. Actually, whoever uses the word "etc." has the right to explain. The legislature that believes that the specific provisions of the civil law include the separate parts of the real right, contract, tort liability, marriage and family, as well as inheritance has the right to explain which specific provisions the word "etc." contains and whether it includes personality rights or not. It is an issue of the power of the legislature, not of theoretical interpretation, to explain how many specific parts are contained in the civil law and which parts of specific provisions the word "etc." includes. Whether personality rights are stipulated in the civil code is subject to the legislative decision-making of the legislature. Others can express their own opinions, but they cannot replace the decision-making by the legislature with their own opinions. It is obviously incorrect to interpret the words "etc." used by the legislature according to one's own opinions and then force the legislature to implement the legislative plan following one's own inclination. It is also wrong that if the word is not interpreted in accordance with one's own opinions, the legislature will be regarded as complying in appearance but opposing in heart.

5.4.2 On the Responsibilities of the Legal Working Committee of the Standing Committee of the National People's Congress and Relevant Units

5.4.2.1 The Legal Working Committee Acts as the Lead Unit for the Compilation of the Civil Code

What is most distinctive in the climax of the debate on the inclusion of personality rights in the civil code is that some scholars accused the legal working committee of the Standing Committee of the National People's Congress of violating its duties and agreeing outwardly but disagreeing inwardly after the exposure draft of personality rights in the civil code was launched.

The legal working committee is the leading unit that organises and bears the responsibility for drafting the civil code. The legal working committee, as the working body of the legislature under the National People's Congress, should be criticised if there is something wrong with the draft of personality rights in the civil code it delivered. However, it is not an independent state organ but a legal working organisation established within the Standing Committee of the National People's Congress. All the work of the legal working committee is carried out in the name of the Standing Committee of the National People's Congress and is subject to the latter. If the legal working committee makes a mistake, the person in charge should bear responsibility, but if a mistake is made by the state organ, the responsibility must be borne by the Standing Committee of the National People's Congress, which is the legal person of this state organ. Therefore, it is worthless to accuse the legal working committee of introducing the draft legislation during the change of the term of office of the Standing Committee of the National People's Congress, and thus criticize the legal working committee for being engaged in petty and two-faced intrigue and not understanding the working system and rules of the organ.

Some scholars also criticised the legal working committee, an internal body of the Standing Committee of the National People's Congress, which could not decide the exposure draft of the law, for getting up to little tricks to challenge the basic principle set by the Party Central Committee. The legal working committee shall, in accordance with its duties, submit a sound legislative draft for the law included in the legislative plan by the legislature to the Standing Committee of the National People's Congress or the National People's Congress for deliberation. In order to ensure the quality of the draft provided, the legal working committee will internally solicit the opinions of experts, scholars and relevant organs on the revision of the draft. This is not only its responsibility but also the principle of democratic and scientific legislation that it has followed for a long time. Since 1990, critics have participated in such activities to provide opinions on the draft law many times, and the legal working committee often solicits opinions from them. It is the normal duty of the legal working committee to solicit opinions on the draft law it is responsible for or to solicit opinions from itself on the revision of the draft law. How could they say the legal working committee, when soliciting opinions on the draft law of personality rights in the civil code, was engaged in petty and two-faced intrigue? The logic behind this statement is incomprehensible.

5.4.2.2 On the Responsibilities of the China Law Society and Other Units Involved in the Compilation of the Civil Code

In the compilation of the civil code, especially the proposed draft for the law of personality rights, it was particularly unjust that the China Law Society was also condemned by scholars who denied the legislative decision-making of the compilation of the law of personality rights. The China Law Society, an academic group in the community of law, is entrusted to manage and coordinate China's legal academic organisations so as to promote the prosperity and development of legal academia. The China Law Society was appointed by the central government to participate in the coordination of compiling the civil code for the mission of the society, but it can't participate in legislation directly. Therefore, during the compilation of the civil code, the China Law Society established a leading group for the compilation of the civil code and coordinated the research forces of the civil and commercial law circles by organising 80% to 90% of the major scholars in these two fields to draft proposals for each part of the specific provisions of the civil code. They provided the proposed drafts of the law of real right, contract, tort liability, marriage and family, as well as inheritance, and also appointed the China Civil Law Society to prepare the proposed draft of the law of personality rights and submit it to the legislature for reference.[28] It is also the responsibility of the China Civil Law Society to solicit opinions on some draft laws on the Internet. Since it did not exercise the legislative power, it has nothing to be criticized for. Over more than 20 years of civil legislation, almost all of us scholars have drafted proposals for law, and many have solicited opinions on the Internet, published monographs and papers, but have never been suspected of exercising legislative power. Why was the China Civil Law Society considered to have exercised legislative power beyond their authority when organising civil law experts to carry out such activities? This is also an abnormal logic of thinking.

Among the coordinating units involved in the inclusion of the law of personality rights in the civil code, the Supreme People's Court, the Supreme People's Procuratorate and the Legislative Affairs Office of the State Council were also accused, but the scholars didn't say what should be criticised. The author would like to say that the Supreme People's Court is most active in advocating for the inclusion of the law of personality rights in the civil code. The essential reason is that the Supreme People's Court is the best qualified to say that more than 30 years of judicial practice has proved the necessity to strengthen the legislation of personality rights. Since basic provisions on personality rights were made in the General Principles of the Civil Law, the civil judge of courts across the country has been the real practitioner in how to protect personality rights in judicial practice and the most qualified to propose the approach to formulating personality rights law. The accusations against them are unreasonable.

5.4.2.3 Two Stages on the Surface and Three Stages in Practice

One of the reasons why some scholars deny the inclusion of the law of personality rights in the civil code is that the legislature made a hidden three-stage plan, opposed to the two-stage legislative plan made by the central government. In fact, the non-existent, so-called two seeming stages and three hidden stages were made up by scholars. The so-called hidden three stages means that specific provisions of the civil code are the integration of the old law rather than the formulation of a new law, while the compilation of personality rights is the formulation of a new law. Therefore, the inclusion of a new law of personality rights in the special provisions of the civil code is considered to be similar to foist some scholars personal views into the official plan. The compilation of the civil code proceeds in two stages, that is, the general provisions first, and then specific provisions. Personality rights, an integral part of specific provisions, are stipulated through overall deliberation, which is the due part of the legislative plan of the legislature. Three hidden stages are false. Personality rights are stipulated in the second stage of the legislative plan and also part of the civil code. The compilation of personality rights is still the authority of the legislature, and any unit or individual has the right to make suggestions and criticism but has no right to interfere with the legislative decisions by the legislature.

5.4.3 *Wrong Interpretation of the Definition of Personality Rights and Wrong Interpretation of the Theory of Personality Rights Law*

5.4.3.1 Personality Rights Are not Indefinable and Unspeakable

In order to deny the legislative decision on the inclusion of personality rights in the civil code, some scholars describe personality rights as defensive, pre-existing, unspeakable and undefined, and then draw the conclusion that the law of personality rights does not need to be compiled independently or even compiled in law. The defensive and pre-existent nature of personality rights has been explained by the author. The unspeakable and undefined nature of personality rights should also be analyzed.

It is really difficult to define personality rights because it has been less than 100 years since personality rights were valued all over the world. It is obviously too short a period of time compared with other concepts of civil rights with an even longer history. However, the difficulty in defining it does not mean that it cannot be defined. Personality rights, if undefined, are not a legal concept at all because any legal concept can be defined, but it is harder to accurately define. The reason why some scholars describe personality rights as unspeakable is that they have not reached a certain degree in the research into the concept of personality rights. The definition of the personality right by law is considered to be only difficult to describe, not to be unspeakable, and the unspeakable concept is not a legal concept. These two proposed attributes of the personality right are not a scientific explanation of the legal attributes of the personality right but show a lack of in-depth research. The right of personality is a kind of inherent necessary civil right that the civil subject enjoys according to law to maintain their own independent personality, with the interest of personality as the object.[29] The correct interpretation of personality interests means that we can accurately define the personality right. As Mr. Zheng Yubo said, the right of personality is the right of the obligee's own personality, that is, social interests, including the rights to life, body, freedom, chastity, reputation, portrait, name, credit and other rights, enjoyed by the obligee and protected by the law due to the inseparable relationship between him and his personality.[30] It is not convincing to deny the legislative decision on the inclusion of personality rights in the civil code for the indefiniteness and unspeakability of personality rights because the argument is untrue.

5.4.3.2 Whether the Right of Personality Needs to Be Confirmed and Can Be Exercised

Another reason for negating the inclusion of personality rights in the civil code is that the purpose of personality rights stipulated by law is to protect and remedy them, not to confirm and exercise them. Therefore, personality rights cannot be exercised and do not need to be exercised. Obviously, such understanding of personality rights is outdated, as this is a statement that people made on personality rights research according to the civil law theory decades ago.

First of all, although the right of personality is pre-existent, there will be difficulties in exercising and protecting it without legal confirmation. The case of the right to privacy mentioned above, for instance, will not be repeated.

Secondly, in modern times, the positive function of personality rights is universally recognised, and personality rights are not just a defensive right.[31] On the one hand, the rules for the right to publicity summarise the positive function of personality rights. Although some personality rights cannot be directly exercised, some other personality rights do have positive functions and can be used for the commercial development of personality interests protected by them so that the obligee can obtain direct property interests. Such personality rights as the rights to portrait, name, privacy and personal information can be exercised. This is the true meaning of Article 4 of the exposure draft of personality rights in the civil code, which stipulates that the civil subject has the right to dispose of their names, portraits, personal information and other personality rights and interests with the content of economic interests, and may license others to use. The domination of the object of these rights, such as name, portrait and personal information, is the exercise of personality rights. The exercise of these personality rights allows the obligee to obtain benefits and realise rights. On the other hand, according to law, the obligee can also exercise some personality rights that cannot be applied to the right to publicity for commercialisation. For example, the donation of one's own body parts to others, and euthanasia, a kind of positive or negative disposition of one's own life interests, are both the embodiment of the positive function of personality rights. It can be seen that these personality rights can be exercised.

5.4.3.3 The Law of Personality Rights Is the Law of the Protection of Rights but First and Foremost the Law of Rights

One of the reasons for negating the inclusion of personality rights and legislative decision-making in the civil code is that they belief that the personality right, which is obtained through birth and naturally disappears when one dies, cannot be included in the framework of the law of rights. It doesn't matter whether the law recognises it or not and whether the law stipulates it or not. There are several mistakes in this interpretation of the law of personality rights. First, the personality right is an inherent right, which is enjoyed but not obtained when one is born. Second, the conclusion that the right of personality is an inherent right that cannot be included in the law of rights is also incorrect because both the inherent right and the acquired right are civil rights and part of the norms of the law of rights. Third, it is completely wrong to believe that it doesn't matter whether the law recognises it or not and whether the law stipulates it or not because the right of personality not recognised or stipulated by the law cannot be protected in judicial practice. As the right to privacy was not stipulated in the General Principles of the

Civil Law described above, the dilemma of privacy protection appeared in judicial practice. In addition, the right to personal freedom, which was not stipulated in the General Principles of the Civil Law, was basically not protected by law in decades of judicial practice. It was not until the Supreme People's Court made a judicial interpretation in 2002 that it was partially protected. The right to personal freedom was not confirmed in the subsequent Tort Liability Law, so it was difficult to have proper legal application for the cases of infringement on the right to personal freedom in reality. All this shows that it does matter much whether the law recognises personality rights or not and whether the law stipulates them or not. Such an interpretation of the law of personality rights does not respect the fact and is wrong in theory.

5.4.3.4 Personality interest of seeking death?

In denying the decision-making on the inclusion of personality rights, some scholars criticised the exposure draft and the indoor draft of the law of personality rights. Some of the criticisms are proper, but the majority of them are groundless. For example, they criticised the statement that civil subjects enjoy personality interests in many parts of the exposure draft and indoor draft and hold that personality rights are not necessarily a kind of personality interest. They think that life, which is painful for some people sometimes, cannot be called enjoyed personality interests, and it is no longer a benefit to a person who is in pain. Because the object of personality rights contains pain or happiness, it is the personality interests enjoyed by the personality rights holder and falls under civil interests.[32] As the object of personality rights, the personality interest does not refer to a specific feeling of the civil subject. Isn't life the object of the right to life for a person who is in pain? The obligee can exercise its personality interests by choosing euthanasia to free itself from pain, which is the embodiment of enjoying personal interests.

5.4.3.5 The Tie between the Law of Personality Rights and Tort Liability Law

The reasons for denying the decision-making on the inclusion of personality rights in the civil code also include the standard for evaluating the protection level of personality rights and the purpose of classifying personality rights in a country. It is believed that the evaluation of the protection level of personality rights depends on whether the country's tort law (protecting personality rights) is developed and progressive and that the classification of personality rights is only to facilitate the labelling of cases of infringement disputes over personality rights according to the cause of action. The former argument seems to be correct but is actually incomplete, and if combined together, these two arguments are incorrect. However, the level of personality right protection depends on the development of both the tort law and personality rights legislation because personality rights should be protected by the claim of both tort and personality, just as the right to property needs to be protected by both tort law and the claim of real right. In addition, the legislation of personality rights should involve provisions on both protection and on the type, content and exercise of personality rights. Therefore, the legislation of personality rights is not perfect, with only personality rights protected by tort law. The classification of personality rights aims to determine the content of different types of personality rights and the rules for the specific exercise of rights. It is obviously a one-sided understanding that is only convenient to label cases concerning infringing personality rights according to the cause of action. The contemporary law of personality rights aims to protect rights, more importantly, to standardise the content and the rule of exercising personality rights. It belittles the value of the law of personality rights to simply identify the labelled provisions of personality rights as the classification of the cause of action of the case of infringement on personality rights. The tort law can protect personality rights but cannot replace the law of personality rights because the former cannot provide for the confirmation and exercise of personality rights.[33]

5.4.3.6 *Query about the Statement That the Dual Application Principle for the Protection of Personality Rights Is Unnecessary*

The dual application principle in law for the protection of civil rights is almost a basic theorem of civil law. The simplest example is the relationship between the claim of real right and the claim of infringement. In a case of the infringement of real right, you can choose either the claim of infringement or the claim of real right for protection. Once the claim of infringement is selected for protection, a dual application mode will be formed; that is, the real right is determined by the Property Law and is also protected by the claim of real right. The protection of tort liability must be regulated by the Tort Liability Law. Can we say the dual application principle is unnecessary, like taking off your pants and farting? It is the same with the protection of the right of personality. The right of personality, if infringed, is protected by both the claim of the right of personality and the claim of infringement. In this regard, why can the dual application principle apply to the protection of real right but not to the protection of personality rights? This statement also shows the critic takes a part for the whole, which is caused by the lack of a comprehensive understanding of the theory and development of personality rights. Besides, it is not scholarly to use such vulgar language for academic discussion.

In this regard, some scholars mentioned that the shortcoming of the inclusion of personality rights lies in incomplete legal provisions and dual application, which shows a misreading of the provisions of the exposure draft. There are indeed some incomplete provisions in the exposure draft, which do not contain a legal effect, but this is to avoid overlapping with the provisions in the Tort Liability Law and reduce repetitive provisions. In addition, rights confirmation is the premise of relief. The exposure draft contains specific provisions on the exercising of rights, stipulating that the personality rights of citizens shall not be infringed upon. The perpetrator who infringes the personality rights of someone needs to remedy the damaged rights in accordance with the Tort Liability Law, which is stipulated in Paragraph 1, Article 6 of the Tort Liability Law. The remedy by the claim of personality rights shall apply to the provisions of the claim of personality rights in Chapter 1 of the exposure draft of the law of personality rights. These are normal applications of the law, and there is no need to criticise them.

5.5 The Draft of the Law of Personality Rights in the Civil Code (Exposure Draft) Is a Relatively Successful Law

One of the important reasons why some scholars deny the legislative decision-making of the inclusion of personality rights in the civil code is that the provisions are similar to definitions, which are either nonsense or fallacies; they are empty articles of "shall not infringe," repeated provisions borrowed from other existing special laws, and incomplete articles on bearing responsibility that make no sense. It is not objective to make such an evaluation on the draft of the law of personality rights in the civil code (exposure draft) because it is an innovation made according to the actual situation of our society and based on the provisions of personality rights in the General Principles of the Civil Law and the General Rules of the Civil Law.[34] Thanks to the combination of innovation and conservation, the draft of the law of personality rights in the civil code (exposure draft) is not only logically consistent in the system but also sufficient and perfect in content, and it can basically meet the legislators' expectation of the function of the civil code. Therefore, it is considered to be a relatively successful draft law.

5.5.1 The Draft of the Law of Personality Rights in the Civil Code Meets the Needs for Social Development in the New Era of Reform and Opening Up in China

We have entered a new era when China is deepening its reform and opening up. With the continuous development of state governance and economy, people's personal dignity has been continuously improved, and China has seen people's status as masters of the country continuously consolidated, and human rights better protected by law. The core of the people's growing demand for a better life is to protect human dignity, status and rights. If this is interpreted with the basic social movement of the contradiction between people's growing demand for a better life and unbalanced and insufficient development,[35] we should focus on solving unbalanced and insufficient development in strengthening legislation. Doing a good job in the inclusion of personality rights in the civil code shows the respect for the movement law of this basic social contradiction—the superstructure must adapt to the development of the economic foundation and meet the needs for social development in the new era. This is how the dignity, status and personality rights of people are protected.

The content of the exposure draft of the law of personality rights in the civil code conforms to China's social development in the new era. First of all, in the movement of basic social contradictions in China, what is primary in meeting people's growing need for a better life is to make them live with more dignity and play a core role in developing productive forces and adjusting production relations. To that end, the civil code as the superstructure must adapt to that and actively play its reaction. The basic idea of said exposure draft is to safeguard human dignity. By improving the system of personality rights, the law of personality rights can ensure that people can play a role in leading the development of production modes, meet the needs for the development of productive social force and production relations and promote the sound movement of China's basic social contradiction. Secondly, said exposure draft meets the need to consolidate the people's status as masters of the country. The exposure draft gives priority to the protection of people's personality rights and interests, which are the most important and essential civil rights and interests of civil subjects. The protection of personality rights and interests means protecting people's qualification as human beings, allowing people to become perfect civil subjects, and best consolidating their status as masters of the country in state affairs. Thirdly, the exposure draft stipulates a relatively perfect system of personality rights, including both general and specific personality rights, turning China's legislative and judicial experience in personality rights since the General Principles of the Civil Law was implemented into a comprehensive and perfect system for the protection of the subject qualification and its constituent elements. As such, in the new era, our people can enjoy more personality rights, better exercise their own personality rights and better protect their personality rights by defending against the infringement of their personality rights.

For the above reasons, it can be confirmed that the law of personality rights in China's civil code represents a declaration to protect the personality rights of civil subjects and a law to confirm, exercise and protect their personality rights, and the exposure draft of the law of personality rights can meet such requirements and accommodate the social expectations for the functions of the civil code. Therefore, said exposure draft is correct in the general legislative orientation, is in line with the needs for China's social development in the new era, and is draft legislation of specific provisions of the civil law reflecting the characteristics of the times.

5.5.2 The Exposure Draft of Personality Rights in the Civil Code Has a Complete and Clear Framework

A look through the current exposure draft of the law of personality rights shows that it has made significant progress compared with the indoor draft. In terms of the overall structure, the indoor draft adopts the lateral-vertical-lateral mode; that is, the draft consists of general provisions, specific personality rights, and provisions on the protection of the personality rights. Such a structure is complex but not concise and clear enough, although it is in line with the internal logic of the legal system of personality rights. The exposure draft changed that into a lateral-vertical structure, which meets the general requirements for designing legislation.

The exposure draft is easy to learn, master and apply in judicial practice for its simple hierarchy, clear structure, distinct general rules and specific rules, and clear system of abstract personality rights and specific personality rights.

Moreover, Chapter 1 of the general provisions and Chapters 2–6 of the specific provisions have a clear framework, with provisions spread in an orderly way, which basically meets the legislative requirements. After further improvement, the exposure draft of the law of personality rights will become civil legislation with a rigorous structure, clear framework, distinct hierarchies and detailed provisions. It will become the highlight with the most distinctive Chinese characteristics in the system of the civil code.

5.5.3 The General Provisions of Personality Rights Stipulated in the Exposure Draft of the Law of Personality Rights Are Perfect and Advanced

As an integral part of the civil code reflecting the characteristics of the new era, the law of personality rights should not only facilitate the social development of the country but also be of significance to the world, reflecting the requirements of the times for the standardisation and development of personality rights.[36] This is clearly reflected in the general provisions in Chapter 1 General Provisions in the exposure draft of the law of personality rights.

Although there are only 12 articles in the first chapter of the exposure draft of the law of personality rights, it is extremely rich and advanced as it is the collection of not only China's achievements in legislation, judicial practice and theoretical research of personality rights, but also the world's main experience in the development of personality rights. That is how the general rules of China's law of personality rights formed.

First of all, the exposure draft of the law of personality rights clearly stipulates the inherent characteristics of personality rights and interests enjoyed by civil subjects. It is stipulated in Article 2 that personality rights and interests shall not be abandoned, transferred, or inherited, indicating that innate personality rights and interests aren't obtained for certain facts or acts. In this regard, the state can impose necessary restrictions in accordance with the law only for the public interest. The isolation and treatment of patients during the SARS outbreak, for instance, didn't violate the inherent characteristics of personality rights and interests.

Secondly, the exposure draft of the law of personality rights stipulates abstract personality rights, including general personality rights and the rights to self-determination and publicity.[37] These general personality rights, in contrast to specific personality rights, are the function of personality rights and the embodiment of enjoying, controlling, exercising and protecting specific personality rights. The general personality rights generalise the nature of specific personality rights and can supplement specific personality rights for the lack of legislation so as to protect personality interests that are not protected by the specific personality right.[38] The right to self-determination is stipulated in Article 130 of the General Rules of the Civil Law on the provisions of right control. This functional right is incorporated into the personality rights law as the right to self-determination of personality rights by Article 3 of the exposure draft. This ensures the distinctively special and exclusive exercising of the personality right; that is, only the obligee has the right to exercise the constituent elements of its own personality.[39] The right to publicity stipulated in Article 4 has shown the most distinctive characteristics over the recent 50 years of development of personality rights. In other words, the obligee has the right to license others to make commercial development and utilisation of some of his inherent personality interests so as to ensure that he can enjoy and control his own personality interests and obtain the greatest interests.[40] These provisions, although recognised and applied in the laws and judicial practice of most countries and regions, are rarely stipulated comprehensively in a law.

Thirdly, the perfect part of the first chapter of the exposure draft of the law of personality rights is the provisions on the protection of personality rights and interests.[41] First, Article 8 stipulates the right of claim for personality rights as the basic method of civil law for the protection of personality rights. It provides for the general methods of relief and also stipulates that the methods of relief for the right of claim for some personality rights are not limited by the limitation of action, which is more conducive to the relief of the infringed personality right. Second, Article 9 stipulates the conditions for exercising the right of claim when the right of personality is infringed, which provides a general legal basis for judicial practice. Third, Article 10 stipulates the prohibition system against the infringement of the right of personality, which is the preventive measure in advance of the infringement of the right of personality. The right subject can apply to the court for an injunction ordering the perpetrator to stop relevant acts so as to protect his personality rights and interests to the greatest extent as long as there is evidence to prove that the perpetrator is conducting or about to conduct an infringement on his rights and interests of personality and will cause irreparable damage to his rights and interests of personality if the conduct is not stopped in time. Fourth, in terms of the specific protection of personality rights and interests, Article 5 stipulates that the close relatives of the deceased have the right to protect a person's rights to name, portrait, reputation, honor, privacy and other personality interests that are infringed. This is connected with the provisions on the protection of fetal personality interests stipulated in Article 16 of the General Rules of the Civil Law, forming a complete protection system for personality rights and interests. Article 10 stipulates that if the breach of contract causes serious mental damage for the infringement on the other party's personality rights and interests, the victim can directly claim mental damage compensation in the litigation of liability for breach of contract instead of exercising an infringement claim alone for relief. Article 11 stipulates the forms of civil liability, such as issuing announcements or publishing effective judgment documents. This is the relief the court actively provides to the victim when the infringer does not bear civil liability, such as an apology. The provisions of these three articles have distinctive characteristics in the world's systems of relief for the damage to personality rights.

It is attempting to say that most of the exposure draft of the law of personality rights is advanced, important and effective institutional rules with characteristics of the times for the protection of personality rights, which is of worldwide significance to the recognition, exercise and protection of personality rights.

5.5.4 The Provisions of Specific Personality Rights Are Basically Complete and Substantial

The main part of the exposure draft of the law of personality rights is the provisions of specific personality rights. This part has the most distinctive characteristics as follows.

First, it stipulates the most important specific personality rights that should be stipulated, including the rights to life, body, health, name, portrait, reputation, honor, privacy and personal information. In addition, some important provisions of more specific personality rights are made in these listed rights in a flexible way. For example, the right to personal freedom is stipulated in the right to body; sexual autonomy is also attached to the right to body; the right to credit is stipulated in the right to reputation for protection; the right to communication confidentiality is specified in the right to privacy. In these different ways, specific personality rights enjoyed by the civil subject in real life are almost made in detail, forming a complete system of specific personality rights.

Second, it specifies the content and rules of exercising various specific personality rights. For example, the provisions on the rights to life, body and health contain the specific contents and general protection methods of the three material personality rights. The main part of the exposure draft also specifies the right to ask for emergency assistance, the right to donate body parts, and the basic requirement for human testing. Most of these rules, although stipulated in different laws and regulations, will be of more important value if they are concentrated, supplemented and included in the basic norms of civil law. The protection of pen names, stage names and online names, as well as abbreviations, style names and literary names, are stipulated in the right to name. In addition to the specific content and general protection provisions of the right to portrait, the provisions of the right to portrait contain those on the partial transfer of the portrait interests by the portrait rightsholder; that is, part of the right to portrait can be transferred to others for use through the contract of portrait license. This is how the general rules for the exercise of the right to publicity of the modern personality right are formed. In addition, provisions for licensing the use of other personality interests are contained. This practice is of significance worldwide and particularly commendable. The provisions of the rights to reputation and honour recognise legitimate news reporting, supervision by public opinion, and literary creation and confirm the conditions for civil liability for acts violating the legitimacy principle. In particular, the right of the obligee to obtain material benefits for his honour is specified for the first time. The provisions of the rights to privacy and personal information comprehensively define the right to privacy and the right to personal information, and specify acts that cannot be conducted to infringe personal privacy, the legal conditions for obtaining other people's information, and acts that don't infringe on the right to personal information. These rules are comprehensive and specific.

Third, the exposure draft is based on the summarisation of the experience in legislation and judicature as well as theoretical research results. It contains many innovations, reflecting the characteristics of the times. The legal regulation of sexual harassment, for instance, involves both rights protection and workplace protection, reflecting the position of giving priority to rights protectionism supplemented by workplace protectionism.[42] The measures for the protection of network names and abbreviations of civil subjects with certain social fame and known to the public are specified in the right to name. In terms of portrait protection, "portrait" is defined as an identifiable external image that can protect the portrait and other parts of the human body image. In particular, with regard to the provisions on the protection of personal information, the newly generated right to be forgotten in Europe is stipulated in Article 47 of the exposure draft in an innovative way. That is, considering the specific purpose of collection or use, it is no longer necessary for the information holder to keep the information, and the natural person has the right to require timely deletion. Such provisions are of great value to the world as they exist in the legislation of only a few countries.

Of course, the above positive evaluation of the exposure draft of the law of personality rights does not mean that it is perfect as it needs to be further improved in many aspects. To keep this thesis compact, I will make suggestions for modification and improvement to the legislature through other channels. Forgive me for not being able to expound on them.

5.6 Conclusions

From the above discussion, we can come to the conclusion that the essential legislative orientation of the exposure draft of the law of personality rights in the civil code is correct, and it is a comprehensive and feasible exposure draft with a clear framework. It is believed that after further modification and improvement, it will become a perfect part of the civil code and play an important part in protecting the people's personality rights.

The criticisms on the legislative decision-making of personality rights in the civil code are largely arbitrary and groundless accusations. In the Ming Dynasty, LV Kun once said in *Moaning Words* about the commandments that critics should abide by,

> When pointing out the mistakes made by a person who has made five mistakes, you had better only point out three or four. Doing so will make him afraid and convinced and stop him from defending. It is unkind of you to point out five mistakes. Doing so, you have no way back. If you point out six mistakes, this will give him an excuse to defend the actual five mistakes

> because one mistake is not that fact. You only point out one extra mistake, and the other five mistakes are pointed out in vain. This is a warning for those who blame people.[43]

Lv Kun (October 24, 1536, to July 24, 1618), styled Xinwu, was also known for his literary name Baodujushi. He was born in Lvdazhuang, Ningling, Guide Prefecture in the Ming dynasty (now Ningling, Shangqiu, Henan Province). He was an upright and honest writer and thinker of the Ming dynasty and one of the three sages in the country during the Wanli period of the Ming dynasty. The above explanation on commandments that critics should abide by hits the nail on the head. In terms of the draft of the law of personality rights in the civil code, we critics have the right to criticise it in order to achieve high quality in the formal legislation. However, the critic may have goodwill or malice in criticising it. The criticism of well-intentioned critics can promote the perfection of legislation. Malicious critics pour criticism on the draft law of personality rights and completely negate it so that it will have no chance to rise again. This violates the commandments that critics should abide by. There are two or three deficiencies in the draft, but some critics pointed out five and even twelve. By pouring on the criticisms, some critics lost their academic face and exposed their weaknesses and malicious purposes. Therefore, they have lost more than they have gained and delayed the legislative process of personality rights in the civil code, which is unnecessary. It is better to focus on how to improve the provisions of personality rights in the civil code than to argue endlessly about whether the law of personality rights can be compiled independently.

Notes

1 Foundation item: This paper is the phased research achievement of the scientific research foundation item of Renmin University of China titled “Research on the Judicial Application and Systematisation of the Basic Principles of Civil Law” (Item No. P17XNQJ04). I would like to thank Jiao Qingyang, Hu Yan, and Li Yiwen for helping me sort out and proofread the manuscript.

2 The Supreme People’s Court promulgated the Reply to the Legal Protection of the Right to Reputation of the Deceased in 1988, the Answers to Some Problems on the Trial of Reputation Cases in 1993, the Interpretation on Several Issues concerning the Determination of Compensation Liability for Mental Damage in Civil Tort in 2002, and the Interpretation on Several Issues on the Application of Law in the Trial of Cases of Personal Damage Compensation in 2004, the Provisions on Several Issues Concerning the Application of Law in the Trial of Civil Dispute Cases Involving the Use of Information Networks to Infringe upon Personal Rights and Interests in 2004, and published eight typical cases involving the use of information networks to infringe on personal rights and interests in the same year, making important contributions to fully realising the protection of China’s personality rights enjoyed by civil subjects.

3 Yang Lixin et al.: Chinese Civil Law over Thirty Years (1978–2008), published in: Chinese Civil Law over Thirty Years, China Renmin University Press, 2008, p. 112, edited by member of executive editorial board Jiang Mingan.

4 On March 10, 2011, when delivering the work report of the Standing Committee of the National People’s Congress to the Fourth Session of the 11th National People’s

Congress, Wu Bangguo, chairman of the Standing Committee of the National People's Congress, solemnly announced that a socialist legal system with Chinese characteristics had been formed. Based on the realities in China, the legal system adapts to the needs for reform, opening up, and socialist modernisisation, and reflects the will of the Party and the people. Subject to the constitution, the system is dominated by relevant constitutional laws, the civil law, commercial law, and laws in other fields, including laws, administrative regulations, local regulations and autonomous regulations, and separate regulations.

5 On June 27, 2016, in the explanation by the chairman's meeting of the Standing Committee of the National People's Congress on the proposal to submit for deliberation the draft General rules of the Civil Law, Li Shishi, chairman of the legal working committee of the Standing Committee of the National People's Congress, said,

> The civil code is to proceed in two phases. First, compile the general rules of the civil code (i.e. the General Rules of the Civil Law) so that it could be adopted by the fifth session of the 12th National People's Congress in March 2017. Second, compile the separate parts of the civil code so that they could be adopted by the session of the National People's Congress in March 2020.

6 Du Tao: The Birth of the General Rules of the Civil Law—An Important Draft of the General Rules of the Civil Law and an Introduction to the Background of the Legislative Process, Peking University Press, 2017, p. 6.

7 See Liang Huixing for negative views: The Most Heated Debate and My Attitude to the Compilation of the Civil Code of China—A Lecture at the Law School of Sichuan University, published in 360doc Personal Library, accessed May 6, 2018, website: http://www.360doc.com/content/16/1215/20/39118872_615098058.shtml. For positive views of many supporters, please refer to Yang Lixin: Rational Thinking on the Major Debate on the Law of Personality Rights Compiled in the Civil Code, China Law Review, 2016, issue 1; Wang Liming: Discussion on the Positive Confirmation Mode of Personality Rights—Also on the Relationship between the Law of Personality Rights and Tort Law, The Jurist, 2016, issue 2.

8 Xi Jinping: Win the Battle to Finish Building a Moderately Prosperous Society in All Respects and Win the Great Victory of Socialism with Chinese Characteristics in the New Era—Report by the 19th National Congress of the Communist Party of China, People's Daily of China, October 28, 2017, edition 4.

9 Yang Lixin: Unifying the Legislative Thought of the Compilation of Personality Rights in the Code in the Spirit of the 19th National Congress, Shengjing Law Review, 2017, issue 2.

10 Sun Xianzhong: Scientific Legislation Required by the 19th National Congress and the Compilation of the Civil Code of China, Journal of Beijing University of Aeronautics and Astronautics (Social Science Edition), 2018, issue 1.

11 Zou Hailin: Why Can't the Right of Personality Be Compiled Separately in the Civil Code, published in WeChat official account of Iolaw.cssn.cn on January 24, 2018; Liang Huixing: The Separate Part of Personal Rights Can Not Be Compiled in China's Civil Code, released in official account, Understanding of the Civil Law, February 4, 2018. During the debate, the official account, Understanding of the Civil Law, published relevant articles and disclosed the unauthorised indoor draft, which was deleted by the author and can't be accessed.

12 The main works of the advocating side include Yang Lixin: Unifying the Legislative Thought of the Compilation of Personality Rights the Code in the Spirit of the 19th National Congress, published on the official account of China Civil and Commercial Law, January 25, 2018; Wang Liming: On the Reasons for the Separate Compilation of Personality Rights; Yang Lixin: Rational Thinking on the Major Controversy over the Compilation of the Law of Personality Rights in the Civil Code; Ma Junju: Discussion

on Personality and the Legislative Model of Personality Rights; Meng Qinguo: The Independent Compilation of Personality Rights is the Only Choice for China's Civil Code; Liu Kaixiang: Debate and Discrimination in the Legislation of Personality Rights; Liu Shiguo: On the Personality of Subject Status and Personality Dignity; Shi Jiayou: On the Relationship Between Human Rights and Personality Rights—Starting from the Independent Compilation of the Personality Right Law, published in the official network account of the China Civil and Commercial Law, January 26, 2018; Wang Liming: Present Efforts Will Benefit Generates—My View on the Law of Personality Rights in the Civil Code of People's Republic of China (Draft), published in the official network account of the China Civil and Commercial Law, February 5, 2018; and Wang Liming: Implement the Report by the 19th National Congress to Strengthen the Legislation of Personality Rights, published in the official network account of the China Civil and Commercial Law, February 11, 2018

13 Liang Huixing: Major Debate in the Compilation of Civil Code—Also on the Two Drafts of Personality Rights Made by the Legal Working Committee, published in: Understanding of the Civil Law, April 26, 2018. The remarks made by the quoted scholars on denying the legislative decision-making of personality rights in this thesis, if not explained with notes, are all from the above article.

14 Wang Liming: What is the Relationship between the Civil Code of Ukraine and the Law of Personality Rights in China's Civil Code, China Civil and Commercial Law, April 30, 2018; China Civil and Commercial Law, May 5.

15 Yang Lixin et al.: Chinese Civil Law over Thirty Years (1978–2008), published in: Chinese Civil Law over Thirty Years, China Renmin University Press, 2008, p. 112.

16 See Article 140 of the Opinions on Several Issues Concerning the Implementation of the General Principles of the Civil Law of the People's Republic of China (for Trial Implementation) issued by the Supreme People's Court in 1988: "Those who publicise the privacy of others in written, oral and other forms, …shall be recognised as acts infringing on the right to reputation of citisens if a certain consequence is caused."

17 See Paragraph 2 of Article 1 of the Interpretation on Several Issues Concerning the Determination of Compensation Liability for Mental Damage in Civil Tort promulgated by the Supreme People's Court in 2002:

> If the victim brings a lawsuit to the people's court for compensation for mental damage on the ground of infringement upon its privacy or other personal interests in violation of social public interests and social morality, the people's court shall accept it according to law.

18 Article 3 of the Constitution of the People's Republic of China stipulates the state organs of the People's Republic of China adhere to democratic centralism.

19 A total of 554,372 disputes over personality rights concluded by the people's court of China can be retrieved from January 1, 1998, to January 1, 2018, through the case database PKULAW of Peking University.

20 Professor Wang Liming also has a full analysis on this. See Wang Liming: On the Independent Compilation of Personality Rights, Studies in Law and Business, 2012, No. 1; Discussion on the Positive Confirmation Mode of Personality Rights—Also on the Relationship between the Law of Personality Rights and Tort Law, The Jurist, 2016, issue 2.

21 Xi Jinping: Win the Battle to Finish Building a Moderately Prosperous Society in All Respects and Win the Great Victory of Socialism with Chinese Characteristics in the New Era—Report by the 19th National Congress of the Communist Party of China, People's Daily of China, October 28, 2017, edition 4.

22 360doc Personal Library: Exclusive Interview with Professor Liang Huixing—From the General Principles of the Civil Law to the General Rules of the Civil Law in the Past 30 Years, accessed on May 8, 2018, website: http://www.360doc.com/content/17/0902/07/1417717_684067918.shtml.

23 Xi Jinping: Win the Battle to Finish Building a Moderately Prosperous Society in All Respects and Win the Great Victory of Socialism with Chinese Characteristics in the New Era—Report by the 19th National Congress of the Communist Party of China, People's Publishing House, 2018, p. 49.
24 Yang Lixin: Unifying the Legislative Thought of the Compilation of Personality Rights in the Civil Code in the Spirit of the 19th National Congress, Reference for the Compilation of Civil Code (internal reference) No. 20, 2017.
25 The Central Committee of the Communist Party of China distributed the Plan for Legislation and Law Amendment Guided by Socialist Core Values in the Construction of the Rule of Law, People's Daily of China, May 8, 2018.
26 Xiong Feng, Xinhua News Agency: What Signals Were Released by the First National Assemble for Training for Leading Political and Legal Cadres after the 19th National Congress? Xinhua Daily Telegraph, May 8, 2018, 3rd edition.
27 Li Jianguo: Notes on the General Rules of the Civil Law of the People's Republic of China (Draft)—at the Fifth Session of the 12th National People's Congress on March 8, 2017, published in: Legislative Background and a Complete Collection of Views on the General Rules of the Civil Law, Law Press, 2017, p. 5.
28 In the group for drafting the proposed draft of each part of the specific provisions of the civil code organised by the China Law Society, Professor Cui Jianyuan is responsible for the law of real right; Professor Wang Liming, the law of contract; Professor Zhang Xinbao, the law of the tort liability; Professor Xia Yinlan, the law of marriage and family; Professor Yang Lixin, the law of inheritance; and Professor Wang Yi, the law of personality rights. Each thematic group includes dozens of civil law experts.
29 Yang Lixin: The Law of Personality Rights, Law Press, 2016, p. 39.
30 Zheng Yubo: The General Rules of the Civil Law, Sanmin Book Co. Ltd., 1998, p. 96.
31 Wang Liming: Discussion on the Positive Confirmation Mode of Personality Rights—Also on the Relationship between the Law of Personality Rights and Tort Law, The Jurist, 2016, issue 2; Liu Zhaocheng: Establishment of Subjective Right Status and the Legislative Choice of Personality Rights, Law Science, 2013, issue 6; Huang Fen: Limited Transfer of Commercialised Personality Rights, Hebei Law Science, 2017, issue 1.
32 Yang Lixin: The Object of Personality Rights is Not Personality but the Personality Interest, Reference to the Compilation of Civil Code (internal reference), 2018, issue 4.
33 Wang Liming: Discussion on the Positive Confirmation Mode of Personality Rights—Also on the Relationship between the Law of Personality Rights and Tort Law, The Jurist, 2016, issue 2; On the Humanistic Care and Independent Compilation of Personality Rights, Journal of Chongqing University (social sciences edition), 2016, issue 1; On the Reasons for the Independent Compilation of Personality Rights, Law Review, 2017, issue 6; On the Promulgation of China's General Rules of the Civil Law and the Establishment of Personality Rights in the Civil Code, Political Science and Law, 2017, issue 8.
34 Shi Jiayou: Pragmatic Combination of Conservation and Innovation: Comment on the Law of Personality Rights in the Civil Law of the People's Republic of China (Draft), Journal of Comparative Law, 2018, issue 2.
35 Xi Jinping: Win the Battle to Finish Building a Moderately Prosperous Society in All Respects and Win the Great Victory of Socialism with Chinese Characteristics in the New Era—Report by the 19th National Congress of the Communist Party of China, People's Daily of China, October 28, 2017, Edition 4.
36 Wang Yi: The Spirit of the Times and Chinese Characteristics of the General Rules of the Civil Law, Ziguangge, 2017, issue 7.
37 Yang Lixin and Liu Zhaocheng: On Abstract Personality Rights and the Construction of the Personality Right System, Chinese Journal of Law, 2011, issue 1.
38 Yang Lixin and Liu Zhaocheng, On General Personality Rights as Abstract Personality Rights, Guangdong Social Sciences, 2010, issue 6.

39 Yang Lixin and Liu Zhaocheng: On the Right to Self-Determination as an Abstract Personality Right, Academia Bimestrie, 2010, issue 5.
40 Yang Lixin and Lin Xuxia: On the Commercialisation of Personality Logo and its Civil Law Protection, Journal of Fujian Normal University (Philosophy and Social Sciences Edition), 2006, issue 1.
41 Yang Lixin and Yuan Xueshi: On the Claim of Personality Rights, Chinese Journal of Law, 2003, issue 6.
42 Yang Lixin: On the Law of Personality Rights, Law Press, 2016, p. 276.
43 Lv Kun: Moaning Words, Volume VI, Human Feelings, China Ancient Book Publishing House, 2008, p. 200.

6 The Formation, Development and Finalisation of the Chinese Experience in Personality Rights Legislation[1]

By Yang Lixin

Since the Law of Personality Rights was stipulated in the General Principles of the Civil Law of the People's Republic of China, the Chinese experience in the legislation of personality rights has been widely praised. In the inclusion of the Law of Personality Rights in the Civil Code, we should correctly interpret the Chinese experience that has been gained in the legislation of personality rights since China initiated reform and opening up in 1978. That is how such an experience can be continuously developed, improved and formalised in China's upcoming civil code. In this way, such experience can continue to be carried forward in China to protect people's personality rights and influence the world.

6.1 The Formation and Development of the Chinese Experience in Personality Rights Legislation

6.1.1 The Initiation of the Concept of the Chinese Experience in Personality Rights Legislation

The Chinese experience in personality rights legislation is also called the Chinese model of personality rights legislation[2] or the Chinese experience in personality rights protection.[3] They are basically the same thing, but they have different focuses.

The concept related to the Chinese experience or Chinese model of personality rights legislation was summarised by me as an initiative of China's civil legislation and a pioneering contribution to the development of world civil law.[4] After the Research Centre of Civil and Commercial Jurisprudence of Renmin University of China completed the Draft Proposal for the Law of Personality Rights in the Civil Code in the spring of 2002, at the Sino–Japanese seminar on the law of personality rights held in Lijiang, Yunnan Province, I proposed summarising the experience in the legislation of personality rights in the General Principles of the Civil Law with the concept of the Chinese model. This proposition was affirmed by Tang Dehua, vice president of the Supreme People's Court, and other participants who thought that this concept accurately summarises the experience in the legislation of personality rights in China.

Careful analysis reveals that there is no substantive difference between the Chinese model of personality rights legislation and the Chinese experience in

DOI: 10.4324/9781003300168-6

personality rights legislation. They are the same, but they are a little bit different from the Chinese experience in personality rights protection. Although the three emphasise the distinctive manifestation of the legislation of personality rights in China's Civil Law and its important position in the history of world civil law, the first two focus on the distinctive and important position of China's legislation of personality rights as a whole, while the third focuses only on the distinctive and important position of China's legislation in the protection of personality rights. In short, it is evident that the first two focus on the overall situation and the third on the local situation.

The author insists on using the concept of the Chinese model of personality rights legislation or the Chinese experience in personality rights legislation to emphasise not only the distinction of China's personality rights law in the protection of personality rights but the distinction in the whole legislation of personality rights. I deliberately avoided the limitations of the concept of the Chinese experience in personality rights protection. The purpose of proposing the concept of the Chinese experience in personality rights protection is to emphasise that the Chinese experience in personality rights legislation lies in the protection of personality rights, rather than the progressiveness of the whole legislation of personality rights.

6.1.2 The Formation of the Chinese Experience in Personality Right Legislation

The Chinese experience in personality rights legislation was formed in April 1986 when the General Principles of the Civil Law was adopted. It stipulates the personality right, which is juxtaposed with the real right, creditor's right and intellectual property right in the chapter on civil rights in the civil law. It also stipulates relatively complete Classification of personality rights, specific content and protection of personality rights.

The Chinese experience in personality rights legislation was formed for the following two main reasons.

First is the painful lessons from a decade of turmoil in the Cultural Revolution from 1966 to 1976. Before the Cultural Revolution, there was no comprehensive protection of personality rights in China, and the legislation of personality rights was almost non-existent. In judicial practice, acts such as fighting causing injury and death that infringe material personality rights are defined as the crime of injury and homicide, and the actor is punished in accordance with the criminal law. In addition, the infringer shall bear the liability for personal damage compensation in accordance with the civil law. In its reply in 1963 to the request for instructions from the Higher People's Court of Heilongjiang Province on compensation for traffic accident damage, the Supreme People's Court noted, "The aggressor shall give the victim for the traffic accident a certain amount of pensions, including but not limited to child maintenance expenses." On May 26, 1965, the Letter on Compensation and Pensions for Traffic Accidents issued by the general office of the Supreme People's Court, the general office of the Ministry of Public Security and the Labor Insurance Department of the All-China Federation of Trade Unions pointed out, "The financial compensation given by the accident causing party to the family members of the employee who dies from a traffic accident is not only a sign of responsibility for the deceased, but also a spiritual comfort." This reply, which did not strictly distinguish property damage compensation from spiritual damage compensation, reflected the basic understanding of the right to personality and personality rights protection at that time. With the spread of left-wing thoughts, legal viewpoints with strong ideological colour that gradually penetrated legal thought, this left-wing ideology denied the spiritual damage compensation and mercilessly criticised the so-called commercialisation of personality rights.[5] These replies reflected the imperfection of personality rights legislation at that time. There was no more declaration and protection of personality rights in the legislation and judicature except that, so personality rights were seriously trampled upon in the ten-year turmoil.

Considering such experience and lessons, the legislature formulated the General Principles of the Civil Law in 1986 and specially stipulated personal rights in a section in the chapter on civil rights. This is how the right of personality was stipulated. What was important in the legislation of personality rights was not how many articles were stipulated but the extreme importance of the legislation and protection of personality rights recognised at that time. In addition, the personality right was given the same priority as the real right, creditor's right, and intellectual property right. That means that the personality right and real right, creditor's right and intellectual property right are the same type of civil rights that should be separately stipulated in the civil law. That is the most important point. Therefore, the legislation of personality rights in the General Principles of the Civil Law is the result of drawing on the painful lessons from ten years of turmoil. For this reason, a good job must be done in the legislation of personality rights to strengthen personality rights protection.

Second, the wisdom and courage of legislators to make innovations and change. People who participated in the legislation of the General Principles of the Civil Law included leaders and staff of legislative organs, civil law scholars and staff of judicial organs. These wise experts and scholars gathered together, summed up the historical experience and lessons, and set aside 8 articles among the 156 articles in the General Principles of the Civil Law for the right of personality. This was a major legislative measure showing great courage and boldness. At that time, there was no civil code but China's that juxtaposed personality rights with real rights, creditor's rights and intellectual property rights in the civil law legislation of all countries in the world. China's Civil Law did so by juxtaposing it with real rights, creditor's rights and intellectual property rights to form the chapter on civil rights. This unprecedented legislation means that the right of personality has the same status as other civil rights in China's civil legislation. This approach has laid a legislative foundation and provided a sufficient historical basis for the legislation of personality rights in the civil code. The legislative precedent of the law of personality rights included in the General Principles of the Civil Law was a legislative achievement that had not been realised in the civil codes of other countries. It was an advanced legislative experience that was proven by practice and also a scientific system generally recognised by civil law scholars.[6] Because of this, it is reasonable to say that the General Principles of the Civil Law has created the Chinese experience and provided a Chinese model in the legislation of personality rights.

To sum up, the Chinese experience in personality rights legislation is that created by the General Principles of the Civil Law. The core value of the experience lies in the systematic provisions of personality rights in the General Principles of the Civil Law and in the establishment of the important position of personality rights in the civil rights system for the first time. In 1986, when the General Principles of the Civil Law was formulated, there was no Civil Code of Ukraine. Although the Civil Code of Quebec of Canada stipulated certain personality rights in a special chapter on persons, it was not a systematic law of personality rights, and its revision was completed later than the General Principles of the Civil Law.[7] In this regard, the General Principles of the Civil Law was considered to be a major breakthrough in the legal system[8] and landmark legislation in personality rights in the civil law in both China and beyond. This is the value of the Chinese experience in personality rights legislation.

6.1.3 The Development of the Chinese Experience in Personality Rights Legislation

The summary of the development of the Chinese experience in personality rights legislation reveals the following four aspects.

6.1.3.1 The Legislation of Personality Rights Has Been Continuously Improved

The General Principles of the Civil Law established the basic system of China's personality rights law, but it also had some shortcomings. Therefore, it needed to be constantly improved in the subsequent legislation. In laws such as the Law of Consumer Protection, the Law on the Protection of Minors, the Law on the Protection of Women's Rights and Interests, the Law on the Protection of the Rights and Interests of the Disabled, the Law on the Protection of the Rights and Interests of the Elderly and the National Compensation Law, personality rights such as privacy, personal freedom and the protection of personality rights such as death compensation and disability compensation were constantly supplemented. In particular, the Tort Liability Law, the revised Law of Consumer Protection, the Food Safety Law and other laws stipulate more personality rights such as the right to privacy and personal information as well as the protection systems for these rights. This has enriched China's Law of Personality Rights and promoted the development of the Chinese experience, forming the state of the legislation today.

6.1.3.2 The Judicial Experience in personality Rights Has Been Accumulating Continuously

Since the legislation of personality rights in the General Principles of the Civil Law, China's judicial practice has continued to promote the development of the Chinese experience in the legislation of personality rights. Before the implementation of the General Principles of the Civil Law, China's judicial practice only protected the right to life and health. In addition to these physical personality rights, China's judicial practice strengthened the protection of spiritual personality rights, resulting in a strong trend of safeguarding rights in China. The judiciary dares to take on the responsibility, constantly summarises the experience, and deepens the theory of personality rights law. In terms of the legal application of personality rights, the Opinions on Several Issues Concerning the Implementation of the General Principles of the Civil Law of the People's Republic of China (for Trial Implementation) stipulates those who publicise privacy in written, oral and other forms openly vilify personality and damage the reputation of others by means of insult and slander, resulting in a certain impact that shall be recognised as infringing on the right to the reputation of citizens. The Supreme People's Court also issued the Answers to Some Issues Concerning the Trial of Cases of the Right to Reputation, Interpretation of Some Issues Concerning the Trial of Cases of the Right to Reputation, Interpretation of Several Issues on the Determination of Compensation Liability for Mental Damage in Civil Tort and Interpretation of Several Issues on the Application of Law in the Trial of Cases of Personal Damage Compensation, forming a complete system for the content and protection of the Law of Personality Rights. The Interpretation of Several Issues on the Determination of Compensation Liability for Mental Damage in Civil Tort, in particular, could be regarded as the second milestone in the legal protection of personality rights in China.[9] All these show that China has established a relatively perfect judicial system of personality rights protection.

6.1.3.3 The Deepening and Refinement of the Theoretical Research into Personality Rights Law

Since the General Principles of the Civil Law established the Chinese experience in the legislation of personality rights, the Chinese academic community of the civil law has provided insights into the legal theory of personality rights, forming a peak of the study of the theory of personality rights. Over the years, articles and work on the law of personality rights have abounded. Before the General Principles of the Civil Law was issued, there was almost no theoretical research into the law of personality rights in China. According to data from China National Knowledge Infrastructure (CNKI), there were only 4 articles on personality rights published before 1986, 5 in 1986, 18 in 1987, 125 in 2001 and more than 200 in 2005 and 313 in 2016. Since 1986, over 4000 papers on the law of personality rights have been published. At present, dozens of monographs and teaching materials on the law of personality rights has been published in China. Over the more than 30 years since the Chinese experience in personality rights legislation established the General Principles of the Civil Law, the theory of personality rights law in China has developed to a considerable extent. It has promoted the progress of China's personality rights legislation and judicature and facilitated the development of the Chinese experience in personality rights legislation. The deepening theoretical research of personality rights law has improved the theoretical basis and value of the Chinese experience in personality rights legislation and has become an important part of the Chinese experience in personality rights legislation.

6.1.3.4 Extensive Reference to Foreign Experience in Legislation and Judicature

Although the General Principles of the Civil Law established the Chinese experience in the legislation of personality rights, the advanced legislative style and system do not necessarily mean perfect legislation. In both theory and practice, the experience must be extensively referred to to solve practical problems in China and be mastered by China. Foreign experience in personality rights legislation, judicature and theoretical research results should be absorbed to form and improve the Chinese experience in personality rights legislation. The general personality rights in Germany,[10] the right to self-determination in Japan,[11] and the right to publicity in the United States[12] can be used for reference to make them an integral part of China's experience in personality rights legislation. These are stipulated in the first chapter of the Law of Personality Rights in the Civil Code (Draft), forming new and systematic general rules of the Chinese experience in the legislation of personality rights. Extensive references to foreign experience have promoted the development of the Chinese experience in the legislation of personality rights. We can quickly borrow new personality rights in the world. For example, the right to be forgotten created by the European Court of Human Rights was borrowed[13] and quickly applied in trial practice.[14]

The continuous development of the Chinese experience in the personality rights legislation mainly relies on the continuous supplementing of legislation, a summary of judicial experience, sublimation of theoretical research and reference to foreign experience. The law of personality rights has a relatively perfect legislative system and rich content and is expected to be shaped in appropriate time.

6.2 Correct Interpretation of the Chinese Experience in Personality Rights Legislation

6.2.1 How to Interpret the Chinese Experience in Personality Rights Legislation

Views are different on how to interpret the Chinese experience in personality rights legislation.

Some scholars believe that when compiling the civil code, China must respect the Chinese experience in protecting the right to personality and take the current Tort Liability Law, which needn't be changed substantially, as part of the civil code. They think it is enough to allocate a special section in the chapter on natural persons in the General Rules of the Civil Law to list the types of personality rights stipulated in the General Principles of the Civil Law, retain the types of personality rights recognised by the judicial interpretation of the Supreme People's Court, and at best, add provisions to general personality rights proposed by scholars. Therefore, China's experience in personality rights protection manifests as follows: firstly, personality rights are protected by tort law; secondly, personality rights are classified by law, and then new types of personality rights are recognised by the Supreme People's Court through judicial interpretation, so as to define the scope of personality rights protection; third, the commercialisation of personality rights is stipulated in Article 20 of the Tort Liability Law.[15]

Attention should be paid to the Chinese experience in personality rights legislation or personality rights protection as follows.

First, the Chinese experience in personality rights legislation cannot be interpreted as the Chinese experience in personality rights protection. The former, established in China's General Principles of the Civil Law, is different from that of other countries, and not just the experience of the protection of personality rights in the civil law of China. Contemporary personality rights law focuses on not only the protection of personality rights but also on the comprehensive standardisation of the content, domination and exercise of personality rights, as does the General Principles of the Civil Law. For example, Article 99 stipulates that citizens have the right to name, which is an enabling provision, the right to decide to use and change one's own name in accordance with law, which is a provision on the content of the right, and the right to prohibit their names from being intervened in, embezzled, and fraudulently used, which is a provision on the protection of personality rights. Therefore, it is incorrect to interpret the Chinese experience in personality rights legislation as the Chinese experience only in the protection of personality rights because the Chinese experience is about the comprehensive legislation of personality rights.

Second, the Chinese experience in personality rights legislation cannot be understood only as the classified provisions of personality rights. The provisions on the classified personality rights mean only highlighting personality rights and specifying specific personality rights the civil subject enjoys. More importantly, they define the content, exercise methods, dominating provisions, protection methods of each specific personality right, the right boundary between specific personality rights, as well as general provisions for the exercise and protection of personality rights. That is why the personality rights law is called a rights law. It is not the original intention of the General Principles of the Civil Law to understand or compile the personality rights law as the law for personality rights protection or to simply identify personality rights.

Third, the basic point of the Chinese experience in the personality rights legislation established in the General Principles of the Civil Law lies in the systematised legislation of personality rights, rather than in the decomposed law of personality rights such as the General Rules of the Civil Law, Tort Liability Law, and judicial interpretation. That is manifested in Section 4 Personal Rights of Chapter 5 set forth in the General Principles of the Civil Law. The legal system of personality rights in the form of the General Principles of the Civil Law, Tort Liability Law, and judicial interpretation was formed because of the imperfect provisions on personality rights in the General Principles of the Civil Law. In the early stage of reform and opening up, when the theory of civil law was not fully prepared, although the provisions of personality rights in the General Principles of the Civil Law were incomplete, the legislative system and status of personality rights were determined. Therefore, provisions for the protection of the right of personality were made in the Tort Liability Law, and in accordance with the General Principles of the Civil Law and the Tort Liability Law, the Supreme People's Court issued a number of supplementary interpretations to improve the legislation on personality rights. Both the provisions of the Tort Liability Law and the General Principles of the Civil Law on the protection of personality rights are a supplement to the normative system of personality rights in the General Principles of the Civil Law, rather than a new system outside it.

Fourth, even the protection of personality rights alone is not a task that the Tort Liability Law can accomplish independently. The protection of civil rights can be realised often through two different claim systems: claim of infringement and claim of the absolute right, which constitute a perfect system for the protection of civil rights. It is the same with the protection of the right of personality. The Tort Liability Law stipulates the claim of infringement for the protection of the right of personality, which is applicable to Article 3 of the law. Similarly, Paragraph 1 of Article 6 is about general provisions for the protection of personality rights, and Article 20 stipulates the protection of the property interests contained in the mental right of personality. These provisions, although important, cannot replace the claim of personality rights to protect personality rights. Although the General Principles of the Civil Law does not stipulate the claim of personality rights in the provisions of personal rights, the subsequent research theory recognised that the personality right needs the protection of both the claim of personality right and claim of infringement and that the claim of personality rights is of great importance to the protection of personality rights.[16] Article 8 of the Law of Personality Rights in the Civil Code of the People's Republic of China (Exposure Draft) stipulates that in accordance with the provisions of this law and other laws, whoever infringes upon the personality rights and interests of others shall bear civil liabilities such as the cessation of the infringement, removal of obstruction, elimination of danger, restoration of reputation and apology not be limited by the limitation of action. This is the stipulation of the claim of personality rights. In particular, the claim of personality rights stipulated in Paragraph 2, which is not limited by the limitation of action, is of more significance for the protection of personality rights. The protection of these personality rights must be stipulated in the law of personality rights, not in the Tort Liability Law. If the protection and the claim of the right of personality are only stipulated in the Tort Liability Law, not in the law of personality rights, such protection is not perfect. These are not the characteristics of the Chinese experience in personality rights legislation.

6.2.2 Correct Interpretation of the Main Aspects of the Chinese Experience in Personality Rights Legislation

The necessary, correct interpretation of the Chinese experience in the personality rights legislation focuses on the following aspects.

6.2.2.1 The Form of Personality Rights Legislation Reflected in the Chinese Experience

The first interpretation of the Chinese experience in the personality rights legislation is the form of personality rights legislation reflected in the Chinese experience. This is the focus of the Chinese experience in personality rights legislation.

Personal rights are stipulated in Section 4 of the chapter on civil rights in the General Principles of the Civil Law. In terms of its legislative value, as scholars say, the independent compilation of the law of personality rights represented a summary of China's existing experience in civil legislation and an inheritance of China's fine legislative tradition. The establishment of Chapter 5, Civil Rights, Section 4, Personal Rights in the General Principles of the Civil Law showed a major breakthrough in the legal system. In particular, the General Principles of the Civil Law gave the same priority to personal rights as the real rights, creditor's rights and intellectual property rights, which had never been seen in the civil legislation of various countries. This legislative system means that the personality rights system is juxtaposed with other legal systems in China's civil legislation, which can provide a sufficient historical basis for the independent compilation of the Law of Personality Rights in the Civil Code.[17] The legislative form of the personality rights law in the General Principles of the Civil Law established the independent status of the personality rights law in the civil law of China, which is the core of the Chinese experience in personality rights legislation.[18] It is contrary to fact that turning a blind eye to such legislative experience and insisting that the separate compilation of personality rights was by no means the initiative of Chinese scholars but of Ukraine.

It should be noted that the reason the personality right was put in Section 4, close to the end of the General Principles of the Civil Law, was that it was incorrectly considered that the social relationship mainly adjusted by civil law was property relationship. Article 2 of the General Principles of the Civil Law stipulates that the civil law adjusts the property relationship and personal relationship between equal subjects, showing that the property relationship was put before personal relationships. Consequently, the General Principles of the Civil Law first stipulates real rights, creditor's rights and intellectual property rights, and stipulates personal rights at the end when stipulating civil rights in Chapter 5. However, in any case, the personal right is stipulated as a separate section, which is juxtaposed with real rights, creditor's rights and intellectual property rights. This shows the law of personality rights is not a fragmented part of the General Principles of the Civil Law but a complete system.[19] The fragmented legislation of personality rights is reflected in the Civil Code of Germany for historical reasons. It can be seen that the Chinese personality rights legislation was not fragmented but a systematic expression from the beginning. That is an indisputable fact. Since the General Principles of the Civil Law was promulgated, China has carried out systematical legislation of personality rights, which is the essence of the Chinese experience in personality rights legislation. Since then, the development of the Chinese experience has also been on a systematic basis. Therefore, it can be said that the form of personality rights legislation in China is systematisation. Similarly, the General Principles of the Civil Law systematically stipulates personality rights, real rights, creditor's rights and intellectual property rights, all of which are juxtaposed together. It can be said that the chapter on civil rights herein is a mini, separate law of civil law, of which the law of personality rights is an integral part. This legislative system is an achievement superior to that of the civil code of other countries. It is an advanced legislative experience that has been proven by practice. It is also a scientific system generally recognised by civil law scholars. Since the General Principles of the Civil Law has constructed an unprecedented new system of provisions of civil rights, which has a far-reaching impact on China's civil practice in judicature and civil law theory, nothing can justify us abandoning such precious experience.[20] The personality rights hereof is to be further spread to become a Law of Personality Rights in the Civil Code, in the same position as the laws of real rights, contract and tort liability.

6.2.2.2 The Law of Personality Rights Is a Law of Rights, Not Just a Law of Right Protection

Another important problem in interpreting the Chinese experience in personality right legislation is whether the personality right law is a law of rights or law of rights protection. As has been mentioned before, this is the essential difference between the Chinese experience in personality rights legislation and the Chinese experience in personality rights protection.

Whether the personality rights law is a law of rights protection or law of rights involves the basic understanding of the nature of this law. This must be confirmed according to the basic content of personality rights stipulated in the General Principles of the Civil Law. If the General Principles of the Civil Law established the Law of Personality Rights as a law of rights protection, not a law of rights, there is a certain basis to define the personality rights law as a law of rights protection. The General Principles of the Civil Law, however, stipulates the protection of personality rights in Articles 119 and 120 in the chapter on civil liability and provides for the system and content of personality rights only in the section on personal rights, excluding the provisions of protection here. Therefore, it is wrong to think that since the Chinese experience in personality rights law recognises that the personality rights law is a law of rights protection, it is enough to provide the protection of the personality rights and there is no need to contain provisions granting and exercising rights in the law and so on. China's personality rights law embodies the characteristics of the modern era, which enables the function of personality rights to transform from active rights exercise to negative rights defence. Thanks to the continuous development and change in the positive function of personality rights, the obligee can actively exercise its personality rights and dominate its specific personality interests to obtain greater financial interest. As China's legislation of personality rights has continued to develop and improve since the General Principles of the Civil Law was promulgated, the personality right has increasingly more extensive and powerful positive functions. Therefore, the law of personality rights is both a law of rights protection and a civil law of rights that stipulates the exercise of personality rights and the domination of personality interests and personality rights granting, of course, including the protection of personality rights, such as the claim of personality rights. The protection of personality rights is only a part of the law of personality rights, so the Chinese experience in personality rights legislation must not be interpreted as a law of rights protection but a law of rights.

6.2.2.3 Correct Interpretation of the Relationship between the Law of Personality Rights and Tort Liability Law

To interpret the Chinese experience in personality rights legislation, we must also understand the tie between China's law of personality rights and Tort Liability Law. It is also wrong to interpret the Chinese experience in personality rights legislation as the integration of the law of personality rights and Tort Liability Law.

This requires us to observe the legislative system of the General Principles of the Civil Law. The General Principles of the Civil Law stipulates personal rights, namely personality rights, in the chapter on civil rights and the tort liability in the chapter on civil liability. It can be seen that the law of personality rights and the Tort Liability Law have completely different legal positions in the General Principles of the Civil Law. The General Principles of the Civil Law takes the Tort Liability Law as the law of rights protection by separating it from the debt law and stipulates it separately in the chapter on civil liability.[21] Such a legislative arrangement can enable us to correctly interpret the relationship between the law of personality rights and Tort Liability Law and realise that tort liability is separated from debt law to be an independent part of civil law. Judging from the General Principles of the Civil Law, the Law of Personality Rights is the law of civil rights and the Tort Liability Law is the Law of Rights Protection. The two are not integrated.

The protection of personality rights in Tort Liability Law is mainly reflected as follows: first, Paragraph 2 of Article 2 of the Tort Liability Law includes personality rights in the protection by tort liability; second, the claim of infringement stipulated in Article 3 includes the claim of infringement on the personality right; third, the general provisions of tort liability stipulated in Paragraph 1 of Article 6 include fault liability for infringement on personality rights; fourth, the compensation for personal damage stipulated in Articles 16 and 17, the compensation for property damage against personality rights and interests stipulated in Article 20 and the compensation for spiritual damage stipulated in Article 22 are all applicable to the protection of personal rights. Such protection of personality rights, however, is the protection of the claim of infringement provided by the Tort Liability Law. All these provisions cannot replace protection by the claim of personality rights, nor can they replace the complete law of personality rights, including rights granting, the content, exercise and domination of personality rights. It is obviously wrong to interpret the integration of the law of personality rights and Tort Liability Law as the core of the Chinese experience in personality rights legislation.

6.2.2.4 Correct Interpretation of the Dual Protection Mode of Personality Rights

The correct interpretation of the Chinese experience in personality rights legislation means how we treat the dual protection of personality rights.

The personality right is indeed protected in two ways: the claim of personality rights and the claim of infringement. This is also related to the Chinese experience in personality right legislation. In fact, this is not only the advantage in the protection of personality rights but also a general rule for the protection of all civil rights because almost all civil rights are double protected. The most typical example is that the Property Law stipulates the claim of real rights. However, isn't the real right protected by the Tort Liability Law? It is protected by both the claim of real rights and the claim of infringement. It does not mean that if it is protected by the claim of real rights, there is no need to protect it through the Tort Liability Law and vice versa. In the Draft Proposal of the Civil Code of China, the third section of the general provisions of the Law of Real Rights specifically stipulates the claim of real rights, including the claim for return, the claim for confirmation of real rights, the claim for elimination of obstruction, the claim for elimination of danger and the claim for compensation for damage, forming a complete system of the claim for real rights.[22] The Property Law stipulates both the claim for real rights and the claim for infringement—a dual protection mode—which is a completely normal legal principle. The specific application depends on the actual situation and the choice of the litigant. Since it is legitimate to implement dual protection for the real right, why can't we do so for personality rights? China's legislative experience in personality rights has proven that the personality right should be protected by both the claim for personality rights and the claim for infringement. The thought that the claim for personality rights is stipulated in the law of personality rights shows a repetition of the provisions of the law of tort liability is, in essence, confusing the boundary between the claim for personality rights and the claim for infringement. The first chapter of the Law of Personality Rights in the Civil Code (Draft) contains five articles stipulating the claim for personality rights, which is an advisable approach with both theoretical value and practical significance.

The dual protection for civil rights is almost the basic method of civil rights protection. Any right needs to be protected by both the claim of the absolute right and claim of infringement to realise the sound protection of civil rights.[23] The same is true of the personality right. It is wrong not to adopt the mode of dual protection.

6.2.2.5 Correct Interpretation of the Tie between Personality Rights Legislation and Its Judicial Interpretation

The correct interpretation of the Chinese experience in the personality rights legislation also involves the relationship between the legislation of personality rights and its judicial interpretation. Some scholars think that the protection of the right of personality in China is characteristic of the classification of personality rights; that is, various types of personality rights are expressly stipulated by law, and then the Supreme People's Court recognises new types of personality rights through judicial interpretation, so as to define the scope of the protection of the right of personality.[24] This has been the practice in China—the last resort since the implementation of the General Principles of the Civil Law. However, this is not a manifestation of the Chinese experience in the legislation of personality rights but is caused by the deficient types and contents of personality rights stipulated in the General Principles of the Civil Law. As some scholars say, judging from the circumstances in China, it is obviously better to include these provisions in the civil code rather than leave them to future judicial interpretation or guiding precedents. Obviously, it is difficult for judicial interpretation or guiding jurisprudence to form a complete system because they are fragmented, which makes it very difficult for the relevant subject to find and apply law. In addition, there may even be contradictions between judicial interpretations drafted at different times and by different departments. The formulation process of judicial interpretation is more arbitrary and opaque than the legislative process, and its draft is often not exposed for comment in advance. Therefore, it is obviously a better choice to incorporate valuable rules into law than to leave it to the judicial organ to summarise the experience and innovate.[25] These opinions show that judicial interpretation is judicial interpretation after all and cannot replace legislation. It is unwise to regard judicial interpretation as the Chinese experience in personality rights legislation and maintain it in the long term.

In summary, the correct interpretation of the Chinese experience in personality rights legislation refers to the Chinese model of personality rights legislation established by the General Principles of the Civil Law, known as the original version of the Chinese experience in personality rights legislation, rather than the "General Principles of the Civil Law + Tort Liability Law + judicial interpretation." Laws and judicial interpretations on the right of personality issued after the General Principles of the Civil Law were the continuous development of the Chinese experience in the personality rights legislation, rather than the change of the legislative experience in the personality rights in the General Principles of the Civil Law.

6.3 The Finalisation of the Chinese Experience in the Legislation of Personality Rights in the Civil Code

The compilation of a civil code is a once-in-a-century legislative opportunity in the history of Chinese civil legislation. It is particularly important whether we can grasp this good opportunity to further develop the Chinese experience in personality rights legislation and fix it as part of China's Civil Code. If this legislative plan can be realised, the Chinese experience in personality rights legislation will benefit the Chinese people in the protection of personality rights and promote the development of the world's civil law. To finalise and upgrade the Chinese experience in personality rights legislation in compiling the civil code, I think the following important problems should be considered.

6.3.1 Sublimation of the Chinese Experience in Personality Rights Legislation

The Chinese experience in personality rights legislation was formed in the General Principles of the Civil Law 30 years ago. To upgrade and finalise the developing Chinese experience into China's Civil Code is to meet the political requirement to protect people's personality rights and the historical requirement to promote China's Civil Law, especially the legislative experience in personality rights, to stand out among the civil codes in the world. Therefore, it is important that we should absorb the theoretical research results on personality rights, summarise the judicial experience in personality rights protection and formulate the Law of Personality Rights in the Civil Code on the basis of the Chinese experience in personality rights legislation created by the General Principles of the Civil Law. That is how we can formulate a personality rights law with Chinese characteristics and finalise the Chinese experience in personality rights legislation.

It should be noted that it matters much how we can make use of this opportunity before us. The General Principles of the Civil Law has constructed an unprecedented new system of provisions on civil rights, which has had a far-reaching impact on China's civil judicial practice and civil law theory.[26] Both the Law of Personality Rights stipulated in China's Civil Law (Draft) in 2002 and the Law of Personality Rights in the Specific Provisions of the Civil Code (Draft) in 2017 developed the Chinese experience in the legislation of personality rights created by the General Principles of the Civil Law, instead of learning from the independent compilation of personality rights in the Civil Code of Ukraine. In terms of inheriting and developing the Chinese experience in personality rights legislation, I think it is up to the state whether to choose to advance or retreat. However, the state, on its part, must make a careful and rational choice. The legal working committee of the Standing Committee of the National People's Congress insists on compiling personality rights separately in the civil code, which shows an inheritance and development of the Chinese experience in personality rights legislation as well as the finalisation of said Chinese experience in the civil code.

It should be noted that the independent compilation of personality rights in the civil code is only part of the efforts to upgrade the Chinese experience in the legislation of personality rights. In order to upgrade the Chinese experience in the legislation of personality rights, personality rights must be listed in the first part of the specific provisions of the civil code, closely following the general provisions of the civil law. This is determined by the importance of personality rights to people and by the sequence of provisions in Article 2, which puts personal relationships before property relationships, and in Chapter 5, which stipulates civil rights, of the General Rules of the Civil Law. The sequence of each specific civil law should be the law of personality rights, marriage and family, property rights, contract, tort liability and inheritance, rather than property rights, contract, personality rights, marriage, adoption, inheritance and tort liability in the 2002 Civil Law (Draft). Only this approach can reflect the important role of personality rights.

6.3.2 Stipulation of the System of Personality Rights

To stipulate personality rights and finalise the above Chinese experience in the specific provisions of the civil code, we must adhere to the systematic legislation of personality rights determined in the General Principles of the Civil Law. This is reflected in the draft Law of Personality Rights in the Civil Code. The draft contains the system of abstract personality rights, such as general personality rights stipulated in Article 7, the right to self-determination stipulated in Article 3, the right to publicity stipulated in Article 4 and the system of specific personality rights, such as the rights to life, body, health, personal freedom and sexual autonomy in Chapter 2, the right to name in Chapter 3, the right to portrait in Chapter 4, the rights to reputation, honor and credit in Chapter 5, and the rights to privacy, personal information and communication confidentiality in Chapter 6. Such an arrangement shows an upgrading and finalisation of the Chinese experience in personality rights legislation stipulated in the General Principles of the Civil Law. It is also wrong to think that with the provisions on the compensation for property losses caused by infringement on personality rights and interests stipulated in Article 20 of the Tort Liability Law, China does not need to recognise the property value of personality rights or create the right to commercialisation through precedents or theories like Germany and the United States. Only when Article 4 of the draft law of personality rights stipulating that the civil subject has the right to dominate his personality rights with economic interests such as the rights to name, portrait, personal information and allowing others to use them, except the right to publicity that cannot be permitted according to its nature or according to the law, is combined with Article 20 of the Tort Liability Law can a complete system be formed for the protection of the right to publicity and the claim of infringement on it. Only one of them is not sufficient.

6.3.3 Stipulation of the Content of Personality Rights

To finalise the Chinese experience in personality rights legislation in the Law of Personality Rights in the Civil Code, the comprehensive stipulation of the specific content of the abstract and specific personality rights is required. The content and exercise of each abstract and specific personality right must be stipulated in the law of personality rights so that the obligee can know the right scope and boundary of each personality right and understand the way to exercise and dominate relevant personality rights and interests. Only in this way can each obligee know what kind of personality rights he enjoys, what content each personality right contains and how it should be exercised. Otherwise, except for its negative defence function, the obligee doesn't know how to use the right's positive function to obtain benefits. The negative defence function of personality rights can play a role in relieving the damage to rights only when the personality right is infringed. The modern personality right has not only negative functions but also more positive functions, which are embodied by the rights to name, portrait, personal information and even the right to life. Euthanasia, for instance, is the embodiment of the positive function of the right to life. Even if the personality rights law does not stipulate the positive function of euthanasia, the obligee can also receive euthanasia in a negative way or volunteer to dominate its own right to life by means of euthanasia. For example, Xia Suwen, Wang Mingcheng's mother, suffered from liver cirrhosis and ascites in October 1984. On June 23, 1986, she was sent to a hospital for infectious diseases in Hanzhong city by Wang Mingcheng and his sisters. The hospital issued a notice of critical illness on the day of her admission. Xia Suwen was in intolerable pain and wanted to die. Wang Mingcheng and his sisters asked the attending doctor Pu Liansheng for euthanasia for their mother and expressed their willingness to bear all responsibilities after confirming that there was no hope for their mother being cured. Pu Liansheng gave Xia Suwen a prescription of 100 mg of the compound chlorphomazine, on which was written "The family members asked for her euthanasia," and Wang Mingcheng also signed the prescription. After the injection, Xia Suwen died on the morning of June 29. Later, Wang Mingcheng and Pu Liansheng were prosecuted by the procuratorial organ for intentional homicide and acquitted by the court in 1992. In November 2000, Wang Mingcheng was operated upon after being diagnosed with gastric cancer. As his cancer cells spread to other parts of the body in November 2002, he was hospitalised again on January 7, 2003. On June 7, he asked for euthanasia, but no doctor dared to do it. In despair, Wang Mingcheng was discharged from the hospital on July 4 and conducted negative euthanasia at home.[27] He died in pain in the early morning of August 3. From this case, we can see that if euthanasia or negative euthanasia had been stipulated in the law of personality rights, the doctors and the patient's family who carried out the euthanasia would not have been put in prison. In the modern era, the law of personality rights should clearly stipulate the positive function of personality rights so that the obligee can know how to exercise their personality rights. Some scholars think that provisions on the right to body in the draft law of personality rights are those pieced together from other laws and regulations. In fact, this shows exactly that all provisions on the right to body are systematised and finalised in the civil law. This is an inevitable way to finalise the Chinese experience in personality rights legislation. It is absolutely necessary to combine the provisions on the rights to the body such as organ transplantation, human experiment and compulsory medical treatment in the draft law of personality rights and refine them in the civil code. In this opportunity of compiling the civil code, it is the best choice to centralise, unify and upgrade all the provisions related to personality rights in the civil code as the highest provisions in civil law.

6.3.4 Stipulation of the Object of Personality Rights and Rules of Dominating Said Object

The object of personality rights is not stipulated in China's General Rules of the Civil Law. The finalisation of the Chinese experience in personality rights legislation means defining the specific object of personality rights and making specific provisions for the obligee to dominate the object of personality rights in the Law of Personality Rights of the civil code.

The object of personality rights is personality interests, which include a variety of material and spiritual elements of personality. In the modern era, specific personality rights have their own objects, and the obligee has control over most of them. Life, body, personal information, name, portrait, privacy, name and so on, as the objects of the rights to life, body, personal information, name, portrait, privacy and so on, can blimitedly dominated by the obligee at their own will. The provisions on the rights to self-determination and publicity in the abstract personality rights are those on dominating the object of these rights, which is reflected in the draft Law of Personality Rights in the Civil Code. The draft Law of Personality Rights also makes provisions for controlling the specific personality interests while stipulating specific personality rights. For example, the provisions of the right to portrait involve the portrait license contract. It is stipulated in Article 30 that if the boundary and mode of portrait use are not clear in the portrait license contract, an explanation in favour of the portrait rightsholder shall be made and that the right to the portrait of the rightsholder in the portrait license contract shall not be exercised by the other party without the consent of the portrait owner. Article 31 stipulates that if the person concerned does not make an agreement or makes an unclear agreement on the terms of the licensed use of portrait, either party may terminate the portrait license contract at any time but shall notify the other party before a reasonable deadline. In addition, if there is a clear agreement on the terms of the licensed use of portrait, and the portrait obligee has legitimate reasons, he may terminate the portrait license contract but shall notify the other party in advance. If the other party suffers losses due to the termination of the contract, the portrait obligee shall compensate for the losses, except for the reasons that cannot be attributed to the portrait owner. Article 32 also stipulates the right to the proper use of another person's portrait without the consent of the portrait owner. These rules are for the exercising of the right to portrait. Such rules shall be observed by the portrait owner when he exercises his own right or by others when they use the portrait of the portrait owner. If the law of personality rights does not stipulate rules for the exercise of these personality rights, it is impossible to effectively protect the right to portrait. This is the specific rule for the obligee of personality rights with modern characteristics to dominate the objcct of its rights. On top of that, the rules of the right to portrait contain the provision that the portrait license contract can be referred to in the licensed use of other personality rights and interests. The characteristic of contemporary personality rights is that the object of specific personality rights can be dominated in accordance with the law so that the obligee can obtain more interest. To formulate the Law of Personality Rights in the Civil Code and upgrade and finalise the Chinese experience in personality rights legislation, we should stipulate the complex law system of personality rights, rather than only stipulate the protection of personality rights.

6.3.5 Stipulation of the Claim of Personality Rights and Its Corresponding Rules

To finalise the Chinese experience in the legislation of personality rights, the claim of personality rights and its corresponding rules should be stipulated in the law of personality rights. The claim of personality rights, combined with the claim of infringement, can provide perfect protection of personality rights. The claim of personality rights means the civil subject can request the perpetrator or the people's court to conduct a certain act or not to conduct a certain act when the personality right of said civil subject is impaired or is about to be impaired, so as to restore his personality right or prevent the obstruction.[28] At present, there are five articles on the claim of personality rights in the draft Law of Personality Rights in the Civil Code, of which Article 8 stipulates the claim of personality rights; Article 9, the conditions for exercising the claim of personality rights; Article 10, the prohibition required by the civil subject who has evidence to prove that another person is committing or is about to commit an act infringing his personality right; Article 11, the ways to bear the claim right to eliminate influence, restore reputation, or make an apology; and Article 12, if a breach of contract damages the other party's personality rights and interests and causes serious damage, the victim may request compensation for mental damage in addition to bearing the liability for breach of contract. These well-designed advanced provisions with modern characteristics reflect the advantages of the claim of personality rights in the protection of personality rights and are convenient for judges to apply in judicial practice correctly.

6.4 Conclusions

The Chinese experience in personality rights legislation formed when the law of personality rights was compiled in the General Principles of the Civil Law of China in 1986. The law of personality rights of China is very different in legislation from the civil codes of other countries in the world. It has unique advantages compared with the French model, the German model, the Swiss model and the Quebec model of Canada. This original version of the Chinese experience is definitely not only different in the protection of personality rights but also has distinctive characteristics in the expression of its form, system, content, domination and exercise of personality rights. Only the correct interpretation of the Chinese experience in personality rights legislation can ensure that the law of personality rights stipulated in the civil code can inherit, upgrade and finalise the advantages of the Chinese experience and allow the law of personality rights in our civil code, with a Chinese style, to play an important role in protecting people's personality rights and in the legislation of personality rights affecting the world.

Notes

1 Foundation Item: the scientific research foundation item of Renmin University of China: Research on the Application and Systematization of the Basic Principles of Civil Law (Item No. 17XNQJ04).
2 Yang Lixin: On the Necessity and Reality of Formulating the Law of Personality Rights in China, Guangming Daily, 11th edition, May 15, 2012.
3 Liang Huixing: Personality Rights Can't Be Established in China's Civil Code, Academic Journal of Zhongzhou, 2016, issue 2.
4 On The Law of Personal Rights, China Procuratorial Press, 1996, p. 2.
5 Chen Xianjie: The Judicial Dimension of the Protection of Personality Rights in China, published in: The Collection of Essays from the Seminar on the Law of Personality Rights in the Civil Law of China over 40 Years, the Research Centre of Civil and Commercial Jurisprudence of Renmin University of China, 2018, pp. 43–44.
6 Wang Liming: Perfection of the Law of Personality Rights in China's Future Civil Code—Comments on the Fourth Part of the Draft Civil Code in 2002, Journal of China University of Political Science and Law, 2013, issue 1.
7 Xu Guodong: Introduction to the Civil Code of Quebec, translated by Sun Jianjiang, etc., attached to the Chinese version of the Civil Code of Quebec, Renmin University of China Press, 2005, p. 27.
8 Wang Liming: Perfection of the Law of Personality Rights in China's Future Civil Code—Comments on the Fourth Part of the Draft Civil Code in 2002, Journal of China University of Political Science and Law, 2013, issue 1.
9 Yang Lixin: Interpretation and Comment of the Interpretation of Several Issues on the Determination of Compensation Liability for Mental Damage in Civil Tort issued by the Supreme People's Court, The Jurist, 2001, issue 5.
10 Yao Hui: On General Personality Rights, The Jurist, 1995, issue 5.
11 Yang Lixin and Liu Zhaocheng: On the Right to Self-Determination as an Abstract Personality Right, Academia Bimestrie, 2010, issue 5.
12 Jiang Jifei and Wang Shengli: Enlightenment from the Right to Publicity on the Legislation of Personality Rights in China, Forward Position, 2010, issue 22.
13 Yang Lixin and Han Xu: Localization of the Right to Be Forgotten in China and Its Law Application, Journal of Law Application, 2015, issue 2.
14 Duan Weili: On the Judicial Relief of the Right to Be Forgotten—Taking the Judgment of the First Case of the Right to Be Forgotten in China as the Starting Point, Journal of Law Application, 2017, issue 16.
15 Liang Huixing: Personality Rights Can't Be Established in China's Civil Code, Academic Journal of Zhongzhou, 2016, issue 2.
16 Yang Lixin and Yuan Xueshi: On the Claim of Personality Rights, Chinese Journal of Law, 2003, issue 6.

17 Wang Liming: Improvement of Personality Rights in China's Future Civil Code, Journal of China University of Political Science and Law, 2013, issue 1.
18 Liang Huixing: Personality Rights Can't Be Established in China's Civil Code, Academic Journal of Zhongzhou, 2016, issue 2.
19 Zou Hailin: Further Discussion on the Civil Law Expression of Personality Rights, Journal of Comparative Law, 2016, issue 4.
20 Wang Liming: Improvement of the Law of Personality Rights in China's Future Civil Code, Journal of China University of Political Science and Law, 2013, issue 1.
21 Wei Zhenying: Research on the Separation of Civil Liability and Debt, Peking University Press, 2016, p. 32.
22 Liang Huixing (ed.): Proposal for the Draft Civil Code of China, Law Press, 2003, pp. 52–53.
23 Tang Zhaohong: On the Establishment of the Claim of Personality Rights and the Claim of Intellectual Property Rights—Another Challenge to the Civil Liability System of Infringement, Studies in Law and Business, 2002, issue 2.
24 Liang Huixing: Personality Rights Can't Be Established in China's Civil Code, Academic Journal of Zhongzhou, 2016, issue 2.
25 Shi Jiayou: Pragmatic Knot of Conservation and Innovation: Evaluation and Analysis of the *Law of Personality Rights in the Civil Law of the People's Republic of China (Draft)*, Journal of Comparative Law, 2018, issue 2.
26 Wang Liming: Improvement of the Law of Personality Rights in China's Future Civil Code, Journal of China University of Political Science and Law, 2013, issue 1.
27 Yang Lixin: Civil Law Thinking and Judicial Countermeasures (Part I), Peking University Press, 2017, pp. 606–607.
28 Yang Lixin and Yuan Xueshi: On the Claim of Personality Rights, Chinese Journal of Law, 2003, issue 6.

7 Interest Re-Measurement Theory and Institutional Arrangement

From Privacy to Personal Information

By Zhang Xinbao[1]

7.1 Introduction

Personal privacy, also known as confidentiality of private life, means that the peace of private life is free from illegal interference by others and confidential private information is free from the illegal collection, spying and disclosure by others. Privacy includes peace of private life and confidentiality of private life.[2] Personal information[3] refers to any information related to a natural person who has been identified or can be identified,[4] including personal name, address, date of birth, ID number, medical record, personnel records, photographs and other specific personal information that can be identified alone or in contrast with other information.[5] There is an overlap between personal privacy and personal information; that is, some personal privacy falls under personal information, while some don't. Some personal information, especially sensitive information related to one's personal private life, is classified in personal privacy, but some personal information isn't due to it being widely known. The traditional privacy law (or the civil law system protecting the right to privacy) protects the right to privacy as one of the personality rights, focusing on personality interests, especially personal dignity and personal freedom. Since human beings entered the information society, stakeholders related to personal information and their interest relations have become diverse and complex, and equal attention has been paid to the protection and utilisation of personal information in legislation. Information operators (i.e., natural persons, legal persons and other organisations engaged in activities such as personal information collection, processing, storage, transmission and utilisation) have emerged as independent stakeholders. The state is no longer an irrelevant legal rule maker and executor, but the largest collector, processor, storer, and user of personal information.

In terms of the legislation of personal information protection, the EU adopts the state-led model of directives[6] and Member State law, while the United States adopts the model of supplementing existing laws (mainly privacy protection laws) and industry self-discipline. This has been studied by Chinese scholars for more than ten years, and the main achievements include the research on the legal basis and theory of personal information protection in China,[7] the expert proposal for the personal information protection law,[8] and the research on some specific

DOI: 10.4324/9781003300168-7

systems of personal information protection (such as the network real name system).[9] In terms of legislative progress, China has also formulated some normative documents on the principle and framework of personal information protection, but it has not yet developed a systematic legal system for personal information protection.

Based on the observation of the social and legal change from privacy protection to personal information protection, this chapter will provide insights into the changes of various subjects relevant to personal information protection and utilisation and the interest relations between various subjects and explore the main interest demands of these relevant subjects. The chapter seeks to balance the interests of all parties by using the principle of interest measurement in legislation. Then, the author will propose the basic theory of two strengths and tripartite balance for the legal protection and utilisation of personal information and explore the main path to realise this theory in the legislation of personal information protection.

7.2 Legal Protection of the Right to Privacy and Interest Measurement of Related Parties

7.2.1 Legal Protection of the Right to Privacy

7.2.1.1 The Right to Privacy Is Recognised as the Right of Personality

The demand for privacy protection, as a natural human emotion, comes from human shame instinct,[10] but the rise of privacy interest as a personal right and in connection with the law came from the article "On the Right to Privacy" written by Samuel D. Warren and Louis D. Brandeis in 1890. The authors believed that with the development of social life, the common law should recognise the personal right to be alone,[11] proposed by Judge Thomas Cooley, and protect the right to choose one's own life without external interference or infringement unless there is a clear social need and legal basis. Since then, the right to privacy has made great progress in the United States. In the field of tort law, four types of privacy infringement summarised by William Prosser were systematised.[12] To protect privacy from public power, the Supreme Court of the United States recognised that the right to privacy was a basic right not expressly listed in the Constitution, leading to the gradual formation of the self-determined privacy and information privacy in the Constitution. The United States also regulated the protection and utilisation of personal information privacy by formulating relevant written laws. In short, the right to privacy exists in the Constitution, tort law and various written laws in the United States. Some American scholars even liken the right to privacy to a chameleon, whose meaning varies according to the circumstance and context.[13]

The right to privacy has a history of more than 100 years in the United States, and similarly, in European countries,[14] the European Convention on Human Rights listed the protection of citizens' private life as one of their basic rights. After World War II, the domestic laws of European countries also responded to human rights protection. In Britain, although it protected citizens' privacy, the law did not recognise the infringement of privacy as an independent cause of action for a long time but included the case of infringement of privacy in other violations. This made privacy protection in Britain underdeveloped and fragmented.[15] In Germany, privacy was the source of the birth and development of the general personality right and was protected through the recognition of the general personality right. After World War II, illegal interference in people's private lives, such as eavesdropping and secret recording, became increasingly widespread. Under such circumstances, the constitutional court introduced the general personality right in the "Case of the Reader's Letter" to provide relief to the victim.[16] As a framework right, the typical category of concretised general personality rights was the private field that provided protection for personal privacy. After that, the German Constitutional Court held in the census case[17] that personal data is the outline of the personality of natural persons, the self-determined value and dignity and the personal life fact that a person decides when and to what extent to disclose.[18] That was how the right to information self-determination was determined and became the theoretical basis of privacy protection in Germany. In France, the concept of early French law and the practice of personality protection dominated by this concept did not involve the privacy and personal life of natural persons.[19] Amid restrictions on press freedom, France paid much attention to privacy, which was reflected in the constitutional provisions against insulting or slandering others' private life. In the 1850s, some famous cases established the protection of the right to personal image. The right to private life being respected was stipulated in Article 9 of the Civil Code of France, amended in 1970.

7.2.1.2 Main Legal Principles of Privacy Interest Protection

The humanism and liberalism generated by the bourgeois revolution and the material civilization brought about by the industrial revolution and the electrical revolution have made the awareness of privacy deeply rooted in the hearts of people in Western society and led to the formation of two different privacy cultures. Overall, the United States understands privacy from the perspective of liberty, while the European continent roots privacy protection in personal dignity. Professor Whitman of Yale University also believes that the two privacy systems have two different value cores. One is the personal dignity mainly threatened by the mass media in Europe. The other is the liberty mainly threatened by the government in the United States.[20] In the United States, due to the special independence and founding of the country, political and social ideas have mainly focused on the distrust of the police and other government officials for a long time.[21] Therefore, their awareness of privacy is more reflected in the pursuit of the negative freedom of prohibiting state intrusion. Many American scholars emphasise the importance of privacy protection through a terrorist-centralised government monitored by an authority in the novel *1984*. As the law protects personal privacy, individuals can withdraw from public life and sight, still enjoy the time and space of solitude amid the expanding public power and increasingly tense social life, live truly and develop their personality without being dominated and manipulated by others. Privacy is considered to be the epitome of human values, which can be summarised as personal self-determination and personality.[22] The protection of privacy helps promote individual independence, maintain social democracy and restrict state power.

The European continent has always had a tradition of maintaining personal dignity, which, early on, only protected for a small number of people such as aristocrats. As humanism spread, the protection of personal dignity gradually extended to every member of society. After World War II, the profound reflection on the Nazi trampling on personal dignity prompted personal dignity to be taken as the core value and ethical basis of the legal system. Compared with the legal principle of protecting privacy interests in the United States, the European continent was more inclined to confirm the necessity of protecting one's personal private life from the perspective of personal dignity. It was declared that when our privacy is illegally exposed to the public, our self-esteem is also destroyed, and the relationship between us and others is also damaged, and that is the reason why the law protects privacy.[23]

7.2.2 Interest Measurement in the Protection of the Right to Privacy

As the society advances, there will be more focus and attention attached to the protection of the privacy. When the social structure, living environment, technological progress and the development of mass media make the relationship between people and society increasingly tense, people have a growing demand for the right to protect their private life from being exposed to the public so as to resist the intrusion of mass media, public comments and public desire into their private life. After the creation of humanism and liberalism, respect for the individual has been valued as never before. If the personal needs of free and dignified survival and life are to be met, we must recognise the legal protection of the privacy and peace of private life. Thus, the right to privacy is also shaped as an absolute and exclusive defensive right. However, it is unrealistic for individuals who are always part of society to be alone. The law also protects individuals' freedom to know and obtain information and express their own ideas. The protection of personal privacy by the law means the restriction of such freedom of others. This reflects the conflict between the right to privacy and the right to learn the truth and the right to freedom of speech.

The right to learn the truth is a personal right to approach and understand public affairs and matters that are related to or are of interest to people, including the right to know about political power, society and personal information.[24] Individuals do not want their private life to be known or interfered with by others but desire as much information as possible to meet their political and spiritual needs. Privacy protects the freedom of individuals to withdraw from public life and sight; private life has nothing to do with public and group interests. The core of constructing privacy law is the distinction between the public and private spheres.[25] When the right to learn the truth involves the public interest or the reasonable interest of the public, the law recognises the superiority of this public interest over individual privacy. The public right to know political affairs and personal information constitutes the restriction on the privacy of government officials and public figures. The conflict between the right to privacy and the right to know personal information mostly occurs between individuals with a special relationship in fact or law. What one party wants to know according to its right to know personal information is exactly what is protected by the other party's right to privacy. At this time, through rights coordination, the law recognises the legitimacy of the right of an individual to know affairs related to him, while requiring the other party exercising the right to know personal information not to disclose the privacy of the other party, so as to protect the privacy holder. Freedom of speech, also known as freedom of opinion or expression, means that citizens have the right to express their ideas in language or any other way. The core of freedom of speech is that everyone has the right to freedom of opinion or expression.[26] In addition, the law must also ensure the freedom of individuals to obtain and disseminate information to realise the freedom of speech. Freedom of speech and the right to learn the truth are interdependent and mutually reinforcing. The protection of freedom of speech by law is applicable to not only the generally accepted speech that does not involve value judgment but also speech that can make people unhappy, disturb the state, or do harm to a certain group. The protection of information privacy cannot infringe on the freedom of speech and hinder the dissemination of information with news value and of public concern.[27] Thus, there is an inevitable conflict between the freedom of speech and the right to privacy. Generally speaking, freedom of speech constitutes a reasonable defense against the infringement on the right to privacy when speech involves the public interest and the reasonable interest of the public. When speech only involves personal life but not public life, the coordination of the conflict between the two is up to the law. The United States, for instance, has always taken the value of freedom of speech to democracy seriously. In legal practice, infringement on the right to privacy is constituted only when the plaintiff proves that the defendant's speech has true malice toward him. This is how more restrictions are given to the right to privacy.

The right to privacy, the right to learn the truth and the freedom of speech, as the basic rights and freedom enjoyed by individuals, are all necessary to maintain personal dignity and freedom and enhance the diversity of a democratic society. Faced with conflicts between different individuals over basic rights and freedom, the state, as a neutral third party irrelevant to the conflict of personal rights, coordinates the conflict of interest by means of legislation and judicial judgment. On the one hand, the right to privacy, increasingly valued as an absolute and exclusive personality right, means that it has been recognised by the will of the state embodied in the form of law. On the other hand, the law also recognises that the public interest constitutes a reasonable restriction on the individual's right to privacy in order to coordinate the conflict between the right to privacy and the right to learn the truth and between the right to privacy and the right to freedom of speech. When the right to learn the truth and the freedom of speech conform to the purport of the public interest, the restriction on news value and public figures constitute an effective defense against the infringement on the right to privacy.

In the design of the right to privacy system, only one conflict needs to be balanced between the privacy interest of the privacy subject (individual) (which can also be expressed as the personality interests in personal freedom and dignity) and freedom of expression and right to learn the truth of the other party (i.e., natural persons, legal persons, or organisations with negative omission obligations). The state, as a social manager in a neutral position irrelevant to the interest contradiction between the two parties, adjusts the interest relationship between the two by formulating and implementing laws. The conflict is adjusted through the applicable rule of public interest: personal privacy that does not involve public interests shall be protected, while that involving public interests is not protected but restricted.

7.3 Legal Protection of Personal Information and Interest Measurement Among Related Parties

7.3.1 Legal Protection of Personal Information

The digitalisation of personal information processing allows people to enjoy many conveniences while facing risks brought by this personal information digitisation. For nearly half a century, the legislation of personal information protection has emerged as one of the most remarkable legislative campaigns in the world. So far, over 90 countries worldwide have formulated personal information protection laws. In responding to the collection and use of personal information in modern ways, continental European countries made special legislative attempts to regulate such acts in order to make up for the lack of privacy protection. The Hessian Data Act formulated by the Hessian state of Germany in 1970 was the first specialised personal data protection law in the world. The Data Act of Sweden promulgated in 1973 was the first national law of personal data protection in the world. In 1977, Germany also formulated the Federal Data Protection Act. In 1978, France passed the Information, Archives and Freedom Act. In 1984, the UK passed the controversial Data Protection Act. The legislation of personal data protection of these countries had a wide and far-reaching impact on the data protection of the whole of Europe. In 1995, the European Union adopted the Personal Data Protection Directive to realise the unified legislative protection for personal data.[28] Due to the economic strength of the EU, the Directive has had a substantial impact on the legislation of personal information protection all over the world.

In terms of information protection, the United States has a relatively perfect legal system of privacy protection. It initially revised the concept of the right to privacy through the theory of the right to control information and provided support for individuals' active control of their information. The exposure of the Watergate incident touched sensitive nerves in American society about the police government and gave birth to the Privacy Act in 1974. The Privacy Act emphasises the fairness and legitimacy of the federal government in the collection and utilisation of personal information and also urges the federal government to provide active protection for citizens' personal information and avoid the improper disclosure or abuse of personal privacy. In the private sector, considering the belief in market regulation and the support for the development of information technology, the United States adopted a decentralised legislative model to legislate separately for the collection and utilisation of personal information in specific industries or fields.[29]

As information technology advanced, China's laws also responded to the protection and utilisation of personal information. On December 28, 2000, the Decision on Maintaining Internet Security issued by the Standing Committee of the National People's Congress was the beginning of China's legal regulation of the Internet. The Decision takes information security as an important part of Internet security and safeguards the right of information subjects by means of criminal sanctions. It is stipulated in Article 4 that illegally intercepting, falsifying, or deleting other people's email or other data or infringing on citizens' freedom of communication and communication secrets can constitute a crime. The Decision on Strengthening Network Information Protection adopted by the Standing Committee of the National People's Congress on December 28, 2012, clearly stipulates in Article 1 that the state protects electronic information that can identify citizens' personal identity and privacy and also provides for a number of basic principles for the protection and utilisation of personal information in accordance with international practices. In terms of branch law, the crime of stealing, buying and illegally providing credit card information was added to the Criminal Law Amendment (5) adopted by the Standing Committee of the National People's Congress on February 28, 2005. The crime of selling and illegally providing citizens' personal information and illegally obtaining citizens' personal information was added to the Criminal Law Amendment (7) adopted by the Standing Committee of the National People's Congress on February 28, 2009. The Tort Liability Law promulgated on December 26, 2009, stipulates the protection of privacy and network tort liability. The Consumer Protection Law revised on October 25, 2013, also values the protection of consumers' personal information.[30] The revised Regulations on the Administration of Credit Investigation issued by the State Council on January 21, 2013, is administrative regulations and departmental rules that provide detailed provisions on the collection of personal information in the credit investigation industry. The Ministry of Industry and Information Technology, as the responsible department of China's information industry, also formulated many normative documents, among which the Regulations on the Protection of Personal Information of Telecom and Internet Users issued on July 16, 2013, is the most targeted. It specifies the personal information collection, use and security by telecom business operators and Internet information service providers. The Guide to Personal Information Protection in Information Security Technology Litigation and Commercial Service Information System (hereinafter referred to as the Guide to Personal Information Protection) jointly issued by the General Administration of Quality Supervision, Inspection and Quarantine and the Standardization Administration that took effect on

February 1, 2013, is the first national standard for personal information protection in China. The Interpretations on Several Issues Concerning the Application of Law in Handling Criminal Cases such as Defamation through Information Networks issued on September 5, 2013, by the Supreme People's Court and the Supreme People's Procuratorate defines the act of spreading fabricated facts and falsified information to damage the reputation of others through the Internet as slander by fabricating facts. On June 23, 2014, Article 12 of the Regulations on Several Issues Concerning the Application of Law in the Trial of Civil Dispute Cases Involving the Use of Information Networks to Infringe upon Personal Rights and Interests issued stipulated the identification of tort liability for the use of networks to disclose personal information. In spite of so many normative documents on personal information protection, overall, there are still the following problems in China's legislation of personal information protection: first, systematic special legislation is still in short supply, and fragmented legislation is prominent; second, the interest balance in personal information protection is not clearly or accurately expressed; third, most normative documents were issued by organs irrelevant to law formulation and enforcement, and normative documents issued by the judicial organs are a mere formality or declarative provisions, lacking operable specific rules; fourth, the positioning and authority of relevant administrative law enforcement departments are not clear, and the administrative management and law enforcement activities of the Cyberspace Administration of China lack the necessary legal basis.

7.3.2 Interest Measurement in Personal Information Protection and Utilisation

Since the middle of the 20th century, the wave of information technology dominated by microelectronics, electronic communication and computers has triggered a new round of the technological revolution, pushing mankind gradually into the information society. As social informatisation advances, information is being widely developed and utilised at an unprecedented speed. As it has become as important as material and energy, information is increasingly relied upon and needed by the whole of society. While enhancing social welfare, the use of personal information may also threaten and infringe the rights and interests of information subjects. That has generated the need for the protection of personal information. Faced with diversified and conflicting interests, the law is the best mechanism to strike a balance between unlimited demands and limited resources and realise the reasonable arrangement of different interest subjects.

7.3.2.1 Analysis of Personal Information Value

7.3.2.1.1 PRESENTATION OF PERSONAL DIGNITY AND FREEDOM

Personal information is something that can identify personal identity. As the data represents personal and behavior status, it is a record of the natural traces and social traces of a person. Personal information targeted at the information subject can show the person's personal life track and personality image. As the external symbol of the personality of the information subject, information forms a personal information image. In the information society, people have been used to referring to personal information image as real individuals. Modern information technology will enable almost all personal behaviors to leave information traces related to all aspects of personal life, resulting in the recording of individuals from the cradle to the grave. Modern information technology can also integrate fragmented personal information. As information accumulates in quality and quantity, fragmented personal information gradually forms a personal personality profile. As Maslow said in his theory of hierarchy of needs, the integrity and authenticity of personality identity are the basic conditions for the subject to be respected by others.[31] Individuals, in a purposeful existence, can live with self-esteem and respect from others only by eliminating their doubts and fears that their information image is being manipulated by others and keeping the consistency between their information personality and themselves from being distorted. Therefore, priority should be given to the personal information value of the information subject to his personal dignity and freedom in the legislation of personal information protection.

7.3.2.1.2 COMMERCIAL VALUE

The exploration of the commercial value of personal information is closely related to the change of business operation, especially the marketing mode, based on an accurate grasp of consumer demand. The transformation from early large-scale marketing to targeted marketing and database marketing is accompanied by the improvement of operators' ability to collect and use consumers' personal information. The popularisation of computers, the Internet and interactive digital media has greatly facilitated operators in obtaining consumer information and made it possible to accurately understand consumer needs and preferences. This enables operators to publish advertisements more efficiently and enjoy the economic returns brought by the increase in the marketing response ratio. The further development of information technology has turned business intelligence analysis into a reality. Business intelligence technology, applied to the consumer information mastered by operators, helps operators upgrade their future products and services, target the overall needs of consumers, has greatly improved the efficiency and rationality of their decision-making, and realised the targeted interaction between consumers and operators.

Personal information is also crucial to the healthy operation of the business environment. The market economy is a credit economy. Credit, on which all links of social reproduction are based, has become a key element in maintaining market order and economic development. Against the background of the credit economy, the establishment of a sound social credit system is related to the economic operation of society. This is obviously inseparable from the massive collection, processing and utilisation of personal credit information throughout China and beyond.

The massive demand of public and private institutions for personal information has also generated special personal information service providers. They have established a variety of personal information databases by collecting a great deal of personal information, providing information services such as information queries or leasing and even sales, including telephone yellow page service, credit investigation by private institutions, credit consulting, information query and so on. Other information service providers also rely on the collection and processing of personal information.

As informatisation advances in every aspect of society, information resources have emerged as important production factors, intangible assets and social wealth. Informatisation is intertwined with economic globalisation, which promotes the global industrial division of labor and economic structure adjustment and reshaping the world's pattern of economic competition.[32] As a rising country of informatisation, China needs to improve the development and utilisation of information resources as a whole not only in the information transformation of traditional industries and traditional service industries but also in the development of information service industries and contribute its due share to the development and utilisation of personal information when it seeks to surpass the world in informatisation.

7.3.2.1.3 SIGNIFICANCE TO PUBLIC MANAGEMENT

As the saying goes, the state must know the needs of the people first if it wants to win their support. Since the beginning of ancient times, it has been a common practice of the government to implement social management and provide public services by collecting and using personal information. As the most basic method for governments to obtain population data and master national conditions and strength in various periods, the census has a history of thousands of years.[33] In the information society, the government can more fully explore the significance of personal information to public management with the help of modern information technology. The combination of information technology with statistics and data analysis technology enables the government to collect and store more personal information at low cost and provide more extensive analysis samples for determining social conditions and public opinions. The processing and utilisation of personal information can also help the government make scientific and rational decisions and better promote public management and services. In addition to the initiatives of the responsible government and service-oriented government, the digital government has become a basic symbol of the modern government.[34] The promotion of public order, public safety and public welfare is inseparable from the support of the database with personal information as the base.

Since the September 11 terrorist attack, anti-terrorism and national security maintenance have become the international mainstream. Terrorism is regarded as the main force threatening the survival of mankind in the 21st century. The world is witnessing an increasingly serious anti-terrorism situation and normalised anti-terrorism efforts. Personal information related to crime is an important social management resource and forces for improving the efficiency of government law enforcement, combating crime and protecting human rights. The National Security Agency of the US learned of Osama Bin Laden's location through telephone monitoring records and finally killed him. In the 2011 London subway terrorist attack, the British police also quickly arrested the terrorists related to the attack and eased the social panic by analyzing the retained communication data. Nowadays, coerced by political purposes, terrorist crimes, increasingly crazy and extreme, have become a huge hidden danger to the international community. Therefore, personal information, applied to government investigation and intelligence analysis, will certainly help prevent and investigate global terrorist activities and contribute to the stability of the whole international community.

The promotion of e-government has always been the strategic focus of China's information development. Since the 1970s, China has begun to explore the application of computers to economic and social statistics, the census and so on. In 2002, China listed the national database of basic population information as one of the four key databases[35] for the national e-government. Over the past decade, China has made fruitful achievements in the government database construction, with the most types of personal information databases held by the Ministry of Public Security, including the system of population information management, the entry–exit certificate information database, national crime centre, DNA database and so on. In addition, national statistics, social security, taxation and other management departments have also established corresponding personal information databases. Since 2004, China has begun to promote the sharing of basic population information by integrating the population information resources of government departments. Relying on the population information of public security departments, China is gradually integrating the information resources of the departments of family planning, statistics, civil affairs, social security, taxation, education and others. According to the e-government Survey 2014 issued by the United Nations, China ranked 70th in the world in e-government development,[36] indicating a medium level. To further promote the construction of the digital government in China, we must make full and proper use of personal information resources.

7.3.3 Interest Identification in Personal Information Protection and Utilisation

Legislation is a process of understanding and expressing interest. To adjust different interests, we must first understand them.[37] In interest measurement, interest identification is taken as the starting point. In the protection and utilisation of personal information resources, the interest needs are as follows.

7.3.3.1 Information Subjects' Demand for Personal Information Protection

Personal information carries the information subject's personality interests, which are based on human freedom and dignity. The information subject requires the law to protect such personality interests, and we cannot treat personal information as pure material. On the one hand, individuals have a stronger demand for privacy protection because other individuals are still likely to infringe on the confidentiality of private life (which is the same as the problems facing us in privacy protection), and because of the virtual network environment as well as the convenience and universality of network communication. On the other hand, due to the technology of modern information processing, the public management value and commercial value contained in personal information will become a huge incentive for public and private institutions to improperly collect, process, use and transmit personal information. Besides, such information is not limited to the confidentiality of private life related to the traditional right to privacy and involves all identifiable information of individuals. Compared with the demand for traditional personal privacy protection, individuals have stronger and more common demands for the protection of their personal information. Therefore, personal information protection has become a common social problem.

The remarkable sign of an information society is the change of society from tangible material value creation to intangible information value creation. Society is depending more on information resources, and individuals in the process of social informatisation are no exception. In everyday life, individuals use relevant information services provided by public and private institutions all the time. The most common search engine service actually involves a huge Internet information retrieval and query system, and its effective operation depends on massive personal information collection and processing. Various identity verification services and credit consulting services are the result of personal information utilisation by society. In traditional privacy protection, individuals meet their needs by hiding or disclosing their privacy. The satisfaction of individual demand for information utilisation calls for the supply of information resources, information products and services by the society, which has penetrated the daily production and life of individuals in the information society. This shows that individuals have the need to protect their personal information and use information, including the personal information of others.

7.3.3.2 Information Industry's Demand for the Use of Personal Information

As society is being informationised, large quantities of information operators have appeared. There are not only traditional industry operators that collect and process massive amounts of personal information to improve the marketing response rate and grasp the market demand, but also information service providers specialising in the collection, processing, storage, utilisation and transmission of information. In traditional privacy protection, whether the disclosure or use of privacy was justified depended on the interest measurement of the conflict in a specific case between the right to know the truth and the right to privacy as well as between freedom of speech and the right to privacy. The use of others' private data was not generally recognised by society. In the information society, the legitimacy of information providers' collection and utilisation of personal information has been generally recognised by legislation and society. Therefore, it is equally important to promote the rational utilisation of personal information and protect personal information through legislation. The availability of information, including personal information, has brought business opportunities never seen before to human society. The basic interest demand of the information industry is to grasp this business opportunity and create more wealth.

Information providers cannot blindly pursue the maximum use of personal information, and appropriate protection of personal information also conforms to their interests. Only when personal information can be properly protected can it be possible to cultivate consumers' trust in providing their personal information and use personal information in the business industry. In addition, the legal protection of personal information aims to set legitimate provisions for the collection, storage, processing, utilisation and transmission of personal information by the information providers, maintain legitimate and fair competition among them, and avoid bad money driving good money out of circulation due to improper competition.

7.3.3.3 Government Demand for the Use of Personal Information

The government has always been the largest collector, processor, depositor and user of personal information. It can be said that the public power of the government must involve the collection, processing and utilisation of personal information. Different from the detached, neutral position in traditional privacy protection, the government participates in the protection and utilisation of personal information as both user and manager. On the one hand, as the undertaker of social management and social welfare, the government relies on the mastery of residents' personal information to promote public safety, public management and public welfare. On the other hand, the government will continue to actively explore the limits and value of the use of personal information for administrative efficiency.

Meanwhile, the government, as the undertaker of state power, has the responsibility to protect the basic rights and freedom of citizens. Human rights are the product of our times and the only political and moral concept that has been widely accepted.[38] The government cannot collect and use personal information wantonly. The development of the legal system of personal information protection has always been accompanied by the restriction of government power because the legal system of personal information protection is not only established to protect citizens but also necessary to maintain the legitimacy of the government's own political power. The principle of human rights protection established in the constitution needs to be realised by departmental law. The state should promulgate laws to limit the ability of the government and information providers to collect, process and use personal information in order to ensure human rights protection and maintain the legitimacy of its own political power. It should also take all necessary means, including the rule of law, technical and physical measures, to ensure the security of personal information.

7.3.4 Interest Measurement in Personal Information Protection and Utilisation

The above interest identification analysis of personal information protection and utilisation clearly shows that interest subjects and interest content involved in personal information protection and utilisation are more diversified than in traditional privacy protection. First, the interest measurement in personal information protection and utilisation is put out to society when the information industry and the government appear as information users. The social aspect of the protection and utilisation of personal information makes it different from the interest measurement at the individual level in traditional privacy protection. As the traditional industry is being informationised and the special information service industry is emerging in the informationisation of society, the information industry has emerged as a new independent interest subject. In addition to its status as a neutral and detached judge in traditional privacy protection, the government participates in the collection, processing and utilisation of personal information in order to complete public management and services as both manager and user at the same time. The emergence of new interest subjects and roles represents the demand of society for the use of personal information. Therefore, different from traditional privacy, which calls for protection only for individuals, personal information needs to be protected and used. Secondly, when the protection of personal information is considered in the context of personal information utilisation, the conflict of interest still exists in traditional privacy protection, and personal privacy interest is still an important part of the interest measurement in personal information protection. In the context of informatisation, the information industry and the government, as new stakeholders, may infringe the privacy of the information subject when using personal information. The demand for personal privacy protection internally limits the information industry and the government in using personal information. The booming information industry and increasingly complex information technology have accelerated the balancing of the four elements advanced by Professor Westin and promoted the development of privacy law.[39] The new social interest pattern requires interest re-measurement in personal information protection and utilisation.

7.4 The Theory of Two Strengths and Tripartite Balance

7.4.1 New Win-Win Thinking on Personal Information Protection and Utilisation in the Era of Big Data

The diversification and conflict of interest have made it necessary to adjust the interest relationship with the help of interest measurement in legislation so that each interest subject can get his due and secure his position. In terms of interest measurement, legislators need to follow certain value guidance. In addition to fairness and justice universally applicable to the law, the historical stage of social development actually constitutes the primary factor affecting the interest measurement by legislators.

As the application of new technologies such as business intelligence, social networking sites, wireless sensors, cloud computing and the semantic web has become increasingly popular over the past 20 years, data has grown and accumulated at an unprecedented rate, leading to the formation of big data.[40] Professor Nicholas Negroponte, an American technology activist, calls this stage the post-information age in his book *Being Digital*. The development of networks promoted by information technology has expanded people's living space from physical space to electronic space and digital space, gradually creating a virtual world.[41] The Internet has changed people's way of expression and recognition. In the online world, any individual behavior will leave data traces. The application of data mining, integrating and analyzing technology to data traces, as well as the invisible data and privacy exposure brought by aggregated data traces, poses more threats to personal privacy protection and makes personal information protection more urgent in the post-information age. On the other hand, in the post-information age, data, a large amount of which is generated and flows all the time, has been a direct wealth and social resource. The application of data technology can help discover new knowledge and create new value. To realise the leap from data to knowledge and action, the public and private fields have a more urgent demand for data utilisation than in any previous era.

Data privacy has also become a top-level issue in the era of the digital economy.[42] The key to solving the problem still lies in the interest measurement in personal information protection and utilisation: as new interest subjects, also one party of interest measurement, the information industry and government represent the demand for using personal information interest. The urgent demand for effective protection of personal privacy still exists and constitutes another party of interest measurement. When both personal privacy protection and personal information utilisation need to be strengthened, the feasible scheme is to provide differential protection and utilisation of personal information according to certain standards so as to realise the win-win outcome.

7.4.2 The Connotation of the Theory of Two Strengths and Tripartite Balance

7.4.2.1 Two Strengths

"Two strengths" means when the concept of sensitive personal privacy is established and differentiated from general personal information, the protection of sensitive personal privacy and the utilisation of general personal information are strengthened to reconcile the demand conflict between the protection and utilisation of personal information and realise the balance between interests.

It is not unheard of in the legal protection of personal information to distinguish different personal information to establish different degrees of protection and utilisation. In 1981, the Convention for the Protection of Individuals with Regard to the Automatic Processing of Personal Data issued by the European Council established in Article 6[43] a special type of data protection system for the first time, which prohibited the collection and utilisation of such data in principle. This system was also followed by the later EU Personal Data Protection Directive.[44] In addition, the laws issued by Switzerland, Norway, Iceland, Canada, Macao and Taiwan also prohibit or restrict the processing of specific types of information. In 2003, Professor Zhou Hanhua provided an in-depth study of sensitive personal information in China's Law of Personal Information Protection (expert proposal draft) drafted by him, but the concept of sensitive information wasn't adopted because much of the wide range of sensitive personal information mentioned in extra-territorial legislation was not suitable for China's national conditions.[45]

The risk of data processing to personal data privacy varies from data sensitivity to data sensitivity.[46] The concept of a special type of data is established to apply rules. Special types of data and general data are differentiated to apply different rules of protection and utilisation, warn that some special types of personal information need special protection by law and loosen the use of other general personal information. This is how the conflict of interest between the protection and utilisation of personal information is better reconciled. Considering that different types of personal information have different effects on the realisation of the interest need of the subject, personal information is categorised to balance the interest among multiple subjects in the protection and utilisation of personal information. The author believes that China's future law of personal information protection should classify personal information based on the concept of sensitive personal privacy.

7.4.2.1.1 STRENGTHEN THE PROTECTION OF SENSITIVE PERSONAL PRIVACY

Sensitive personal privacy refers to highly private personal information of which the disclosure or utilisation will have a significant impact on individuals, such as sexual life, genetic information, medical records, financial information and so on. In China's Guide for the Protection of Personal Information, sensitive information is defined as personal information that will have an adverse impact on the identified personal information subject once it is disclosed or modified.[47] The author believes that taking the adverse impact on the subject of personal information as the defining standard is turning a blind eye to bad behavior, which also greatly reduces the significance of distinguishing sensitive information from general information. The law of personal information protection does not provide thorough protection for all privacy-related information but only for sensitive personal privacy. There is an overlap—the confidentiality of private life—between personal information and personal privacy. With the application of digital technology, more and more confidential, personal, private life information can be recorded as personal information. The application of data mining, analyzing and integrating technology makes almost all personal information related to privacy. If personal privacy is used as the standard for differential protection, it will substantially restrict the use of personal information and lead to the improper suppression of freedom of speech and suppression of disclosure to society. As everyone is inseparable from information products and services in the information society, the use of non-sensitive private information will ultimately benefit every information subject.

The concept of sensitive privacy is highly localised. When enumerating the types of sensitive privacy in China, we should pay attention to China's cultural tradition, universal social values, legal tradition, customs and so on. The Law of Personal Data Protection of Taiwan provides a valuable reference. Considering the relationship between sensitive personal information and personal core privacy, Article 6 of this law lists the types of sensitive personal information, including personal data related to medical treatment, genetics, sexual life, health examination and criminal record. As sensitive personal privacy is dynamic, its enumerated types should be flexibly revised in line with the current scientific and technological progress and social development. In the General Data Protection Regulation issued by the EU in 2012, genetic information is included in special types of data and given special protection in line with the development of modern biotechnology.[48]

7.4.2.1.2 STRENGTHEN THE USE OF GENERAL PERSONAL INFORMATION

In May 2011, McKinsey & Company, a world-renowned consulting company, released *Big Data: The Next Frontier for Innovation, Competition, and Productivity*, which was the world's first thematic research achievement to interpret the development potential of big data from the perspectives of the economy and commerce. The report notes that data that has penetrated into every industry and the field of business has gradually become an important production factor. People's use of massive data will herald the arrival of a new wave of productivity growth and consumer surplus.[49] The application of big data and big data technology will make human decision-making as intelligent and accurate as never before.[50] The "big" is used to describe both the scale and value. More and more people consider data as an economic asset. The government can better understand the operation of the national economy and society and make better decisions through accurate data quantification. Operators can understand consumers' hobbies, traits and psychological characteristics from the data, so as to provide more personalised products and services and achieve a win-win relationship between operators and consumers. Besides, personal activities in the real, physical world have been recorded as never before. For instance, news posts, interactive records of social platforms, web browsing records and so on. have all provided large quantities of data for the research of social sciences. Social sciences in the 21st century may get rid of the title "quasi-science," realise quantitative research and become a real science. Therefore, strengthening the use of general personal information and promoting its commercial and public management value to the greatest extent has become an inevitable choice for all countries to occupy the discourse power in the post-information age. The law of personal information protection to be promulgated in China must give the information industry great freedom of collecting, processing and using personal information. The power and ability of state organs to collect, process and use personal information must be guaranteed for national security and social management.

7.4.2.2 Tripartite Balance

Tripartite balance refers to the balance among the individual's interest in the protection of personal information (the core is personal freedom and dignity), the information industry's interest in the use of personal information (the core is obtaining economic interests through business activities) and the state's public interest in the management of society. Balance is a tension state in which the core interest of each interest subject is protected and realised, and the non-core interest is transferred as the condition and basis for other parties to realise their core interests. Specifically, the protection of sensitive privacy in personal information should be strengthened, and personal freedom and dignity should be better protected. The information subject should transfer some of its interests of non-private information so that the information industry can have greater freedom to collect and use the processed information to facilitate its operation. The information industry realises its main interests through the interest transferred by individuals and through the good information management environment guaranteed by the state while respecting the individual's right to privacy and management regulations issued by the state. It should consciously protect the core privacy of the information subject in collecting, processing, storing, transmitting and using personal information, respect privacy and resist the R&D and application of information technology for the purpose of violating privacy, realising the core interest of the information subject and the public management interest of the state in the personal information protection. It is the various information products and services provided by the information industry that allow individuals to have more opportunities to meet the needs for daily life and realise the right to know the truth. The state, on the one hand, should obtain the power and ability to collect, process, store and use necessary personal information in order to administer society. On the other hand, the exercise of public power, such as the collection and use of personal information, needs to be constrained. The state cannot use technical means and state machinery to intervene in private life. The state, as the holder of public power, also needs to formulate laws to define the boundary for the protection of privacy, formulate management norms for fair competition in the business activities of information operators and provide all necessary support and institutional guarantees for the construction and security of personal information databases, including physical security and information security. It must also crack down on crimes seriously infringing on personal information and punish the information industry for the improper collection, processing, storage, utilisation and transmission of personal information.

7.5 Realisation of the Theory of Two Strengths and Tripartite Balance

7.5.1 The Theoretical Basis of the Legislation of Personal Information Protection in China

The legislation of personal information involves models of the European Union and the United States. The United States adopted the model of operator self-discipline due to its relatively complete protection in its original privacy law, while Europe adopted a national (government)-led legislative model due to its legislative tradition. At present, as China has not fully established a general system of privacy protection but has scattered and chaotic legal provisions on personal information protection, it is necessary to formulate a comprehensive law of personal information protection to standardise the basic problems of personal information protection and utilisation.

One of the main functions of law is to adjust and reconcile various conflicting interests, including both personal and social interests.[51] Under the modern state system, the main task of legislation is to balance interests. Solving the interest conflicts behind norms constitutes the internal system of law,[52] and the theoretical basis for the law of personal information protection must be the theory of interest measurement aimed at reconciling multiple interest conflicts in the protection and utilisation of personal information.

In the information society, individuals, information operators and the state are three interest subjects related to personal information resources. The concept of sensitive personal privacy is used to distinguish the types of personal information. The protection of sensitive personal privacy should be strengthened to safeguard the core interests of individuals in personal information protection. The use of general personal information should be strengthened to meet the legitimate needs of the information industry and the state to use personal information and realise the tripartite balance. In the future, China's Law of Personal Information Protection should be based on the theory of two strengths and tripartite balance to establish the relevant system of personal information protection and utilisation.

7.5.2 Establish a Rule of Law Model Characteristic of State Domination, Industry Self-Discipline and Individual Participation

7.5.2.1 State Domination

The state domination referred to in the Law of Personal Information Protection is reflected in legislation and law enforcement: first, a unified personal information protection law is formulated as the basic law of personal information protection to adjust the relationship between personal information protection and utilisation in the public and private fields. The authority, compulsion and universal applicability of laws are unmatched by informal systems, such as self-discipline regulations, because laws can establish stable expectations for institutions and individuals to regulate their behaviors more effectively.[53] When a sufficient market of self-discipline has not formed in China, it is particularly necessary for the state to regulate it by unified legislation. Specifically, guided by the theory of two strengths and tripartite balance, the state should establish the threshold standard for personal information protection in China by making basic principles of personal information protection suitable for China's national conditions, and stipulating the rights of information subjects, and the obligations and legal responsibilities of the information industry and government. Secondly, state domination also means that there are special agencies responsible for the implementation and supervision of the law of personal information protection. Special data protection institutions originating in the European Union[54] were established in Switzerland, Norway, Canada, as well as in Hong Kong and Macao SAR. The author believes that China should establish an independent special management organisation to ensure the implementation of China's Law of Personal Information Protection. Amid global economic integration, the special management organisation will facilitate China's better participation in international cooperation in the cross-border circulation of personal information and safeguard China's information sovereignty and citizens' information interests. In terms of the current institutional establishment in China, we can consider taking the existing Cyberspace Administration of China as the platform and properly integrating some functions of the information industry and the industrial and commercial administration department to construct the special management organisation. This agency will supervise the implementation of the law of personal information protection, conduct law enforcement investigations, research personal information protection and utilisation, and put forward legislative opinions and suggestions to the legislature in time.

7.5.2.2 Industry Self-Discipline

Guided by the state, we should also fully encourage the information industry to implement self-discipline management. The self-discipline mechanism means that social organisations spontaneously regulate their own behavior and achieve self-discipline by establishing self-discipline norms beyond national legislation.[55] As an internal mechanism, industry self-discipline can interact with the national law as an external coercive mechanism in a positive way. The unified personal information protection law is often not flexible or targeted. The legislation may only reach a consensus on the minimum standard of personal information protection when multiple interests are balanced and compromised. Therefore, there is more room for industry self-discipline in personal information protection. We should fully encourage the self-discipline enthusiasm of operators in the same industry and motivate them to bear social responsibility beyond the law.[56] Specifically, on the one hand, the information industry can formulate more targeted and detailed guidelines for the protection and utilisation of personal information by referring to the principled provisions of the basic law issued by the state on personal information protection and considering its own business characteristics and business practice experience. When processing specific personal information in a manner that is concise and easy to understand, the information industry should give explanations and tips to the information subject to provide more convenient, sufficient and high-level protection for the information subject. On the other hand, industry self-discipline is also an effective way to alleviate the lack of legislative supply caused by the rapid development of information technology. The ongoing informatisation of society requires that legislation should be rational and restrained and should not hinder the technological innovation of the whole market. The information industry should be encouraged to formulate self-discipline norms to provide certain protection for the information subject. Legislators should formulate laws to regulate them after fully summarising the useful experience of the information industry. That is a good policy to avoid blind and advanced legislation stifling the vitality of technological innovation. Also, the driver and pressure from the market provide sufficient dynamics for industry self-discipline: the level of information protection will affect choices of consumers, who vote with their feet, resulting in the survival of the fittest in the information industry; reputation also provides reverse incentives for the self-discipline of the information industry.

7.5.2.3 Citizen Participation

With the innovation made by China in its social management mode, the government has transformed from a regulator to a service provider. In terms of the governance of social problems, China no longer simply emphasises national regulation but the combination of national governance, social coordination and citizen participation. Citizens have massive enthusiasm and need for participation in personal information protection, and the development of modern information technology also provides convenience for more citizens to participate. Opacity and lack of participation will generate doubt in the rationality of the rules themselves, make it difficult to keep up with the pace of social progress and eventually lead to more special rules and government intervention as well as less order and autonomy, a so-called antinomy.[57] Therefore, in the formulation, implementation and relief of relevant laws and policies, we can broaden the participation channels of citizens and strengthen their interest expression and supervision as well as relief to them through the network platform. First, when making laws and policies, the legislature and administrative departments can also solicit public opinion through an open network platform, in addition to the traditional legislative hearing. As it is difficult for elected representatives to fully express the public interest demands due to the increasingly diversified interests in modern society, soliciting opinions through the network platform can bring more interest demands into the consideration of legislators so as to formulate more just laws and policies. Second, special institutions for personal information protection can also establish a network platform for more convenient reporting, complaint, appeal and supervision from information subjects, ensure the practical implementation of laws and policies and make long-term preparations for further improving relevant laws and policies. Finally, the government and information industry should also listen to public opinion and give timely feedback by establishing network platforms and citizen hotlines so as to better solve problems in time.

7.5.3 The System of Real Names of the Information Industry and the System of the Verifiable Real Identity of Network Users

In order to purify the network environment and maintain network security, China has gradually expanded the system of real names of telecom value-added service providers and network service providers[58] to cover all network users.[59] While the necessity and justice of the system of real names of information providers such as telecom value-added service providers and network service providers are obvious, the system of real names of all network users has aroused great debate. The author believes that the practical implementation of the above two systems and the rational construction of the system of the verifiable real identity of network users will eventually help the protection and utilisation of citizens' personal information.

7.5.3.1 The System of the Real Names of the Information Industry

While telecommunications and the Internet have greatly facilitated the release of information, the subsequent spam messages and emails sent by phishing websites, pseudo-base stations and fraudulent telephone communications have seriously disrupted the social order and people's daily lives. The most serious among them are telecommunications and network fraud through[60] virtual number dialing (pseudo-base stations) and phishing websites, which can cause citizens' property losses and even personal injury and damage the prestige of public power organs and the trust in the whole market environment. The appearance of both virtual number dialing and phishing websites results from the weak dynamic supervision by telecom operators and the China Internet Network Information Centre of the real identity of information operators. The success of virtual number dialing is due to the use of IP address phone service loopholes of telecom operators to set the calling number as the number of credible state organs and social institutions. In terms of anti-phishing websites, organisations such as the China Anti-Phishing Alliance and Anti-Fraud Alliance compare suspected malicious websites with those in the open database of their allied units so as to reduce the online fraud probability of users of allied units. However, the China Centre for Internet Network has a limited role in establishing a coordinated dynamic anti-phishing mechanism and in authenticating website identity integrity. The effective implementation of the system of real names of the information industry requires relevant regulators to intercept unqualified subjects in the network and effectively implement dynamic supervision in order to maintain the credibility of network order.

7.5.3.2 The System of the Verifiable Real Identity of Network Users

The system of the verifiable real identity of network users is related to the system of real names of network users and can be regarded as an upgraded version of the latter. Both aim to establish the connection between the virtual network identity and the real physical identity and solve the difficulty in tracking and the accountability of network violations and crimes caused by the virtual and mutable network identity. The network world also needs to be managed through legislation by the state to maintain the peace of network order. That is what the legitimacy of the real name system lies in. The system of the verifiable real identity of network users has the same effect on network management as the system of real names of network users. However, the former can better maintain the security of citizens' personal information, avoid the deterrent effect on freedom of speech caused by the real-name system, minimise the restrictions on citizens' rights and freedoms and achieve the balance between regulation and freedom. Specifically, the system of the verifiable real identity of network users means verifying the real identity of citizens by uniformly issuing and authenticating the network identity code in the established national official website to replace the real identity of citizens under the real-name system.[61] Under the system of the verifiable real identity of network users, the real identity of network users is only controlled by the national website. Therefore, the information of network users is less likely to be disclosed to a national website than to all kinds of Internet information service providers under the real-name system. Compared with Internet information service providers providing uneven services, national websites can better maintain security. In addition, under the system of the verifiable real identity of network users, the user's real name only exists on the national website, and the real identity can be authenticated only for legitimate reasons and in accordance with procedures. This can maintain the user's anonymity state in cyberspace to the greatest extent and avoid the deterrent effect on citizens' freedom of speech. State organs can only check the real name of network users involved in illegal and criminal acts on a legal basis and in line with their authorisation and shall not abuse their power to check the real identity of network users. For moderately improper network speech and behavior, the state's public power should not be frequently used to check the real identity of network users.

7.5.4 Strengthen the Dual Functions of the State in the Protection and Utilisation of Personal Information

In the context of big data, the way to maximise the state's use of personal information is to establish a central database of the state, solve information isolation between databases and maximise the efficiency of government administration. It was noted in Article 10 of the Opinions on Strengthening the Construction of Social Security Prevention and Control System (hereinafter referred to as the Opinions) issued by the General Office of the Communist Party of China (CPC) Central Committee and the General Office of the State Council on April 13, 2015, that China would establish a unified and shared national database for basic population information with a citizen ID number as the only code, improve the real-name registration system, establish a unified social credit code system for citizens and explore the system of smart cards containing all the citizen's information.

The central database of the state is necessary for the progress of informatisation, and the primary problem we need to face is how to ensure information security and protect citizens' legitimate rights and interests noted in the Opinions. The author believes that the solution to this problem involves the security of personal information and the restriction of state power. We should ensure the safe sharing and proper use of personal information resources through both technical guarantees and legal regulation. The state must increase technological investment in an effort to promote innovations in technology, improve China's information security, ensure the security of China's information sovereignty and ensure the security of the central database of the state and all state organs' databases involving citizens' personal information. More importantly, the government's public power should be strictly limited by law to ensure the proper use of the central database of the state-by-state organs and avoid the nightmare of data monitoring. The establishment of the central database of the state is, in nature, the intervention of expanded public power in citizens' private life, which must comply with the principle of legitimate use, the principle of legitimate purpose and the principle of minimal intervention. First of all, the central database of the state must be established in accordance with clear provisions formulated by the legislature because its establishment involves the basic rights and freedoms of citizens. The key to legislation is to strictly restrict the use of the database and specify the specific circumstances and preconditions for the use of the database. It can be used only for legitimate reasons such as major social and public interest. Second, the collection and utilisation of personal information in the central database of the state must conform to the purpose of establishing the database, and personal information shall not be collected and utilised illegally. Third, the use of the central database of the state must be necessary and important to achieve its purpose and should intervene in the freedom of the related parties as little as possible.[62] The state should have an inclusive attitude to acts that have not yet constituted illegality and crime or do not seriously deviate from the social public order and good customs, give people full freedom and pursue kind governance rather than blindly monitor and control. Finally, personal information in the central database of the state must be collected and used in accordance with the basic principles for personal information protection and utilisation, including data quality, restriction on collection, disclosure principle and information subject participation, so as to ensure citizens' right to know the truth and right to participation. The operation of the central database of the state should be made public as an important part of the openness of government affairs to facilitate public and social supervision.

7.5.5 Information Industry: Depersonalised Information Processing and Utilisation

Personal information is information that can identify personal identity. The identifying function will affect the protection of the rights and interests of information subjects and restrict the use of it by information providers. On the one hand, more restrictions should be imposed on the use of personal information by information operators when they use personal information of specific information subjects in direct selling.[63] On the other hand, the information industry should carry out depersonalisation in collecting, storing, processing and using personal information when it does not use the personal information of the single target subject. For example, the information industry's focus on the group characteristics of consumers and removal of the clear identification elements of a single individual does not affect its analysis of the group characteristics of consumers when personal information is used in targeted marketing, database marketing and business intelligence analysis. Unless refused by the information subject, the identifiable factors of personal information should be generally removed by the information industry through code or encryption to cut off the identification elements between the information and specific individuals. Such depersonalisation of information can reduce the impact of possible security events such as information disclosure on the information subject in the future.

Depersonalisation will lead to a slight rise in the information processing cost of operators, but the risk of improper processing, transmission and utilisation of personal information will be significantly reduced after de-personalisation. This can avoid the direct identification infringement on the information subject, which is of positive significance to the information subject. This also meets the need to maximise the protection and utilisation of personal information between operators and information subjects.

7.5.6 Individuals: Special Protection of Minors and Their Sensitive Privacy

7.5.6.1 Strengthen the Protection of Minors' Information

According to the 2013 Survey of Chinese Teenagers' Internet Behaviors released by the China Internet Network Information Centre, as of December 2013, the number of Chinese minor Internet users reached 140 million, accounting for 22.65% of the total. More teenagers under 12 used the Internet, and their online behaviors involved information acquisition, communication, online entertainment, business transactions and so on.[64] In 2014, China noted the 20th anniversary of its access to the interpersonal Internet. Today's minors are the generation who have really grown up in the era of the Internet. The Internet has become an important part of their lives and has a profound impact on their lifestyle and even ideology. Minors, who are not mature in mind, do not have enough ability of cognition, control and self-protection like adults. Their rights and interests are undoubtedly more vulnerable to infringement. In terms of personal information protection and utilisation, special attention should be given to minors.

In strengthening the protection of minors' personal information, the United States is a pioneer in legislation. As early as 1998, the United States enacted the Children's Online Privacy Protection Act to restrict website operators from collecting children's personal information through the Internet. The act stipulates that website operators bear the responsibility to protect children's online privacy and security and shall not collect personal information of children under 13 without the consent of their parents or guardians. By 2012, the restriction on website operators was expanded to the collection of photos, videos and geographic information of children. In addition, the laws enacted by some states in the United States also embody the awareness of strengthening the protection of minors. For example, the Eraser Act issued by California in 2013 requires that social networking sites should allow minors to erase their Internet traces so as to avoid being troubled in the future for Internet traces left when they are not mentally mature.[65] The General Data Protection Regulation issued by the European Union in 2012 also made extra provisions on the special protection of children's personal data by learning from the legislative experience of the United States.[66]

China's Guide for Personal Information Protection also embodies the concept of special protection for minors' personal information. It stipulates that sensitive personal information shall not be directly collected from minors under 16 or other persons with limited civil capacity or without capacity. If it is really necessary to collect their sensitive personal information, clear consent shall be obtained from their legal guardians. It can be said that the Guide for Personal Information Protection is more advanced than the acts issued by the United States and the European Union as it is not only applicable to the network environment but uniformly enhances the protection of minors' personal information being collected. With the development of new digital media platforms and TV shopping, minors' personal information will certainly not be collected or used only through the Internet. However, the enhanced protection of minors is limited to the collection of their sensitive information in the Guide, which actually limits the effectiveness of the enhanced protection. In the future legislation of personal information protection in China, an age boundary suitable for the development of teenagers in China should be determined through abundant empirical social research to strengthen protection.

7.5.6.2 Strengthen the Protection of Sensitive Personal Privacy

The concept of sensitive personal privacy is proposed to enhance its protection. The collection, processing and utilisation of sensitive personal information and general information apply to different legal rules. The experience from comparative law shows that on the basis of a clear distinction between the two, the EU prohibits the collection and processing of sensitive personal information in principle. Although there is no clear classification of sensitive personal information in the United States, there are some similar restrictive provisions. For instance, it is stipulated that sensitive information shall not be used as the basis for making a certain decision that otherwise shall be regarded as discriminatory. For example, in the US credit investigation industry, the credit investigation organ shall not disseminate, consider, or calculate sensitive information such as race, nationality and marital status in credit scoring, although it can collect such information. Otherwise, it will be punished by the Federal Trade Commission for making a discriminatory decision.

The enhanced protection of sensitive personal information still involves both protection and utilisation. Protection is reflected in the prohibition of information processing in principle, while utilisation is reflected in the exceptions to the prohibition of information processing. The principle of prohibiting information processing shall apply to the whole process of personal information processing, including collection, storage, processing, utilisation and dissemination. The exceptions to the prohibition are limited to the explicit consent or self-disclosure of the information subject, the express provisions of the law, the necessity for the public organ to perform its statutory duties or the non-public organ to perform its statutory obligations and the necessity for the public organ or research institution to conduct statistical or academic research for the purpose of medical treatment, health, crime prevention and so on. In the case of the above exceptional use of information, public and private institutions dealing with sensitive personal information shall better protect sensitive personal privacy.

7.6 Conclusions

In the information society, everyone is a person of information. An individual is both a producer and a consumer of information. No one can live without information. Accordingly, every social relationship in human society is directly or indirectly branded with informatisation, so laws regulating these social relations should also adapt to informatisation. Personal information is inextricably linked to privacy, but the interest re-measurement in the protection and utilisation of information will inevitably become the starting point and foundation of the law of personal information protection in theory due to values of personal information such as personal freedom and dignity, commercial value and significance to public management.

The result of the zero-sum game for the interest and profit is always a life and death struggle, while interest measurement in legislation aims to achieve a win-win and harmonious outcome. Therefore, it is necessary to identify the interest needs of various parties in the protection and utilisation of personal information and promote the realisation of their core interests. The parties should transfer their own non-core interests and allow other parties to realise their core interests.

By strengthening the protection of sensitive personal privacy, as well as the use of general personal information by information operators for commercial purposes and by the state for public management, we can achieve the balance of interest among individuals, information operators and the state. This theory of two strengths and tripartite balance should be the theoretical basis of China's Law of Personal Information Protection. The full realisation of this theory needs institutional arrangements, including the rule of law model characteristic of state domination, self-discipline and individual participation, the system of real names of the information industry and the system of the verifiable real identity of network users, the role of the state as both a user and social manager of personal information, the depersonalised use of personal information by the information industry and the special protection of minors' personal information, and sensitive personal privacy.

Notes

1 Chief scientist of the 2014 major project of the National Social Science Foundation of China, Research on the Legislation of Major Issues of Internet Security (project approval No.: 14ZDC021), Professor of the School of Law at Renmin University of China, and chief editor of this journal. This paper is the phased achievement of the subproject Research on the Legislation of Personal Information Security Protection, written by Zhang Xinbao, Ge Xin and Zhang Le. Members of the subproject team include Li Changxi (director of Policies and Regulations Bureau at the Cyberspace Administration of China), Wang Xu (associate professor of the School of Law at Renmin University of China), Jiang Qiang (judge of the first civil court of the Supreme People's Court), Chen Pu (associate researcher of Renmin University of China), Zhang Le (associate professor of the School of Law at Henan Normal University) and Ge Xin (doctoral candidate of the School of Law at Renmin University of China).

2 Zhang Xinbao: Legal Protection of the Right to Privacy, People's Publishing House, 2004, Pp. 7. For the same view, see Wang Liming: Redefinition of the Right to Privacy, The Jurist, 2012, issue. 1.

3 Some scholars also call it personal data, personal information, information privacy and other titles, but there is no essential difference in the research object and content. This paper follows the consensus of the current academic and practice circles and adopts "personal information," which has the same meaning as personal data.

4 General Data Protection Regulation, Article 4.

5 Article 9 of the Personal Information Protection Law of the People's Republic of China (Expert Proposal), quoted from Zhou Hanhua's Personal Information Protection Law of the People's Republic of China (Expert Proposal) and Legislative Research Report, Law Press, 2006, page 3.

6 See Directive 95/46/EC (Personal Data Protection Directive, revised as General Data Protection Regulation in November 2012), Directive 2000/31/EC (Electronic Commerce Directive), Directive 2002/58/EC (Privacy and Electronic Communications Directive), Directive 2006/24/EC (Data Retention Directive).

7 For relevant research results, see Qi Aimin, Research on Principles of Personal Data Protection Law and on Legal Issues of Cross-Border Circulation, Wuhan University Press, 2004; Kong Lingjie, Legal Protection of Personal Data Privacy, Wuhan University Press, 2009; Jiang Po: Legal Protection of Personal Data, China University of Political Science and Law Press, 2008; Guo Yu: Research on the Personal Data Protection Law, China University of Political Science and Law Press, 2012.

8 See the previous citation (4) by Zhou Hanhua; Qi Aimin: Draft of the Model Law of Personal Information Protection of the People's Republic of China (Scholar's Proposal), Hebei Law Science, 2005, issue 6.

9 Qi Enping: On the Game between the Real Name System and Private Right Protection, Law Science Magazine, 2013, issue 7; Ma Yanhua: Analysis of Legal Issues Related to the Network Real Name System, Hebei Law Science, 2011, issue 2; Yang Xiaonan: Management of Network Real Name System and Protection of Citizen Personal Information, Information Science, 2012, issue 11; Wang Xiuzhe: Identity Certificate and Personal Information Protection—Research on the Legal Regulation of China's Resident Identity Card, Hebei Law Science, 2010, issue 5; Wang Rui, Xiong Jian and Huang Guiqin: Legal Thoughts on Improving China's Personal Credit Investigation System, China Legal Science, 2002, issue 4; Sun Ping: Protection of Citizens' Privacy in the Era of Huge Government Database, Law Science, 2007, issue 7.

10 Carl D. Schnlelder: Shame, Exposure and Privacy, W. W. Norton & Co. Inc., 1992.

11 Thomas M. Cooley: Law Of Torts, Calllaghan & Company, 2nd ed., 1888, p. 29.

12 William L. Prosser, Privacy, California Law Review, 1960, issue 3.

13 Deckle McLean: Privacy And Its Invasion, Praeger Publishers, 1995, p. 3.

14 Article 8 of the European Convention on Human Rights stipulates that everyone has the right to make his private and family life, family and communication respected.
15 Wang Zejian: Concretization of the Right to Personality and Its Protection Scope: the Right to Privacy (Part I), Journal of Comparative Law, 2008, issue 6.
16 BGHZ 13, 334.
17 BVerfGE 65, 1.
18 Previous quotation (14) from the article by Wang Zejian.
19 Long Weiqiu: On the Personality Right of Natural Persons and its contemporary approach—Also on Constitutional Order and Civil Law Positivism, Tsinghua University Law Journal, 2002, issue 2.
20 James Q. Whitman: The Two Western Cultures of Privacy: Dignity Versus Liberty, Yale Law, Journal, 2004, issue 6.
21 Id 19.
22 Arita L. Allen and Richard C. Turkington: Privacy Law: Cases and Materials, edited and translated by Feng Jianmei, China Democracy and Legal Publishing House, 2004, p. 17.
23 Ruth Gavison: Privacy and the Limits of Law, Yale Law Journal, 1980, issue 89.
24 See the previous citation (1) by Zhang Xinbao, pp. 85–87.
25 Richard C. Turkington and Anita L. Allen: Privacy, 2nd ed., West Croup, 2002, p. 1.
26 Article 19 of the Universal Declaration of Human Rights stipulates that everyone has the right to freedom of opinion and expression and this right includes freedom to hold opinions without interference and to seek, receive and impart information and ideas through any media and regardless of frontiers.
27 Matthew C. Keck: Cookies, The Constitution, and the Common Law: A Framework for the Right of Privacy on the Internet, Albany Law, Journal of Science & Technology, 2002, issue 1.
28 See Directive 95/46/EC, Article 3.
29 For example, the Fair Credit Reporting Act of 1970, Right to Financial Privacy Act of 1978, the Cable Communication Policy Act of 1984, the Video Privacy Protection Act of 1988, the Telephone Consumer Protection Act of 1991, the Driver's Privacy Protection Act of 1994, the Children's Online Privacy Protection Act of 1998, the Financial Service Modernization Act of 1999 and Controlling the Assault of Non-Solicited Pornography and Marketing of 2003.
30 See Articles 14, 29, 50 and 56 of Consumer Protection Law of the People's Republic of China.
31 Abraham Maslow: Motivation and Personality, translated by Xu Jinsheng, China Renmin University Press, 2007 edition, p. 31.
32 See the General Office of the CPC Central Committee and the General Office of the State Council: National Strategy of Informatization Development (2006–2020), accessed on April 30, 2015, website: http://www.gov.cn/test/2009—9/24/content_1425447.htm.
33 Lu Lixin: A Brief Discussion on Population and Environment, Yellow River Water Conservancy Press, 2010, p. 54.
34 Jiang Po: Research on Legal Issues of Personal Data Protection in Public Management Affairs, published in: Legal Protection of Personal Data in Mainland China, Hong Kong, Macao and Taiwan edited by Chen Haifan and Zhao Guoqiang, Social Science Academic Press, 2014, p. 139.
35 See the General Office of the CPC Central Committee and The General Office of the State Council: Guidance by the National Informatization Leading Group on E-government. The other three databases are the basic database of legal entities, the basic database of spatial geography and natural resources and the basic database of macro economy, accessed April 30, 2015, website: http://www.e-gov.org.cn/ziliaoku/news004/201305/140983.html.
36 The 2014 UN E-Government Survey was released in Beijing, accessed April 30, 2015, website: http://politics.people. com.cn/n/2014/0812/c1027-25452028.html.

37 Guo Daohui: On Interest Distribution and Regulation in Legislation, Xiangjiang Law Review (Volume II), Hunan Publishing House, 1997, p. 10.
38 L. Hengjin: The Era of Rights, translated by Xin Chunying, Wu Yuzhang and Li Lin, Knowledge Press, 1997, p. 1.
39 Martin E. Abrams: Privacy, Security, and Economic Growth in the Emerging Digital Economy Era, translated by Wen Zhenkui, published in: Research on Frontier Issues of Personal Information Protection, edited by Zhou Hanhua, Law Press, 2006, p. 5; In his book, *Privacy and Freedom*, Professor Alan F. Westin, an American scholar on information privacy, proposed four mutually restrictive privacy elements in society, namely, solitude, exposure, curiosity and government monitoring, to maintain public order.
40 There is no generally accepted definition of big data. The more typical is the 3V definition, that is, it is considered that human data needs to meet three characteristics: volume, variety and velocity. See Meng Xiaofeng and Ci Xiang: Human Data Management: Concepts, Technologies, and Challenges, Journal of Computer Research and Development, 2013, issue 1.
41 Zhang Kangzhi and Xiang Yuqiong: Construction of Policies in Cyberspace, Social Sciences in China, 2015, issue 2.
42 He Zhile and Huang Daoli: Background and Impact of European General Data Protection Regulation, Information Security and Communication Privacy, 2014, issue 10.
43 Article 6 of the Convention for the Protection of Individuals with Regard to the Automatic Processing of Personal Data stipulates that personal data disclosing race, blood, political opinion, religion or other beliefs and personal data related to health or sexual life shall not be processed automatically in principle, unless appropriate protection measures are provided for in domestic laws and regulations. The same applies to criminal records.
44 Directive 95/46/EC, Article 8; General Data Protection Regulation, Article 9.
45 Previous citation (4) by Zhou Hanhua, p. 79.
46 Kong Lingjie: Legal Protection of Personal Data Privacy, Wuhan University Press, 2009, p. 213.
47 General Administration of Quality Supervision, Inspection, and Quarantine and Standardization Administration: Article 3.7 of the Guide for the Protection of Personal Information in Public and Commercial Service Information Systems through Information Security Technology.
48 General Data Protection Regulation, Article 9.
49 McKinsey Global Institute, Big Data: The Next Frontier For Innovation, Competition And Productivity, accessed April 30, 2015, website: http://www.mckinsey. com/.
50 In 2008, for example, Google launched the "influenza trend" service. The server calculated the data retained in the Google server through a mathematical model to predict influenza. The calculation was even 7–10 days faster than that made by the US Centers for Disease Control and Prevention. See: Google Launched the Influenza Trend Service to Predict the Influenza Epidemic, accessed April 30, 2015, website: http://tech.qq.com/a/20081112/000333.htm. Baidu launched the Baidu Migration service in 2014. Through mining and analyzing the request data of the Baidu map, Baidu visually and dynamically displayed the track and characteristics of population migration before and after the Spring Festival. The new version of Baidu Migration in 2015 also had new query functions such as real-time flights, airport heat and railway station heat, so as to facilitate the life and production of Internet users and enterprises. See "Baidu Migration" for Spring Festival Travel in Place, News of Innovation of Big Data broadcast in CCTV, accessed April 30, 2015, website: http://it.sohu.com/20150215/n40y037209.shtml.
51 E. Bodenheimer: Jurisprudence: the Philosophy and Method of the Law, translated by Deng Zhenglai, China University of Political Science and Law Press, 1999, p. 398.

52 Philipp Heck: Begriffsbild ung und lnteressenjrisprudenz, Tubingen, S. 139ff; quoted from Zhu Yan: Change of Social Foundation and Construction of Dual System of Civil Law, Social Sciences in China, 2010, issue 6.
53 James G. Match and Johan P. Olsen: Rediscovering Institutions: The Organizational Basis Of Politics, The Free Press, 1989, p. 178.
54 See Directive 95/46/EC, Article 28.
55 Qi Aimin: Research on Personal Information Protection Law, Hebei Law Science, 2008, issue 4.
56 It refers to the responsibilities borne by the enterprise that exceed the mandatory obligations of the law and meet the social values and expectations. See Zhou Linbin and He Qidan: On Corporate Social Responsibility Beyond the Law, Modern Law Science, 2008, issue 3.
57 Zhou Hanhua: On Internet Law, China Legal Science, 2015, issue 3.
58 The Measures for the Administration of Internet Information Services issued by the State Council in 2000 stipulates that a licensing system shall be adopted for commercial Internet information service providers. In 2005, the Ministry of Information Industry issued the Administrative Measures for the Filing of Non-Operating Internet Information Services, which stipulates that the filing system should be implemented for non-operating Internet information service websites. In 2002, the Ministry of Information Industry issued the Measures for the Administration of Internet Domain Names in China to regulate domain name registration services and related activities in China. In 2005, the Ministry of Information Industry issued the Measures for the Administration of Internet IP Address Filing and the Detailed Rules for the Administration of Internet Websites, which stipulate the filing of Internet IP addresses and websites.
59 Since September 2010, the Ministry of Industry and Information Technology has promoted the real name registration system for telephone and mobile phone users and the Regulations on the Registration of Real Identity of Telephone Users in 2013 institutionalized the real name of telecom users. In 2015, the Cyberspace Administration of China issued the Regulations on the Management of Internet User Accounts and Names, Article 5 of which specifies that Chinese network users can use real names in the background and voluntary names at the foreground.
60 A virtual number is mostly dialed by criminals who set the calling number as a credible subjects such as finance, telecommunications and even national administrative and judicial organs, so as to obtain the trust of the victims and commit fraud. Phishing websites, usually well-known shopping websites, are fake websites by criminals, who send the content containing the website address to the victims in the form of an email, SMS, web advertising and so on. Because the counterfeit website and web content are very similar to the original websites, the victim may suffer losses by providing personal information such as bank account numbers and passwords based on misinformation.
61 Specifically, network users first provide their real identity information on the official website of the state or use the second-generation identity card to make the identity card information read for registration. The official institution will identify and verify the personal information of network users. After verification, network users will obtain a unique and random sequence identification code and corresponding password. The identification code, as the network identification code of the network user, can replace the real identity information to apply for other registration services. Then, when the network user registers with other websites, it only needs to provide the identification code to the network service provider. The network service provider verifies the user's identification code and password by visiting the official website of the state, and provides services to it after the verification is passed.
62 Chen Xinmin: Basic Theory of German Public Law (Volume II), Shandong People's Publishing House, 2001, p. 358.

63 See Directive 2002 /58/EC, Article 13.
64 China Internet Network Information Centre: 2013 Survey of Chinese Teenagers' Internet Behaviors, accessed April 30, 2015, website: http://www.cnnic.net.cn/lilw-fzyj/lilwxzbg/. The 2014 survey of Chinese teenagers' Internet behaviors has not been released.
65 Pei Honghui: The United States Issued the Eraser Act to Erase Minors' Internet Negligence, Law and Life, 2014, issue 1.
66 General Data Protection Regulation, Article 8.

8 The Relationship Between Human Rights and Personality Rights

Also on the Deficiencies of the Relevant Provisions of the General Rules of the Civil Law

By Shi Jiayou[1]

Personality marks the characteristics of a particular person and their personal traits. Therefore, the personality referred to in personality rights differs from a legal personality: the former refers to the unique characteristics of each person, while the latter refers to the qualification of the subject to enjoy rights and undertake obligations. The former is the individual's unique traits, while the latter is common to all people.

Personality rights are subjective rights given by civil law and other private laws, a kind of private right whose obligation subjects are parties concerned with private law. Human rights are rights stipulated by the constitution, international conventions on human rights and other public laws. The subject of the obligation of human rights is mainly the state. The vertical effect occurs in the vertical relationship between the state and the individual. In the modern era, fundamental rights themselves, which are also recognised as having horizontal effects, can also play an effective role among individuals. If the basic right of an individual is infringed in a civil contract, the victim can directly oppose the other party by claiming that the contract is invalid. Therefore, there is an overlap between personality rights and the obligation subjects of human rights. Personality rights and human rights have similarities also in the subject of rights. Besides natural persons, legal persons can also become the subject of rights. When the existence of a legal person is damaged, spiritual damage occurs. As a result, it has lost what it owns, and the economic losses of the legal person have also arisen. This view is obviously different from those of some conservative scholars in China.[2] In terms of content, personality rights are a kind of non-property right, including the rights to life, health, name, reputation, privacy and so on, while human rights include non-property rights, property and economic rights, as well as political rights, cultural rights and so on. Therefore, human rights contain a broader range of rights than personality rights. Some scholars believe that not all human rights are personality rights, but all personality rights fall under human rights.[3]

The relationship between personality rights and human rights is, in essence, the relationship between civil law and the constitution. In this regard, it is widely recognised that the civil code does have a constitutional function, which is the

DOI: 10.4324/9781003300168-8

important spillover effect of the civil code in modern society. In the 1980s, Professor Jean Carbonnier, one of the greatest post-war civil law scientists in France and the leading undertaker of the revision of the Civil Code of France in the 1960s to 1970s, drew a widely quoted authoritative conclusion that the civil code was the real constitution of France. Because the civil code has brought together the main ideas formed during the French Revolution, which French society depends on and are still being enriched but have never been denied, the civil code, like the Palace of Versailles and Marseille, has become the collective memory of the French nation.[4] In China, some civil law scholars also advocate that the civil code should give full play to the role in limiting and protecting rights and serve as a partial constitution. Specifically, the constitutional function of the civil code is fully realized through normative rights on the basis of the constitutional text and its interpretation. This approach can make constitutional norms vital and maximise the function of the civil code.[5] Such a claim is obviously reasonable, especially in terms of the provisions of respect for and the protection of human rights in China's constitution. A large number of civil rights stipulated in civil legislation are the implementation and concretisation of basic rights stipulated in the constitution and the concrete manifestation of the state's obligation to protect these rights. Therefore, the interpretation and application of basic rights (personal dignity, right to life, ownership, etc.) by civil judges should be based on the norms of basic rights stipulated in the constitution. This is also inevitably required by the horizontal effect of basic constitutional rights in civil relations. In this sense, a comprehensive understanding of the close internal relationship between human rights and personality rights helps provide new dynamic sources, open up new ways to better protect human rights and provide a more sufficient legitimate motivation for the development of personality rights.

Based on the General Principles of the Civil Law of 1986, the Tort Liability Law of 2009 and relevant judicial interpretations, the General Rules of the Civil Law of 2017 stipulates the personality rights system in Articles 109, 110 and 111. Some of them still have limitations in terms of the relationship between human rights and personality rights. On the other hand, this also has put forward requirements for the design of relevant systems in the specific provisions of the civil code.

8.1 The Interaction Between Human Rights and Personality Rights

The right of personality relies on the protection of the Tort Liability Law. However, the Tort Liability Law aims to protect the civil (subjective) rights confirmed by the law and cultivate new types of civil rights. Article 2 set forth in the Tort Liability Law of China in 2009 emphasises that civil rights and interests protected in the Tort Liability Law include both rights and interests, which highlights the function of Tort Liability Law to create new civil rights.

The Tort Liability Law protects basic rights such as personal rights and property rights, and one of the basic functions of basic rights is to provide the basis for the state to bear tort liability for public power and individuals under some special circumstances.[6] Therefore, the Tort Liability Law, as a remedy for private delicts, is the basic composition of the modern liberal constitutionalism governance structure. The right to relief enjoyed by citizens for having their rights infringed by others has constitutional value. In this sense, the system of tort damage compensation, which is considered to have constitutional significance, is the key to the protection of basic constitutional rights. Civil judges can directly apply constitutional provisions in tort law when necessary.[7]

8.1.1 State Obligation to Protect Basic Rights

The protection of basic constitutional rights by civil tort law is mainly reflected in tort law providing effective tort compensation and relief when basic rights (especially the right to freedom) are infringed. For example, the state, if considered to have the positive obligation to protect the right to life, should take necessary positive measures in advance. If it fails to take any preventive measures due to negligence, causing the murder of the victim, the government violates its obligation to protect the right to life. The judge can rule that the government should be liable for tort compensation to the families of the victim in accordance with the right to life stipulated in the constitution.[8] For the "case of wrong birth" in which infants are disabled due to a fault in the prenatal examination by medical institutions, the court can directly award damages without requiring them to prove the existence of mental damage in accordance with the basic right to reproductive autonomy enjoyed by parents.[9]

8.1.2 Application of Constitutional Principles to Improve Tort Law

Another manifestation of the constitutionalisation of tort law is that judges can apply constitutional principles to improve the tort liability system. First, the principle of complete compensation in tort law is considered to be the inevitable requirement for the rule of law in the constitution because legal order should be fully restored after being destroyed. Therefore, there is doubt about the rationality of the limited compensation system in special civil law.[10] In China, the limited compensation system established by some special civil laws other than the Tort Liability Law should be excluded in the application by civil judges in accordance with the basic constitutional rights involved, when necessary.[11]

Secondly, due process, a basic constitutional right, requires the improvement of many systems of tort law. For example, the tort prescription system directly restricts the exercise of the right to claim compensation, and the tort law protects the basic constitutional rights such as property rights and personal rights. Therefore, the tort prescription can have a greater impact on basic rights than the contract prescription. If the tort prescription unreasonably restricts basic rights, the judge can exclude the application of it according to due process. In China, the one-year limitation of actions established by the current law for personal injury compensation is obviously too short, which is not beneficial for the victim to exercise his right of relief. When necessary, the judge can make appropriate adaptations by reasonably determining the starting point and the interruption of prescription.

In another example, the court can expand the application of mental damage compensation according to due process.[12] China's mental damage compensation system was also established by civil judges for human rights protection,[13] then confirmed by judicial interpretation, and finally fixed in Article 22 of the Tort Liability Law. It is worth noting that this article adopts personal rights and interests as the expression of the infringed object. Personal rights and interests obviously contain more than traditional personality rights. Therefore, in view of the infringement on some new personality interests, the judge can creatively rule spiritual damage compensation based on the victim's right to relief.

Third, civil judges can give equal protection to infringed victims in accordance with the constitutional right to equality. The right to equality means that the same treatment should be applicable to the same situation. Thus, different treatments for the same situation or the same treatment for different situations can be considered as discrimination.[14] The primary object restricted by the constitutional right to equality is public power institutions, including legislative and judicial institutions. The stipulation of discriminatory treatment in civil legislation by the state constitutes a violation of the constitutional right to equality. In accordance with the state's obligation to protect the right of citizens, the court should give relief to the victims. It is worth noting that Article 17 of China's Tort Liability Law represents a response to the criticism from the public on the judgment of the same life with different prices in the previous judicial interpretation.[15] However, in the expression of this article that if the same tort causes more than one death, the death compensation can be determined in the same amount; the word "can" seems to be the norm of advocacy and has no rigid binding force on judges, but reserves room for discretion. This seems to violate the constitutional principle of equality. Therefore, judges should, rather than may, determine death compensation in the same amount based on the principle of equality in the constitution as far as possible.

8.1.3 The Interaction Between Basic Constitutional Rights and Civil Personality Rights

Unlike property rights, which concern the ownership of persons, personality rights concern the existence of persons.[16] The traditional civil code did not recognize the existence of personality rights as an independent type of civil right.[17] An important feature of the modern civil code is the establishment of the personality right system. As the right of personality contains all the necessary intrinsic elements inseparable from persons, some elements of the right of personality in civil law have also become the objects protected by the constitution, such as personal dignity, the rights to life, health and body, private life and so on.[18] The right of personality in the constitution (the core of which is personal dignity and free development of personality) is the foundation for the development of the human rights system in civil law.[19] The general right of personality itself is directly derived from the personal dignity and free development of personality in the constitution. Personality rights in the constitution and personality rights in the civil law are unified for the judicial protection of the all-round and free development of persons. The picture of the two together looks like a mosaic patchwork on the surface, but actually, they form a complete picture.[20] In France, for example, when Professor Perreau proposed the systematic theory of personality rights in the early 20th century, the Declaration of Human Rights, a constitutional document in 1789, was its logical starting point and philosophical origin.[21]

Therefore, personality rights in civil law must bear the imprint of basic rights in the constitution in a specific way. This internal tie determines an inevitable interaction between the two. The interaction between basic rights in the constitution and personality rights in civil law is specifically manifested as follows.

First, there is a trend of the fundamentalisation of personality rights. Basic rights are the reservoir of the legal order, which provides reference and enlightenment for the whole legal order in terms of legal concepts, classification and reasoning.[22] The right to private life, for example, obtained the status of constitutional rights in the 1950 European Convention on Human Rights. The European Court of Human Rights held that private life cannot be defined in a detailed and exhaustive way due to it being a very broad concept. The right to private life at least includes the right to self-determination, the right to personal freedom of action, the right to personal development and the right to establish and maintain relations with others and the outside world.[23] This obviously contains more than the right to privacy in civil law. The judge can deduce many new personality rights in civil law based on the constitutional personality right, including the right to personal information protection, the right to voice, the right to personal private space and so on. As a kind of basic right, personality rights have become the pioneer in promoting the development of the personality right system in civil law.[24]

The human right to know one's life experience, for example, has become a personality right in the civil law of Switzerland, which is a parental system independent of the relationship between parents and children.[25] Actually, this right was first established by the International Convention on Human Rights. In 1989, Article 3 of the United Nations Convention on the Rights of the Child established the maximization of the interest of children. It is stipulated in Paragraph 1 of Article 7 of the Convention that a child shall be registered immediately after birth and shall enjoy from birth the right to name, the right to nationality, the right to know as far as possible who its parents are and the right to be cared for by his parents. Article 8 of the 1950 European Convention on Human Rights stipulates the right to protection of private life and family life. In this regard, scholars generally believe that the right to know one's identity includes the right to know one's parents, which falls under private life.[26] More importantly, the European Court of Human Rights made a series of judgments in this regard, such as *Mikuli v. Croatia* on February 7, 2002,

Odievre v. France on February 13, 2003,[27] *Jaggi v. Switzerland* on July 13, 2006, *Godelli v. Italy* on September 25, 2012, and so on, that have had a far-reaching impact on the family law of the Member States. On June 22, 2001, the government of Switzerland ratified the Hague Convention on the Adoption and Protection of Children that provided for the right of children to know their life experience. Since the convention took effect in Switzerland in 2003, the right to know one's own life experience has been recognized as a basic human right by Swiss law. Accordingly, Switzerland amended its civil code. It is stipulated in Paragraph 1, Article 268c of the revised Civil Code of Switzerland that children have the right to obtain relevant information about their biological parents from the age of 18. Before reaching the age of 18, children also have the right to obtain such information if it is proven that it has a legitimate interest. Therefore, the right to know one's own life experience was officially recognized as a personality right by the Civil Code of Switzerland. Besides, in accordance with the theory of positive obligations developed by the European Court of Human Rights (the state not only has an obligation to respect human rights but also should take positive measures to protect them), the Swiss court held that the right to know one's own life experience can also produce positive obligations.[28]

Secondly, the constitutional right of personality provides the basis of interpretation and the source of enlightenment. As the constitutional personality right is broader than the civil law personality right, the judge can directly use the constitutional personality right as the source of enlightenment and dynamic to develop civil law personality rights.

Third, when dealing with the conflict between personality rights and basic rights, we can use the proportionality principle to measure the necessity to restrict basic rights. The four-prong proportionality test is as follows: (i) whether the purpose of making rules is legitimate; (ii) whether the means chosen in legislation to achieve the purpose are suitable; (iii) whether the means adopted are necessary—they must cause a minimum disturbance to the basic rights of others in order to achieve the purpose; (iv) whether the means of restriction are reasonable. Judges take conflicting principles into balanced consideration to determine whether the restriction is reasonable. China's civil judges also use this proportionality principle to deal with cases of disputes between personality rights and freedom of speech and the press.

On the other hand, there is a trend of civilization in human rights themselves. First, much of the content of personality rights is the specific implementation of the provisions of basic constitutional rights. For example, the constitution stipulates the right to life. In terms of personality right, civil law stipulates that violations of the right to life will bear civil liability for compensation. The specific implementation of the norms of basic constitutional rights by personality rights also embodies that basic rights have the dual attributes of objective law and subjective rights. Infringement on basic rights will lead to the same legal consequences as an infringement on civil rights. Secondly, civil rights have the characteristics of certainty with a clear and definite connotation, while the norms of basic rights are general principles with uncertainty rather than rules. Only by referring to the personality right in civil law can judges fully understand the constitutional personality right. Third, the right of personality provides a paradigm for the application of the norms of human rights. The presumption of responsibility, prescription, punitive damages and the principles of good faith, sincerity and honesty in civil law, for example, all provide a reference for the application of the constitutional norms of human rights.

It should be noted that the constitutional personality right is not satisfied with being only a higher law overlapping with the personality right in civil law but gradually infiltrates into the latter when conveying its value to the latter. The result of the constitutionalization of personality rights in civil law is that civil norms are endowed with higher effectiveness. The direct application of the constitutional personality right as the basis enables the personality right in civil law to obtain support and approval from a higher authority and higher effectiveness. The promotion of effectiveness can better protect the beneficiaries, especially when the object of a civil right is also protected by the basic right; the exclusive effect of said civil right will be significantly enhanced compared with that of other rights.[29] That was why, in a judgment, the French Supreme Court noted,

> Considering the provisions of Articles 8 and 10 in the European Convention on Human Rights and Article 9 in the civil code, the right to protect private life has the same normative value as the right to express freedom. This requires the judge to strike a balance between them and protect the most legitimate interest when necessary.[30]

8.2 On the Lack of Relevant Provisions in the General Rules of the Civil Law from the Perspective of the Relationship between Human Rights and Personality Rights

It is the inevitable logical consequence of the modern governance model to recognize and protect the effectiveness of fundamental constitutional rights in private law relations. From the perspective of human rights protection, private law also has the same obligation to protect basic constitutional rights as public law.[31] In 2004, an important provision that the state respect and protect human rights was introduced into China's constitution, which marked major progress in the protection of human rights in China's constitution. The state's solemn commitment to respect and protect human rights means that the state has both the negative obligation (defensive function) to respect human rights and not to interfere with individuals' exercise of basic rights, and the positive obligation (protective function) to protect human rights and promote the realization of human rights by means of legislation. In terms of the source of violations of fundamental rights, China's constitution does not distinguish between state infringement and private infringement of fundamental rights. Therefore, the same attention should be paid to the protective function and defensive function. This was also why the constitutional amendment gave equal priority to the respect for and protection of human rights.[32] From the perspective of the interaction between human rights and personality rights in civil law, many deficiencies exist in the provisions of personality rights in the General Rules of the Civil Law. They are as follows.

8.2.1 The General Rules of the Civil Law Fails to Invoke the Provisions of Constitutional Human Rights in the Part on Legislative Purpose

The respect and protection of basic constitutional rights stipulated in the provisions of the civil code are of great help for the effective protection of basic rights in civil justice. In this regard, the model of the Civil Code of Quebec deserves particular attention. It is clearly declared in the first paragraph of the preamble of the Civil Code of Quebec, which came into force in 1994, that the Civil Code of Quebec adjusts persons, things and the relationship between persons in harmony with the Charter of Human Rights and the general principles of law. This paragraph is of great significance as it reveals the harmonious and consistent interaction between the Civil Code of Quebec and the Charter of Human Rights. It should also be noted that the Civil and Commercial Code of Argentina, which took effect in 2015, also contains similar provisions. It is stipulated in Articles 1 and 2 of the Civil and Commercial Code of Argentina that the provisions on basic rights in the constitution and the International Convention on Human Rights are the legal sources of civil and commercial law. These provisions play an important role in the interpretation of civil and commercial law. As some scholars have pointed out, the openness of basic rights in the civil code is an important feature of the modern civil code influenced by human rights philosophy.[33] This interaction between civil code and public law is called a dialog between legal sources.[34]

First, the article declares the unity of civil law rights and basic constitutional rights. As some scholars said, the harmony between civil law and human rights is reflected in the consistency of their goals from a macro-perspective. From a micro-perspective, there is also consistency in the legal subject practising its law in both fields. In terms of the relationship between civil law norms and what is required by human rights, the hierarchical, pyramid-like, or simple Kelsen logic has been weakened and replaced by a new compromise between the autonomy of the private law and the hierarchy of norms.[35] This compromise is the inevitable requirement for the supremacy of the constitution and the objective value of basic rights.

Second, this article contains the constitutional interpretation. In other words, the interpretation of the provisions of the civil code must be consistent with those of the Quebec Charter of Human Rights. There is no hierarchical conflict in provisions between the Civil Code and the Quebec Charter of Human Rights, as this has drawn the vigilance of legislators. The above wording clearly expresses the legislator's intention to coordinate the two. If any problem occurs, the legislator knows how to solve it.[36] Accordingly, considering this clause, the Supreme Court of Canada recognized that enlightenment must be sought for civil tort liability from the values protected by the basic rights system, but the method and principle of civil law should still be followed in specific applications.[37] Of particular importance, it is necessary to refer to the provisions of Paragraph 2 of the preamble of the Civil Code of Quebec that the civil code is composed of all rules regulating relevant matters; the text, spirit, or object of these provisions have established their jus commune explicitly or implicitly in the field of what they regulate; the civil code is the basis of other separate laws in these fields, although separate laws can supplement the civil code or make rules of exception. As the common law of private law, the civil code includes significance in deconstruction and hermeneutics. In view of the provisions of Paragraph 2, it is necessary to follow the constitutional interpretation in the whole private law, not just within the civil code.[38]

Third, the infringement of basic rights will lead to tort liability similar to the infringement of subjective rights. It is stipulated in Article 49 of the Quebec Charter of Human Rights that if a right or freedom recognized in this Charter is infringed, the victim has the right to demand the cessation of the infringement and claim compensation for spiritual or material damage. In the case of intentional infringement of basic rights, the court may also impose additional punitive compensation liability on the infringer. Enlightened by this provision in the Charter of Human Rights, Article 1457 of the Civil Code of Quebec stipulates that everyone has an obligation to abide by the obligations imposed on him in accordance with the situation, custom, or law in a way that does not harm others and when he has a reason but fails to perform his obligations, he shall be liable for compensation for the physical, mental, or material damage caused to others due to his fault.[39]

From this point of view, China's civil theory and legislation are obviously conservative and out of date. It is a great pity that Article 1 of the General Rules of the Civil Law in 2017 on the purpose of legislation doesn't contain the provision of respect and protection of human rights set in the constitution. In the future, the words "protect the legitimate rights and interests of civil subjects" and "in accordance with the constitution" can be expanded through interpretations to be connected with the human rights provisions of the constitution. This is of great significance. First, the civil code can invoke constitutional clauses of human rights as one of the grounds for its legislation. Second, the quotation of constitutional clauses of human rights by the civil code also requires judges to respect and protect the basic rights stipulated in the constitution in civil justice, adopt constitutional interpretation when necessary to interpret relevant civil law norms or contracts or obtain enlightenment or an ideological source for interpreting civil norms or contracts from the necessity of the constitutional protection of basic rights. Third, the quotation of constitutional clauses of human rights also fully shows that China's Civil Code, as a new civil code, has distinct characteristics of the 21st century that are obviously different from the classical civil code: upholding social fairness and justice and paying attention to the comprehensive protection of people.

In this regard, it is particularly worth noting that the Standard for the Production of Civil Judgment Documents by the Supreme People's Courts was issued in June 2016. It emphasizes in Article 7 Judgment Basis that the constitution, guiding documents on the trial work issued by the people's courts at all levels, minutes of meetings, replies from trial chambers and documents jointly issued by the people's courts and relevant departments shall not be used as the basis for judgment, but the principle and spirit embodied in them can be described in the reasoning part. That is to say, the constitution shall not be cited in civil judgment documents but can be used as a reason for civil adjudication. Judging from this, China's highest judicial organ seems to tacitly consent to the constitutional interpretation. In other words, constitutional provisions cannot be directly cited in civil judgments, but the provisions and spirit of the constitution can be used to explain the specific applicable civil norms of law. Can this be taken as an indirect application of constitutional norms? There is no doubt that this needs to be further observed through specific precedents in the future. However, the position of the norms of basic rights in the constitution as the substantive source of the interpretation and application of civil rights, especially the right of personality, should not be questioned.

8.2.2 The General Rules of the Civil Law Fails to Establish Human Dignity as a Basic Principle

Human dignity is a basic human right universally recognized in the constitution and the International Convention on Human Rights. It is also stipulated in civil law as a basic civil right in order to effectively protect this basic constitutional right. It is stipulated in Article 38 of the Constitution of China that the personal dignity of citizens of the People's Republic of China is inviolable. The principle of personal dignity is stipulated in civil laws such as the General Principles of the Civil Law and the Law of Consumer Protection and other civil laws. The controversial term "the right to personal dignity" was even directly used in relevant judicial interpretations.[40] Thus, human dignity was established as a subjective right in civil law. In German law, human dignity was deliberately placed at the beginning of Chapter 1 Basic Rights of the Federal Basic Law by the framers. This subjective right is of objective significance as the entry point of the individual status as the right subject.[41]

As science and technology develop, it is particularly necessary to emphasize human dignity today. In the modern era, the rapid development of biomedical technologies such as artificially assisted reproduction, surrogacy, embryonic stem cell research and cloning, as well as artificial intelligence technologies such as speech recognition, face recognition and unmanned driving have seriously impacted human subjectivity, and people are increasingly risking being reduced to the object of legal relationship. To deal with the threat of subject objectification, it is necessary to clearly reaffirm human dignity as the basis and most essential principle of the legal order.

It is stipulated in Article 109 of the General Rules of the Civil Law in 2017 that the personal freedom and personal dignity of natural persons are protected by law. This is interpreted as the clause of general personality rights. Although it is placed at the top of Chapter 5 Civil Rights, this article cannot change the status of dignity as only an ordinary civil right. Dignity, however, has become a cornerstone of civilization in modern society and the basic principle of public law and private law. From this perspective, the understanding of dignity in the General Rules of the Civil Law in 2017 didn't make a progress compared with that in the General Principles of the Civil Law in 1986.

Fundamentally, in German law, the German Federal Supreme Court often expresses the general personality right as a right closely related to personal dignity and the free development of personality, which requires respect from all people. This expression is obviously open and uncertain.[42] The general right of personality is not equal to dignity. The General Rules of the Civil Law regards dignity as part of general personality rights, which, in fact, risks belittling the value of dignity.

8.2.3 There Is an Obvious Lack of Provisions on the Right to Personal Information

In the digital environment, the great progress of technology allows people to change their views on objects, the value of subjects and the relationship between subjects. People's behavior in the virtual world may be mapped to that in the real world. A great danger in the digital age is that people's autonomy may be threatened, and their status as a subject may be dispelled. Digital humanism emphasizes people's position as a subject in the digital environment, and accordingly recognizes individuals' right to dominate personal information in the Internet environment, "If individuals cannot accurately predict which personal information is known by society and who can obtain it, the freedom of individuals to decide their actions without any pressure will be damaged."[43]

For this reason, the Charter of Fundamental Rights of the European Union in 2000 lists in Article 8 the right to personal information as a basic right, in addition to the protection of private life in Article 7. The article stipulates that (i) everyone has the right to obtain legal protection for his personal information. (ii) Such information must be properly processed for the designated purpose and with the consent of the subject or for other legitimate reasons specified by law. Everyone has the right to obtain his own information and request to correct the wrong information. (iii) The implementation of relevant provisions shall be supervised by the independent institution. It is also stipulated in the first paragraph of Article 16 of the 2009 Treaty on the Functioning of the European Union (TFEU) that everyone has the right to legal protection of his personal information.

It is also worth noting that in the General Data Protection Regulation (GDPR) (2016/679/EU) adopted by the European Union on April 8, 2016, there are many amendments and reforms to the Personal Data Protection Directive 1995 (95/46/EC), that was replaced on May 25, 2018.

Article 5 of the 2016 GDPR stipulates the principles on personal information processing, including: (i) legality, fairness and transparency; (ii) purpose restriction; (iii) minimum information; (iv) accuracy; (v) restriction on storage period; (vi) information integrity and confidentiality; (vii) imputation. Articles 12–23 of the GDPR specify rights enjoyed by the information subject, including the right to prohibit the collection and processing of sensitive information, the right to access information, the right to block and prevent others from obtaining wrong information, the right to prevent conclusions based on the automatic processing of personal information (such as credit rating for users by the platform), the right to limit the information storage period, the right to move information and the right to prevent others from making commercial use of personal information and so on.

In contrast, Article 111 of the General Rules of the Civil Law in 2017 is much more careless and fails to reflect any advantage of backwardness. This article stipulates that the personal information of natural persons shall be protected by law; any organization or individual that needs to obtain the personal information of others shall obtain it in accordance with the law and ensure information security, and shall not illegally collect, use, process and transmit, trade, provide, or disclose the personal information of others. This was the first time that China's basic civil law had established the right to personal information. This article is not even as proper as the previous provisions of the Consumer Protection Law and the Network Security Law, as its negative wording is actually a normative mismatch.[44] In particular, this article does not specify the individual's right to control his information; the core right in the right to personal information. Without the right of the information subject to consent, other rights are in vain and become an aerial castle. Besides, Article 111 does not specify the principle of processing personal information (there must be legitimate and specific purposes for processing the data, the company/organisation must collect and process only the personal data that is necessary and relative to fulfil that purpose, the company/organisation must ensure the personal data is accurate, etc.).[45] In addition, the wording "shall not" in the second half of the article is used to prohibit some illegal acts of institutions engaged in information collection and processing (illegal collection, use, processing, transmission, illegal trading, provision, or disclosure of other people's personal information). The wording of illegal trading raises people's doubts whether there is a legal trade in personal information—the information can indeed be transferred in the form of big data after being processed, but such information must be anonymized. That is to say, personal information that can indicate the identity of a specific subject cannot be traded. For this reason, the GDPR 2016 issued by the European Union clearly stipulates that the information subject has the right to prevent others from the commercial use of its information.

8.2.4 The Meaning of the Right to Health Needs to Be Clarified

Among the specific personality rights enumerated in Article 110 of the General Rules of the Civil Law, there is the right to health. This article is derived from Article 98 of the General Principles of the Civil Law in 1986 (citizens enjoy the right to life and health). Generally speaking, the right to health means that people's physical health shall not be illegally infringed. In this case, it is worth noting how to distinguish it from the right to body to avoid the artificial concurrence of laws. The right to body usually contains two meanings: first, the integrity of the body is inviolable; second, the commercialization of the human body and its tissues is prohibited. The infringement of the integrity of the body will generally damage the victim's health. In addition, the integrity of body also includes mental integrity in a broad sense. The two should be distinguished by judicial interpretation or typical cases in the future.

In particular, the right to health in personality rights should be distinguished from that in the constitution. In comparative law, the right to health refers to the latter. It means that everyone has the right to the highest physical and mental health standard, including access to medical services, health facilities, adequate and healthy food, decent housing, healthy working conditions and a clean environment. The right to health especially emphasizes the availability, acceptability and good quality of health services. It is a basic human right established by many international conventions or declarations on human rights. For example, it is stipulated in Paragraph 1, Article 25 of the Universal Declaration of Human Rights that everyone has the right to a standard of living adequate for the health and wellbeing of himself and of his family, including food, clothing, housing, medical care and necessary social services and the right to security in the event of the loss of earning capacity for unemployment, sickness, disability, widowhood, old age, or other circumstances beyond his control. It is stipulated in Article 12 of the International Covenant on Economic, Social and Cultural Rights that:

1. The States Parties to the present Covenant recognize the right of everyone to the enjoyment of the highest attainable standard of physical and mental health.
2. The steps to be taken by the States Parties to the present Covenant to achieve the full realization of this right shall include those necessary for:
   (a) The provision for the reduction of the stillbirth-rate and of infant mortality and for the healthy development of the child;
   (b) The improvement of all aspects of environmental and industrial hygiene;
   (c) The prevention, treatment and control of epidemic, endemic, occupational and other diseases;
   (d) The creation of conditions which would assure to all medical service and medical attention in the event of sickness.

Obviously, as a basic human right in the international law of human rights, the right to health points to the state and the subject of obligation is the contracting state, not the individual subject in private law. That is to say, the right to health in international law and comparative law is a basic human right in public law. If it is used in civil law, the meaning of the right to health should be clarified to avoid confusion.

8.3 On the Limitations of the Traditional Relief Mode of the Tort Liability Law from the Perspective of the Relationship Between Human Rights and Personality Rights

Since the above provisions of the General Rules of the Civil Law list the types of personality rights, it has become a very important issue whether it is necessary to establish an independent law of personality rights in the specific provisions of the civil code. According to the experience from comparative law, some scholars believe that the relief by tort law can effectively protect the right of personality. This proposal actually fails to realize the limitations of the foreign relief mode in tort law and many negative effects that may be caused after it is introduced into China.

8.3.1 Judicialisation of the Constitution Is Likely to Occur if the Protection Mode of Tort Law Is Introduced

On the condition that the civil code lacks detailed provisions on the right of personality, the judge must invoke the provisions of basic rights from the constitution to protect the right of personality.

In France, the protection of personality rights leapt forward in the 1970s against the following important background: first, the landmark judgment made by the French Constitutional Council in 1971 confirmed the effectiveness of the Constitutional integrity (*bloc de constitutionalité*) and determined that the economic and social rights in the 1789 Declaration of Human Rights and in the preamble to the Constitution of the Fourth Republic in 1946 also constituted an integral part of the constitution. This *bloc de constitutionalité* is a collection of all principles and rules with constitutional status, which restricts the legislature, administrative organs, judicial institutions, public power organs and private law subjects. Since then, ordinary courts in France have been able to directly invoke constitutional principles as the basis for adjudication. Second, France approved the European Convention on Human Rights in 1974. According to Article 55 of the Constitution of France in 1958, the international treaty is under the constitution and above ordinary law in effectiveness. It was after France acceded to the Convention that the Civil Code of France was amended in 1971, to which Article 9 on the protection of private life was added. This article was recognized by the Constitutional Council in 1999 as having the same constitutional value as Articles 8 and 10 of the European Convention on Human Rights and Article 11 of the 1789 Declaration of Human Rights. The Constitutional Council also believes that a balance must be struck between these principles when there is a conflict between them.

The Civil Code of Germany only stipulated the right to name in Article 12 because the drafters at that time thought that the uncertain content of personality rights was the main obstacle to its being written in the civil code. From the Bismarck case in 1899, the German court protected the right to portrait, which was written in the Law of Artist Copyright Protection in 1907. The Weimar Constitution in 1919 systematically stipulated the basic rights of citizens for the first time that were not actionable in judicature. These rights were only set as the future political goal of legislators by the framers. The real change took place after the end of World War II, especially after the formulation of the Federal Basic Law in 1949. The cornerstone for the development of the personality right system in civil law is composed in Article 1 on the inviolability of dignity, Article 2 on the free development of personality and Article 13 on the confidentiality of correspondence in the Federal Basic Law. Since the Federal Basic Law is binding on all public authorities, the old civil code must adapt to the new constitution. In this context, the theory of third-party effectiveness of basic constitutional rights came into being. The general personality right was established through the interpretation of Articles 1 and 2 of the basic law.[46]

In China, many documents issued by the Supreme Court have repeatedly stressed that judges cannot directly invoke the constitution in their judgments to avoid disputes over the judicialization of the constitution. Therefore, great obstacles will be posed to the judicial protection of personality rights if the constituent elements and forms of responsibility of various personality rights are not stipulated in the specific provisions of the civil code, and judges are not allowed to invoke the constitution.

8.3.2 The Protection Mode of Tort Law Must Rely Heavily on Precedents or Judicial Interpretation

Articles 109–111 in the preface of the General Rules of the Civil Law only list the types of personality rights. The word "etc." in Article 110 shows the openness of the enumeration and the future recognition of new personality rights by law in practice. In addition, it is impossible for the General Rules of the Civil Law to make specific provisions on the concepts, constituent elements and forms of responsibility of these personality rights due to the limited length of the law. If it cannot be undertaken by the specific provisions of the civil code, this task can only be completed by judicial interpretations and precedents. Such a mission, however, can't be effectively undertaken by either judicial interpretations or typical cases due to their deficiencies: both lack legitimacy; judicial interpretation can only be used to solve the specific application of law in judicial practice; both lack systematicness; the formulation is opaque and arbitrary.[47]

8.3.3 China's Tort Liability Law Is Not Like the Grand Tort Law of France

Article 6 of the Tort Liability Law of China issued in 2009 stipulates the general provision of fault liability, which was inspired by the famous general provision of fault liability in Article 1382 of the Civil Code of France. Of course, the general provision itself is characteristic of its openness. However, it should be noted that China's Tort Liability Law is not completely like the Grand Tort Law presented by Article 1382 of the Civil Code of France and is not unlimited in its openness.

On the one hand, Article 2 of the Tort Liability Law lists 18 types of civil rights and interests protected. Although the words "and other personal and property rights and interests" are used at the end, indicating that it is an open list, judges will be obviously restricted in creating new types of rights and interests freely in the future because the legislator has listed 18 specific types of rights and interests in great detail. The judge will be sure to first take into consideration the list already made by the legislator in Article 2 when applying the general provision of fault liability. For example, the types of personal rights and interests mentioned therein include the rights to life, health, name, reputation, honour, portrait, privacy, marital autonomy and guardianship.

On the other hand, from the perspective of judicial tradition, especially the judge's legal interpretation, Chinese judges are generally cautious and modest in their interpretation of legal texts. Compared with foreign judges, there is more self-restraint in Chinese judges who rarely completely deviate from the legislative texts or make completely free interpretation and judgment from the spirit of the law. French judges could freely develop a complete personality right system through interpretations in accordance with Article 1382 of the Civil Code and with provisions of basic constitutional rights. This is obviously not suitable for China's national conditions.

8.4 Conclusion

In the 21st century, the development of science and technology has profoundly transformed society. Science and technology in the fields of the Internet, biomedicine and artificial intelligence have brought unprecedented convenience to humankind while posing risks never encountered before to humankind. The traditional subject-object structure between man and thing in legal relations has encountered great challenges. Man has the increasing risk of being changed into things, from subject to object of legal relations. In short, the main challenge facing the contemporary personality right system is the objectification of the subject. Just as some Swiss scholars expressed their concerns when describing the developing trend of the personality rights system, in legal reality, it can be seen that due to ubiquitous mobile phones and the Internet, people's willingness to respect others' personality rights is declining (especially the right to portrait), and they even lack the corresponding consciousness. It can be predicted that the social attitude toward personality protection may change toward the weakened legal status of individuals in the long run.[48]

In view of this, the interaction must be strengthened between the systems of personality rights and human rights. Human rights are stipulated by the constitution, which is a public law, and personality rights are stipulated by the civil law, which is a private law, but they have the same mission to protect people's free survival and development. Therefore, there is no isolation but a very rich and dialectical interaction between the two. It is incorrect to think that there is a split between the norms of personality rights in civil law and those of human rights. The two types of norms interpret each other. The norms of personality rights penetrate those of basic rights, and the latter is influenced by the former.[49] Therefore, some scholars emphasize that the personality right is not a civil right similar in nature to real right, creditor's right, intellectual property right and the right to identity, but a basic right entrusted to each individual by the basic law (constitution).[50] Such an argument does disclose the intrinsic close tie between personality rights and human rights. However, the denying of the civil attribute of personality rights for that is obviously one-sided and conservative, and this makes it difficult to respond to new challenges posed to the personality rights system in current times. Law is not only a kind of local knowledge applicable to specific human rights in specific regions but also a kind of knowledge with contemporary characteristics that should respond to the needs of a specific society in a specific era. China's future civil code is bound to respond to the special challenges facing China that is heading for a country ruled by law. It is a typical fallacy of inflexible methodology to treat the codification of contemporary China according to the experience from the classical codification period, which certainly leads to a misunderstanding of the protection of personality right in the present circumstances in China.

In this sense, we need not deny the close internal tie between personality rights and human rights to cover up or even deny the significance of personality rights protection to human rights progress. Human rights protection, after all, is one of the basic objectives recognized in China's constitution and the Decision to Comprehensively Promote the Rule of Law and other programmatic documents, and it is also one of the basic values of the socialist rule of law. China's Civil Code promotes the improvement of China's human rights protection with the high-level protection of personality rights. This itself is an important historical mission that contemporary China should burden in codification and also the only way for the state to truly respect and protect human rights, comprehensively promote the rule of law, and realize social progress!

Notes

1 This paper is the phased achievement of the Renmin University of China–University of Geneva Seed Fund—Scientific Research Fund Project of Renmin University of China on "Reform of the Debt Code of Switzerland and Compilation of the Civil Code of China" (funded by the special fund for basic scientific research business expenses of central universities) (project approval No. 16XNQ021).

2 For example, some scholars exaggerated by saying that there is no basis for legal theory and there is so much harm but no benefit practically when mixing group personality with personality of natural persons, and then deriving the personality right of legal persons. Yin Tian: On Personality Rights of Legal Persons, Chinese Journal of Law, 2004, issue 4, p. 57.

3 Jean-Michel Bruguière and Bérengère Gleize: *Droits de la personnalité*, Ellipses, 2015, p. 66.

4 Jean Carbonnier: Le Code Civil, in Pierre Nora (dir.), *Les Lieux de Mémoires*, vol. 2, La Nation, Gallimard, 1986, p. 307.

5 Xie Hongfei: Constitutional Function of China's Civil Code—Surpassing Constitutional Implementation Law and Civil Law Imperialism, Journal of National Prosecutors College, 2014, issue 6, p. 43.

6 Siewert Lindenbergh: The constitutionalisation of private law in the Netherlands, in Tom Barkhuysen and Siewert Lindenbergh (ed.): Constitutionalisation of Private Law, Martinus Nijhoff Publishers, 2006, p. 120.

7 John C. P. Goldberg: The constitutional status of tort law: due process and the right to a law for the redress of wrongs, The Yale Law Journal, 2005, vol. 115, p. 527. In France, in accordance with Article 4 of the Declaration of Human Rights ("freedom is the right to do all things harmless to others") as the preamble to the constitution, the Constitutional Council declared that the provision of the fault liability in Article 1382

of the Civil Code of France has constitutional value (Conseil Constitutionnel, Décision no. 82-144 DC, 22 oct. 1983, D. 1983, p. 189, note F. Luchaire).

8 ECHR, *Öneryildiz v. Turkey*, No. 48939/99, June 18, 2002. In this case, the Istanbul municipal government failed to take preventive measures against the garbage dump near the plaintiff's residence, resulting in the explosion of waste methane gas from the garbage dump and the death of the plaintiff's family. Therefore, the court ruled that the Turkish state failed to fulfill its obligation to protect citizens' right to life.

9 Supreme Court of Netherlands, Decision dated March 18, 2005, RvdW 2005, 42 (wrongful life).

10 Siewert Lindenbergh: The constitutionalisation of private law in the Netherlands, in Tom Barkhuysen and Siewert Lindenbergh (ed.): Constitutionalisation of Private Law, Martinus Nijhoff Publishers, 2006, p. 122.

11 Zhang Xinbao: Administrative Regulations Should Not Stipulate Specific Tort Liability, The Jurist, 2007, No. 5, p. 137.

12 For example, the Supreme Court of Lithuania expanded the application of compensation for moral damage in the civil code in accordance with the right to relief for compensation in Article 6 Due Process in the European Convention on Human Rights. In the case of violation of the right to life, the civil code only limits the obligee of spiritual compensation to "relatives who have a maintenance relationship with the victim during his lifetime", which has been extended by the court to "all family members who have close and genuine emotional ties with the victim." Supreme Court of Lithuania, September 26, 2007, case No. 3K-3-351/2007.

13 Beijing Haidian District People's Court: "the personal injury compensation case of Jia Guoyu v. Beijing International Aerosol Co., Ltd., Longkou Kitchen Supporting Equipment and Appliances Factory and Beijing Haidian Chunhai Restaurant", Bulletin of the Supreme People's Court of the People's Republic of China, no. 2, 1997, pp. 68–70. Article 14 of the Interpretation of the Supreme People's Court on Several Issues concerning the Application of Law in the Trial of Cases of Compensation for Road Traffic Accidents in 2012 lists the mental damage and loss of work delay of road traffic accident victims as personal injury and death, thus ending the dispute over whether they should be defined as personal injury and death or property loss in past judicial practice. This will undoubtedly help to strengthen the protection of the fundamental rights of life and health.

14 ECJ, *Commission v. Italy*, C-13/63, Judgment ofJuly 17, 1963.

15 Zhang Xinbao: Interpretation of Death Compensation System in Tort Liability Law, China Legal Science, 2010, issue 3, p. 23.

16 Adrian Popovici: Personality rights—A civil law concept, *Loyola Law Review*, 2004, vol. 50, pp. 356–357. In Quebec, Canada, for example, as the 1975 Quebec Charter of Human Rights stipulated some personality rights, the Civil Code of Quebec in 1994 finally stipulated the personality right system of civil law in Article 3. Of course, there are still some differences in the content between the civil law personality right and the constitutional personality right. In terms of the right to privacy, for instance, the constitutional right to privacy actually includes some basic rights such as freedom of residence and communication.

17 The Napoleon Code, for example, stipulated the inheritance system in 174 articles, the marriage system in 194 articles, and the boundary of common real estate in 20 articles. However, the code did not have a word on issues such as the way to protect the right to name. R. Lindon: La creation prétorienne en matière des droits de la personnalité, une approche critique sur la notion de famille, Dalloz, 1974, p. 87.

18 The civil personality rights recognised in the Convention on Human Rights include the right to enjoy legal personality, the right to presumption of innocence, the right to inviolability of residential and communication secrets, the right to reputation, the right to personal information and so on. See H. Oberdorff and J. Robert : *Libertés fondamentales et droits de l'Homme: textes internationaux et nationaux*, Montchrestien, 2007, pp. 189.

19 Lin Laifan and Luo Zhengyan: On the Right of Personality in the Constitution, The Jurist, 2008, issue 5, p. 63.
20 Jean-Christophe Saint-Pau (dir.)L *Droits de la personnalité*, LexisNexis, 2013, p. 465.
21 M.-E.-H. Perreau : *Des droits de la personnalité*, in *RTD. civ.*, 1909, p. 501.
22 M. Samson: *Droit civil et droit de la personne au Québc et en France: conflit et réconciliation*, in *Jurisdoctoria*, 2009, no. 2, p. 108.
23 ECHR, *Pretty v. The United Kingdom*, Application no. 2346/02, April 29, 2002.
24 Jean-Christophe Saint-Pau : *L'article 9, matrice des droits de la personnalité*, in *Recueil Dalloz*, 1999, no. 37, p. 541.
25 Philippe Meier and Estelle de Luze : *Droit civil suisse : Droit des personnes, Articles 11-89a CC*, Schulthess, 2014, p. 277.
26 Marie-Laure Papaux Van Delden: Au nom des droits de la personnalité de l'enfant: facettes choisies, in *Facettes du droit de la personnalité*, Schulthess, 2014, p. 97.
27 In this case, the plaintiff was 38 years old. Born in 1965, she was abandoned by her biological mother at birth, and first adopted by a social institution and later by her adoptive parents at the age of four. Since 1990, she began to collect information about her life experience, but the information she had obtained could not be identified. In 1998, she filed a lawsuit in court and was dismissed. On January 22, 2002, France passed a relevant law, commonly known as the *Acouchement Sous X*, which established CNAOP to help applicants understand their life experience. The institution can contact relevant hospitals, health organisations, and adoption institutions. It can also disclose the relevant information of their biological mothers and fathers after obtaining their explicit consent. The plaintiff believed that the law created an institutional obstacle for her to understand her life experience. The European Court of Human Rights held that the case mainly involved two basic rights: the applicant's right to know her life background and her biological mother's right to request anonymity to protect her private life. In addition, the case also involved the interests of the family of their adoptive parents, family members of their biological parents and so on. The European Court of Human Rights held that French law was in line with the principle of balance of interests and the principle of proportionality and did not violate Article 8 of the European Convention on Human Rights.
28 Philippe Meier and Martin Stettler: Droit de la filiation, 5th edition, Schulthess, 2014, no. 416, p. 271.
29 Jean-Christophe Saint-Pau (dir.): *Droits de la personnalité*, LexisNexis, 2013, pp. 432–434.
30 Cass. 1ère civ., July 9, 2003 : *JCP Edition Générale*, 2003, II, p. 10139, note J. Ravanas.
31 Shi Jiayou: Improvement of the Governance System and the Spirit of the Times Reflected in the Civil Code, Chinese Journal of Law, 2016, issue 1, p. 10.
32 Chen Zheng: The State Obligation to Protect Basic Rights, Chinese Journal of Law, 2008, issue 1, p. 52.
33 Mélanie Samson: *Les interactions de la Charte des droits et libertés de la personne avec le Code civil du Québec: une harmonie à concrétiser*, Collection Minerve, Éditions Yvon Blais, 2013, p. 7.
34 Rémy Cabrillac: Le nouveau Code civil et commercial argentin: l'éclatante réussite d'un audacieux pari, in *Recueil Dalloz*, 2015, No. 41, p. 2399.
35 Bjarne Melkevik: *Le nouveau Code civil du Québec et les droits de l'homme: le paradigme d'un nouveau "droit commun"*, in Jean-Luc Chabot, Philippe Didier, and Jérôme Ferrand (dir.), *Le Code civil et les droits de l'homme*, L'Harmattant, 2005, p. 409.
36 Monique Ouellette: Livre premier : Des Personnes, in *La Réforme du Code Civil : Personnes, successions, biens*, Presses de l'Université Laval, 1993, p. 16.
37 Louis Lebel: *La protection des droits fondamentaux et la responsabilité civile*, 49 McGill Law Journal 246 (2004). For example, in a case trialed by the Quebec Court of Appeal in 2001, Louise Otis, the judge, stated:

> The civil code of Quebec, as a structured and hierarchical legislative whole, establishes human physical integrity as one of the basic principles for enjoying and exercising civil rights in order to conform to the Charter of Human Rights…This is repeatedly emphasised in the preamble, Articles 3 and 10 of the civil code and Article 1 of the Quebec Charter of Human Rights.

Cour d'appel du Québec, l'affaire Montréal (Ville de) c. Tarquini, [2001] R.J.Q., 1405 (C.A.) paragraphe 174 (L. Otis).

38 Ministère de la Justice du Québec: *Commentaires du ministre de la Justice, Le code civil du Québec*, Tome 1, Québec, Les Publications du Québec, 1993, p. 1.

39 Mariève Lacroix: *La relativité aquilienne en droit de la responsabilité civile – Analyse comparée des systèmes germanique, canadien et québécois*, 59 McGill Law Journal 462 (2013).

40 Whether personal dignity can become a personality right is controversial in foreign theories. Opponents believe that dignity is not a personality element of the civil subject, because the subject of dignity is not an individual, and is not owned by a subject with specific individuality, but it is an element shared by all mankind. The right of personality emphasises individuality, while dignity falls under humanity and is common to all human beings. Jean-Michel Bruguière and Bérengère Gleize: *Droits de la personnalité*, Ellipses, 2015, pp. 109–110.

41 Song Xin: On Human Dignity in and Reference to the German Constitution, Oriental Law, 2016, issue 6, p. 128.

42 Yang Fang: Privacy Protection in General Personality Rights in Germany—Restrictions on the Concept of Self-Determination under the Principle of Freedom of Information, Oriental Law, 2016, No. 6, p. 108.

43 Jean-Michel Bruguière and Bérengère Gleize: *Droits de la personnalité*, Ellipses, 2015, p. 178.

44 Shi Jiayou: Legislative Technology of Civil Code—A Critical Interpretation of the *General Rules of Civil Law*, Journal of Comparative Law, No. 4, 2017, p. 136.

45 Agence des droits fondamentaux de l'Union Européenne: *Manuel de droit européen en matière de protection des données*, Office des publications de l'Union Européenne, 2014, p. 67.

46 Gert Brüggermeier, Aurelia Colombi Ciacchi, and Patrick O'Callaghan (ed.), *Personality rights in European Tort Law*, Cambridge University Press, 2010, pp. 16–21.

47 Shi Jiayou: Legal Source System of Civil Code—Taking Article 10 of the General Rules of the Civil Law as an example, Journal of Renmin University of China, No. 4, 2017, pp. 17–18.

48 Bettina Hurlimann-Kaup and Diana Oswald: Protection of Personality Rights in the Civil Law of Switzerland, translated by Jin Keke, Oriental Law, 2013, No. 3, p. 134.

49 Jean-Christophe Saint-Pau (dir.)L *Droits de la personnalité*, LexisNexis, 2013, p. 439.

50 Yin Tian: Re-Criticism of the Independent Compilation of Personality Rights, Journal of Comparative Law, 2015, No. 6, p. 1.

9 The Influence of the Independent Compilation of Personality Rights on the Theory and Practice of Marriage and Family Law

By Sun Ruojun

There has been a debate in the academic circles of civil law for many years over whether personality rights should be independently compiled from civil law, but the marriage law circle has not participated in this discussion. The law of personality rights and the law of marriage and family are being compiled in the current civil code simultaneously. On the surface, whether the law of personality rights is separately compiled has no direct connection and substantive impact on the revision of the Marriage and Family Law. I think, however, the separate compilation of personality rights will greatly promote the development of marriage and family law and judicial practice in the future, and even guide marriage and family relations in China to develop in a more humane direction.

9.1 The Influence of the Independent Compilation of Personality Rights on the Functional Orientation of Civil Law

As civil law has always been known as property law, there is no objection to the incorporation of the Marriage and Family Law, which has always been independent of the General Principles of the Civil Law, into the civil code. However, during the formulation and publicity of the General Rules of the Civil Law, many scholars completely ignored the existence of the Marriage and Family Law, thinking that the civil code aims to adjust the market economic rules. Valuing objects over people in the traditional civil law will not be changed because the Marriage and Family Law is included in the civil code. However, the separate compilation of personality rights is bound to highlight the essence of civil law as law for human beings and really change people's concept of the function orientation of civil law.

9.2 The Independent Compilation of Personality Rights Will Help Reconstruct a Complete Theoretical System of Personal Rights

Although China has established a legal system of personal rights protection based on the Constitution and connected with criminal law, civil law and administrative

DOI: 10.4324/9781003300168-9

law, the concept of personal rights is still very vague and confused in practice. Some civil law scholars interpret personal rights as personality rights combined with the right to identity from the perspective of the General Principles of the Civil Law, but society still uses personal rights as a byword for personality rights. Personal rights include the right to identity only in a broad interpretation. If personality rights are not compiled independently of the civil law, the definition of personal rights as personality rights plus identity rights is also very far-fetched, and the provisions of personality rights can't be considered complete. In fact, the concept of the right to identity is not clear as there is no right to spouse in China's Marriage and Family Law or parental right in law. Therefore, the personality right, if compiled separately and defined as the right of humans to survival and development, will help to promote the construction of a complete theoretical system of personal rights with public and private laws united in China.

9.3 The Influence of the Independent Compilation of Personality Rights on the Implementation of Freedom of Marriage

Freedom of marriage is a constitutional right and the primary principle of marriage law. However, in the 21st century, freedom of marriage in China's legal system still remains in the freedom to get married and prohibits parents from arranging marriages. The ideal of freedom of divorce pursued by the first generation of leaders since they were stationed in the revolutionary base area is far from being realised. At present, China is reforming its domestic relations trial system, requiring the court to stabilise domestic relations. Therefore, in addition to the pilot courts carrying out various all-around emotional tests on the litigants, other courts of domestic relations are also taking action. It is common that judges impose feelings on the litigants. Although the state has made a fundamental design for family problems, the freedom of marriage has always been restricted by politics, economy and the culture at specific times and cannot be simply advocated. The standards for divorce and all-round relief measures for divorce are stipulated in the marriage law. Whether it is necessary to expand the discretion of judges needs to be reconsidered. Many civil law scholars say that whether personality rights are separately compiled, it is necessary to highlight the protection of natural persons' personality equality, freedom and dignity. However, in fact, the implementation of the General Rules of the Civil Law has no impact on domestic relations trials. Therefore, when the separate law of personality rights is in place, only through publicity and learning can judges truly understand the meaning of a person, learn to respect persons and their feelings, and value the litigant's choice of their own life, rather than repeatedly educating, helping and making decisions for them as if they were persons with limited capacity. In modern times, various countries restrict the freedom of divorce moderately in the law of domestic relations and adopt objective standards. Humanistic care in civil law aims to enable individuals to enjoy a dignified life and maintain everyone's dignity. Therefore, humanistic care in marriage and the family should not be excluded. To be sure, there is no contradiction between promoting family virtues and protecting the freedom of divorce. Reluctant marriage and family relations, in name, cannot bring social stability and harmony.

9.4 The Independent Compilation of Personality Rights Will Help Settle the Conflict between the Right to Identity and the Right to Personality

How to deal with the conflict between many rights that should be in marriage and family relations and personality rights is a problem that has puzzled judicial practice for a long time. Although there are disputes about what the conflict of rights is and whether the rank of rights exists, there is a consensus that if a right determined by law represents the most fundamental interests, the protection of said right should be given priority. Therefore, if personality rights are compiled separately, it is theoretically necessary to re-examine and deeply study the boundary and limitation of rights, whether the rank of rights exists or not. This will undoubtedly have a profound impact on the future trial of domestic relations.

9.5 The Independent Compilation of Personality Rights Will Promote the Further Improvement of the Adult Guardianship System in the Future

The guardianship system in the General Rules of the Civil Law contains a newly made system of voluntary adult guardianship, which is regarded as great progress by the academic circles of civil law. Since the end of the 20th century, however, countries around the world have successfully reformed the adult guardianship system profoundly, especially abolishing the traditional act capacity system in civil law. In the guardianship of mental patients and the elderly, transaction security is no longer the only purpose to be sought. Instead, their free will is respected as members of society and their actual needs for personal and property management are met. On the contrary, the adult guardianship system established in the General Rules of the Civil Law still focuses on the acting capacity of the subject rather than physical and mental protection. It measures neurocognitive capacity with act capacity, replaces the neurocognitive capacity system with the act capacity system and denies the independence of neurocognitive capacity. If personality rights are compiled independently, I believe it will help promote the improvement of the adult guardianship system.

Index

For Product Safety Concerns and Information please contact our EU
representative GPSR@taylorandfrancis.com
Taylor & Francis Verlag GmbH, Kaufingerstraße 24, 80331 München, Germany

www.ingramcontent.com/pod-product-compliance
Ingram Content Group UK Ltd.
Pitfield, Milton Keynes, MK11 3LW, UK
UKHW020004200926
475702UK00015B/2476
* 9 7 8 1 0 3 2 2 9 1 3 6 9 *